CHE... COUNTY

VIRGINIA

⚒UNCOVERED⚒

The Records of Death
and
Slave Insurance Records
for the
Coal Mining Industry

1810–1895

To Jennifer H

Nancy C. Frantel

HERITAGE BOOKS
2008

*4-24-12
Nancy Frantel †
To God be
the
Glory!*

HERITAGE BOOKS

AN IMPRINT OF HERITAGE BOOKS, INC.

Books, CDs, and more—Worldwide

For our listing of thousands of titles see our website
at
www.HeritageBooks.com

Published 2008 by
HERITAGE BOOKS, INC.
Publishing Division
100 Railroad Ave. #104
Westminster, Maryland 21157

Copyright © 2008 Nancy C. Frantel

International Standard Book Numbers
Paperbound: 978-0-7884-4902-4
Clothbound: 978-0-7884-7500-9

TO CAROLINE

Although no one heard you when your life was taken at an early age, God made sure your voice was blessed Forever.

If you listen closely, you may hear an angel whisper.

Table of Contents

Acknowledgements

The guidance provided by many individuals was extremely valuable. Archivists, librarians and historians helped make this book a reality. The support from friends and family provided the energy to continue with the research. Research that was filled with pain.

Several individuals deserve special recognition. The dedication shown by Diana Lachatanere and Janice Quinter in preserving the slave insurance information at the Schomburg Center for Black Research and Culture was outstanding. Staff at the Virginia Historical Society Library, under the guidance of Frances Pollard, were consistently extremely helpful. Jenny Namsiriwan, David Angerhofer and the staff at the Maryland Historical Society also provided slave insurance policy documentation so the voices of those who were insured could continue to be heard.

A thank you is extended to several key libraries in the area. The Library of Virginia and the Chesterfield County Main Library have done an outstanding job of preserving their respective historical information. Records at both locations were made readily available with the assistance of knowledgeable staff.

The bulk of the material was housed at the Library of Virginia, where the staff made me feel very welcome. However, appreciation is extended to the individuals who assisted in the county library's History Room, especially the Chesterfield County Historical Society volunteers. My wish is that you will be able to continue providing a sanctuary for those seeking knowledge. Both libraries, by watching over the death records and articles for the benefit of future generations, allowed a portion of each individual's life story to be told.

The dedicated guardians at the University of Virginia Library's Special Collections also provided wonderful direction and support. Manuscripts under their care helped prove key aspects discussed in the book.

Gratitude is extended to Mr. Jerry Hynson, one of the kindest gentlemen I have ever met, who by publishing the *"Baltimore Life Insurance Company Genealogy Abstracts"* allowed the circle of life to be complete. Ms. Sharon Murphy played a key role by providing relevant information in the book's introduction. She also encouraged me to review the BLIC correspondence, which proved to be very productive.

Mr. Ronald Lewis, author of numerous books, provided excellent guides regarding the complexity of industrial slave involvement in the country.

The mining experts and staff at the Virginia Department of Mines, Minerals and Energy patiently answered my questions and willingly shared their Richmond Coal Basin scientific knowledge. Although unaware of the potential for a book, they consistently treated me with respect and helped provide a general mining education.

Archive staff at the United States Department of Labor's Mine Safety and Health Administration Library deserve special recognition. Although the staff was contacted near the end of the research period, their assistance was invaluable. Thank you for opening my eyes and providing a better understanding of how many newspapers across the country printed articles about the Chesterfield County mine disasters.

Preface

Realizing a fainting spell was imminent, I quickly walked to the counter, placed the copy of the recently discovered article down, and asked the gentleman at the desk to call 911. When the paramedics arrived moments later they asked if this had ever happened to me before. The answer was no.

By this point my heart had experienced several shocking discoveries. Why would this unknown short article written in 1991, be any different? Perhaps it wasn't the article. Instead, it was the cumulative effect of my heart breaking over and over again. And Chesterfield County was right at the center.

Deciding to write this book came as a result of an accumulation of several discoveries. The information presented in this book was initially being reviewed for personal education. However, as more public documents were discovered, the path became clearer. The writers from the past were guiding me along the unfolding story.

One of the most powerful events leading to writing the book happened while reviewing a document at the Library of Virginia. Holding the documentary evidence of so much pain and suffering was something I had never experienced before. After all, it was just a piece of paper. Or was it? Although having reviewed the history of Chesterfield County's coal mines, and being aware of their explosive nature and related fatalities, this discovery surprised me.

Inside the folder was a life insurance policy for a slave named Robert Moody. James H. Moody, his owner, insured Robert in 1847. The policy was effective February 16, 1847, and stated the slave would be working at the Clover Hill coal pits in Chesterfield County for one year. His owner, James H. Moody, purchased the policy and was listed as the beneficiary.

I started researching the slave insurance business after learning about Robert. Different aspects of selling the insurance and the financial benefits of the practice were revealed. It is not known if Robert and the other slaves listed in the third chapter of this book knew about the policies on their lives.

This insurance discovery, through a single interaction with Robert, brought a connection to the present and directly to me. The compassion I felt for Robert, knowing his owner would receive a death benefit if he died, was real. I shared the insurance information with a colleague. Several conversations later I was shocked to learn that a corporation in existence today receives a death benefit when I die. The policy purchased on Robert's life was for one year. However, I haven't worked for the company who still holds the insurance policy on my life for over twelve years.

The connection with the past compelled me to search for the rest of the story.

Introduction

An omen was present. Yet the capitalistic desires fulfilled by using the sacrifice of others continued to possess the owners and the lessees of the land in Chesterfield County. The warnings were everywhere, yet they appeared to ignore them. After all, it did not affect them. Only the final product of the labor from those who suffered appeared to be important to the individuals in control.

The screams were piercing. With the sound of the explosions no one above heard them. Except for God. Though they suffered in great pain and bled, they were never alone. God would not stop the pain that other men had intentionally inflicted, however He could make sure the Future never forgot them.

I am sorry for your suffering. May you suffer no more.

Your story will finally be told.

CHAPTER ONE

The Omen

Chesterfield County, Virginia, is a county of many "firsts." Historical markers around the county highlight early discoveries and industrial advances. Included among the list of "trophies" is "the first iron furnace in English America, built in 1619," noted by the Virginia Historical Marker S-4.[1]

Marker O–35 titled "Midlothian Coal Mines" includes the statements, "South of here are the Midlothian coal mines, probably the oldest coal mines in America. Coal was first mined here before 1730." The marker also highlights the fact, "The first railroad in Virginia was built from the Midlothian mines to the town of Manchester in 1831."[2] Railroads were key in transporting the coal to distribution locations (and further transport). After examining the county's history, seeing a train carrying coal and hearing the sound of the familiar train whistle may take on a new meaning.

The commercialization of coal mining heavily influenced the county's growth. As stated in *Virginia's Coal Ages*, "These coals were first mined commercially in 1748." The author also states the "first ones to be mined in the United States are from an area near Richmond...." An additional resource indicates that coal in Virginia was first discovered "along the James River west of Richmond in 1701."[3] The same resource reports, "In 1927 the last major mines closed, 226 years after the initial discovery."[4]

During Chesterfield County's mining era, over twenty companies were involved with the local operations.[5] The *Mining History of the Richmond Coalfield of Virginia* is an excellent resource providing a summary of the industry. This outstanding compilation of information published in 1988 also includes a bibliography of almost two hundred sources.[6]

The early years of Chesterfield County's commercial mining period produced another valuable publication. In 1837 the *PROPOSALS FOR INCORPORATING THE BEN LOMOND COAL COMPANY* was made available for investors to review.[7] The publication concentrated on the corporation's potential for success in Chesterfield County and provided perfect staging for the "rest of the story." The writers probably did not realize the publication's future value as a historical resource, and as an outline of the harmful results of the commercial enterprise.

An excellent snapshot of the capitalistic components of the industry at the time was provided in the publication as well. The coal business was key to the economic development of the county, as exemplified by the number of coal mine lands mentioned in the *PROPOSALS*. Was the growth worth the sacrifices that were made? The omen, which revealed itself even in the publication, foreshadowed the unfortunate series of events that would trouble the business.

As a selling point for investors, the *PROPOSALS* highlighted important background information. The facts described the assets and experiences of those involved in the business. In 1825 A. S. Wooldridge and A. L. Wooldridge formed A. & A. Wooldridge & Co. However, the publication states they, "take this mode of laying before the public, a proposal to embrace all of their property, *real* and *personal*, connected with the coal trade under an act of incorporation, styled the *Ben Lomond Coal Company*, passed by the Legislature of Virginia, on the 27th day of February last." The publication continues by stating that the first company "is about to terminate by limitation...."[8] A specific date is not mentioned for the property to be transferred to the Ben Lomond Coal Company. However, the Chesterfield County personal property tax records for A. & A. Wooldridge & Co. only show activity through 1838.[9]

The February 1837 "Act to Incorporate" for the Ben Lomond Coal Company provided the names of those who requested incorporation as Henry Clarke, Gustavus V. Clarke and Frederick Clarke.[10] However, after incorporation, valuation solicitation requests were sent to certain mining related representatives. Answers to the requests were included in the *PROPOSALS*. Numerous letters were addressed to A. & A. Wooldridge & Co. which specifically pinpointed the brothers' direct involvement in the new company.[11] What was noticeably absent in the correspondence was a detailed listing of the ways the miners could be killed as a result of their endeavor.

Shortly after the Ben Lomond Coal Company was introduced by the publication, it seemed to fade into the background. Coal-related history of the area scarcely mentions the company. In an effort to track their activity, the county's property tax records were studied. Starting with 1837 and checking through 1843, no references to the Ben Lomond Coal Company were found.[12] The Legislative Petition to the General Assembly dated December 13, 1836,[13] indicated the company's desire to operate coal mines in both Chesterfield and Powhatan Counties. Therefore, the records for Powhatan were also checked, and the results were the same.[14]

The Chesterfield County personal property tax records for A. & A. Wooldridge & Co. for 1826 through 1838 listed slaves, horses and mules owned. The only exception was for 1827, where a company entry was not listed.[15] The records showed a minimum of forty-two slaves during the period, with as many as 143 slaves over the age of twelve listed in 1833.[16] Considering this documented slave ownership, the probability of the Ben Lomond Coal Company using non-slave labor seemed highly unlikely. After all, the *PROPOSALS* stated the previous owner's real and personal property would be assigned to the new company.[17]

Why all the discussion about a company that seemed to evaporate in the same year as incorporation? Following the company's trail beyond the tax records was not a priority for this chapter. Although the Ben Lomond Coal Company was given "life" in 1836 through incorporation,[18] the company's greatest contribution may have been the well-written pamphlet. The *PROPOSALS* has served a valuable purpose as an introduction to the coal mine owners' practices in Chesterfield County and helped set the stage for the omens that perpetuated over the years.

Even though the Ben Lomond Coal Company did not show up on the tax records, members of the Wooldridge family were active in the industry. "An Act to incorporate the Mid Lothian Coal Mining Company" proved the incorporation request was passed in January 23, 1835, two years prior to the Ben Lomond Coal Company. The documentation revealed key involvement by Abraham S. Wooldridge and Archibald L. Wooldridge, the "A. & A." of the A. & A. Wooldridge & Co.[19]

Wooldridge connections were also found in the incorporation of the Rosewood Coal Mining Company. They were involved with the chartering of the Persons Coal Mining and Iron Manufacturing and the Chesterfield Coal Mining Company.[20] Therefore, although the PROPOSALS indicated the Wooldridge brothers played a key role with Ben Lomond, the records showed active participation in other companies instead. With this extensive involvement, apparently they understood the industry well.

Early in the PROPOSALS a reference was made that Wooldridge leased coal land once owned and "extensively wrought" by the late Major Harry Heth.[21] Henry "Harry" Heth remained a prominent figure in Chesterfield County history. He was very active in the mine business for many years, especially the first two decades of the 1800s.[22] The county personal property tax records showed slaves listed under both Harry Heth and Henry Heth. Records for 1801 list that Harry Heath [Heth] owned twenty slaves over the age of sixteen. In 1812, his personal ownership increased to 114 slaves.[23] The trail of slaves left a well-worn path.

Another individual mentioned in the PROPOSALS who operated in Chesterfield County was Mr. Nicholas Mills. He owned several coal mines in the area at different times, as well as many slaves. In the PROPOSALS Mills was listed as the owner of the Railey Hill Pits, located in Midlothian.[24] He was also involved with Mills, Reid and Company, another coal company mentioned in the publication.[25]

Nicholas Mills's slave ownership can be easily found by reviewing the Chesterfield County personal property tax records. For example, in 1833, he owned ninety-three slaves over the age of twelve years of age.[26] By reviewing the slave records, as well as the listings of number of horses and mules owned, animals frequently used in the mining industry, his family's coal mine connection was easily traced. In 1837, the year of the PROPOSALS, the Mills, Reid & Co. owned 106 slaves over the age of twelve and twenty-five horses and mules.[27] Mr. Mills's slave ownership will become more relevant in the following chapters of the book.

Nicholas Mills's influence in Chesterfield County was undeniable. Aside from owning coal mines, he was a key investor in the railroad in Chesterfield County that carried coal to the James River for further transport. When he passed away at the age of eighty in 1862, he was reportedly one of the wealthiest Virginians.[28]

Numerous influential individuals were involved with encouraging investors as noted in the *PROPOSALS*. Even with their presence in the community, facts about the company being a safe investment were documented throughout the publication. Although the authors of the publication stated that the coal resources had great potential, they seemed frustrated at having to repeat the obvious. "We think it unnecessary to say much upon this subject, since the public are already well informed of the general character of the resources and advantages now offered."[29]

By providing a summary of the basics, those involved appear to be flexing their corporate muscle.

> Suffice it to say, that we offer the coal-fields and pits, in operation, with the negroes, mules, machines, engines, rail roads, buildings, and fixtures of every description whatever – as well, also, as the coalyard and farm, with the labor and stock thereon, – affording the facilities for foraging and feeding the necessary force required in the mining operations, – which renders the Company or Corporation, independent for supplies, labor and means of almost every kind, and affords a profit nearly nett except the transit of coal upon the rail road.[30]

An impressive array of assets is provided for consideration of the company's worth. The list includes established coal mines and their proximity to many productive mines. "Black Heth Pits," the Grove tract, Union Pits and Stone Henge connections are made several times. References to the coal land and pits sunk by the Midlothian Coal Mining Company indicate success nearby as well.

Additional assets unfortunately included slaves, which as mentioned earlier, was common in the county's coal mines. The

PROPOSALS publication clearly establishes the "slaves as property" status. The names and values of forty-five slaves at Chesterfield County's Mssrs. A. & A. Wooldridge & Company's pits are listed. The ages of the property are also provided, ranging from eleven to sixty, with their value assigned next to their age. Totaling $30,925.00 in 1837 implied great worth. Also included are the slaves' names, ages and a $17,325.00 value for the twenty-eight pieces of human property belonging to Mssrs. A. & A. Wooldridge & Co. at the Falls Farm and Coal Yard. Combining the two entries yields an impressive total of $48,250.00, equating to over $1,000,000 in 2008 dollars.[31]

Several years prior to the 1837 *PROPOSALS* publication, another coal mining company printed its scheme for operation. Upon reviewing the information for the previously mentioned Midlothian Coal Mining Company, similar threads of confidence of success appear. The *CHARTER, SCHEME AND CONDITIONS OF SUBSCRIPTIONS* for the Midlothian Coal Mining Company presented in 1835 did not provide a detailed list of its assets. However, the proprietors seemed to revel in the potential amount of bushels of coal that could be raised from the pits, and very simplistically presented the estimated annual operating expenses for the mines, ending with the conclusion of corporate success.[32]

Was there anything wrong with the company extolling the potential production of the coal seams and resulting projected profits? After all, the purpose of the "*SCHEME*" was to gain investors, as stated in the very first sentence. "The proprietors of the lands chartered under the title of the Midlothian Coal Mining Company, deem it proper to offer a concise statement of the reasons which induce them to apply for a charter, and of the probable advantages and profits, likely to accrue from the purchase of stock in said company."[33] A few pages later a reference is made to "the prospect of immense profits."[34]

The subtle text may provide possible answers to the profit question. As early as page two in the twenty-five-page publication, the slave reference as laborers surfaces in the phrase, "...if judiciously invested in slaves...."[35] Another slave reference is made as part of the "practical" discussion. In determining how to use the extra estimated profits the proprietors suggested, "... forming an accumulating fund for the purpose... of purchasing additional slaves, engines or sinking shafts, as occasion may require."[36]

Why so much attention to the tax records documenting the slaves who worked in the county's coal mines? The fibers of their being will start weaving a golden thread into the future. A trail leads from early mining operations to very prominent players, like the Mid Lothian Coal Mining Company. Personal property tax records first list the corporation in 1837, indicating ownership of forty-one slaves over the age of twelve.[37] Scanning a fifteen-year period revealed the slave ownership peaked at 187 in 1848.[38]

Both the Ben Lomond and Mid-Lothian companies presented information for investors who were considering becoming involved either directly or indirectly with the county's coal lands. However, the point to be remembered is not about the land interests specifically. Instead, what happened on the land as a result of those investments is more important.

Commercialization came with an incentive to succeed apparently regardless of the risk. The potential of increased wealth appeared to be a lure for many. The dangers of coal mining were acknowledged near the end of the *PROPOSALS'* justification to investors: "In conclusion, we would say that the operations in coal mines are precarious, and liable to many casualties, perhaps to a greater degree than some other pursuits...."[39] History has clearly shown the truth of those words, through records of disasters whose toll on human suffering can never be erased.

Just two years after the Ben Lomond Coal Company proposal was published, an explosion occurred in the "Black Heath" coal mine. The March 18, 1839, disaster killed over forty people, with at least one source indicating over fifty were killed.[40] Although black and white perished, only the names of the two whites, the mine superintendents, were provided in the March 23, 1839, article printed in the *Richmond Enquirer*.[41] For reference, the 1839 Chesterfield County personal property tax records for the Black Heath Company of Colliers listed 111 slaves over the age of eleven.[42]

The 1839 article referenced the early explosions in England's coal mines, where over one hundred people were killed between 1812 and 1815. The article denied any future risks locally from explosions by stating, "The discoveries of Sir Humphrey Davy and other contributors to science and benefactors of mankind have since rendered the avoidance of these destructive explosions certain."[43]

Avoidance certain? Apparently the thought was that science could be controlled. "Let the unfortunate event which has just occurred be a lesson and warning, as we are sure it will be; and if possible, cause a more constant and rigid observance of the rules which science and experience have pointed out as the sure and unerring guarantees of safety."[44] As the Records of Death indicate in the following chapter, the discoveries when brought to the United States, were not as helpful as may have been expected. History clearly proved the inaccuracy of being able to predict or control science.

Even Reverend Jeremiah Bell Jeter, a preacher, noticed the gas in the mines. On September 12, 1843, he visited one of the mines owned by the Midlothian Coal Mining Company and preached to the miners, the overwhelming majority of whom were black. Soon after the visit he sent a letter to "Messrs. Editors" of the *Richmond Compiler*. The description of his experience was very vivid in his correspondence. "In some places we had to crawl on our hands and knees, and in others to ascend the banks by vigorous exertion, and the aid of the colliers. We saw the gas bubbling through the small streams which were flowing in some of the drifts."[45] At the time of Reverend Jeter's visit, less than fifteen percent of the total documented mining deaths had taken place. Yet in his role as a simple observer, even he saw the gas.

Several decades later, in 1876, Mr. Heinrich, a "superintending engineer" in Midlothian wrote about an area previously mined under consideration "to get the property in working order again." His recommendation was "to go into new ground adjoining, not infected with the sins of our forefathers in mining, which are at the bottom of all the evils existing in this section of country."[46]

Mr. Heinrich's recommendation was published before the May 20, 1876, gas explosion in another mine in the same part of the county. Several miners were killed in that unfortunate incident. However, the following statements about the actions of those above ground need no further comment. "In a few minutes they heard signals from the bottom for help and immediately turned water in the mine, hoping thereby to drive all the gas from it. Unfortunately, it proved afterwards that two of the men, who were only stunned by the explosion, were drowned by the water."[47]

How many more warnings were needed?

CHAPTER TWO

The Records of Death

When the mining operations were active in Chesterfield County, the laborers, both black and white, were subjected to many deadly hazards.

> He must encounter dangers at every stage, from the falling or crumbling of the roofs and pillars; from accidental fire (a casualty which has twice occurred to the Midlothian Company); from sudden irruptions of water flooding his works; from the fearfully destructive explosions produced by inflammable gas; and from the breaking of ropes and other accidents in ascending and descending the shafts, a danger which will be better appreciated when it is remembered that every laborer employed in mining is at least twice a day suspended over a depth of many hundred feet.[1]

This excellent summary of risks was outlined in a Legislative Petition submitted to the General Assembly of Virginia in January 1851. The petitioners were, "Your memorialists, the President and Directors of the Midlothian Coal Mining Company, on their own behalf and that of the Stockholders, whose constituted agents they are, respectfully ask the attention of your honorable body to the facts and consideration in the following statements...."[2] The president of the company who authorized the facts regarding the dangerous mining conditions was A. S. Wooldridge.[3] Fourteen years after releasing the *PROPOSALS FOR INCORPORATING THE BEN LOMOND COAL COMPANY*, the entrepreneurs finally officially documented the many ways miners could perish.

The death records for Chesterfield County and period newspaper articles together solidified the toll in human lives resulting from the documented hazardous conditions of the coal mines. The finality of the tragic circumstances was permanently written in the death records. When reviewing the death records, combined with the descriptions provided in the newspaper articles, it was not difficult to imagine the sounds of the explosions or the screams of those about to drown.

The death list following this section shows the diversity of workers who perished in the mines. Young and old, slave, white, and free black, death did not have barriers in the depth of darkness. Death came equally to them all. Many were bonded for life in more ways than may immediately be apparent.

Death, mainly as a result of explosions in the mines, did not spare the souls who were forced to work there. All who perished died a horrible death and are due equal respect. The death list documents some of the slave fatalities, although more slaves probably perished than were recorded in the surviving resources.

The United States Department of the Interior's Bureau of Mines published a brief history of the county's explosions in Bulletin 586. Especially noteworthy is the sentence printed on page one, "In the United States the first reported explosion was listed as occurring in approximately 1810...."[4] The location of the explosion? "Heath's pits" in Chesterfield County, where "some" were killed.[5] The government publication also states, "In those mines, methane was encountered that often formed explosive mixtures in poorly ventilated workings."[6] Methane is "an odorless, colorless, flammable gas, CH_4, the major constituent of natural gas, that is used as a fuel...."[7]

The country's second documented explosion resulting in loss of life also took place in Chesterfield County. Occurring in 1818, the location was listed as "Heath's pits," the same as the first explosion. "Previous to the adoption of this (improved) method of ventilation, they experienced great inconvenience from carbonic acid gas; and some of the workmen had been killed by an explosion of carburetted hydrogen gas."[8]

Information Circular 9503, recently released by the National Institute for Occupational Safety and Health, mentioned the volatility of the area mines. "These explosions are caused when buildups of explosive gas and/or dust in the mine are ignited by the presence of a flame or spark. Methane gas is inherently generated and held by adsorption in coal and is normally liberated during mining."[9]

Specifics regarding the character of the Richmond Coal Basin, which would include "Heath's pits," were further described as follows. "Limited information on the gas content of these coalbeds indicates very high methane contents and these early explosions were most likely caused by excess gas emissions related to the faulting and igneous activity."[10]

Moving beyond the scientific discussion, the following newspaper excerpt provided a simple description of how easily the gas exploded in the mines.

> It seems that Mr. Thomas Carrol, the foreman of the mine, was informed that the mine was filling up with gas, and went down the pit to see about it. He held in his hand an open lamp, such as is commonly used by the pit hands. The moment he reached the bottom of the pit and started to go into the mouth of the shaft, the gas communicated with the lamp and a terrible explosion occurred.[11]

Eight people died as a result of this 1876 explosion in the Grove Shaft, sixty-six years after the first documented explosion in the county. Although some improvements in determining the presence of gas over the years were beneficial, flaws in the system still existed. For example, the cause of the explosion in 1810 was listed as "gas – open light,"[12] the same type of ignition source as in 1876.

Who were the victims in the first two documented explosions in the United States? For the answer, a review of the mining practices is important to consider. The owners of Heath's pits apparently used slaves in the mines. The Chesterfield County Personal Property Tax lists provide evidence of the Nicholson, Heth & Company's slave ownership. In 1810, the year of the first explosion, the company owned ninety-one slaves over the age of sixteen.[13] The records for 1811 show Henry "Harry" Heath [spelled both Heth and Heath in county records] with sixty-two slaves over the age of sixteen.[14] In 1818 Henry "Harry" Heth owned fifty-five slaves.[15]

Henry "Harry" Heth, through Nicholson, Heth & Company, also hired slaves to work in the mines. The following 1810 advertisement was apparently intended for slave owners:

> WANTED, on hire for the balance of the year, 30 or 40 able bodied Negro Men, for whom a liberal price will be given – they will be employed in the Coal Mines– Apply to the Subscribers in Manchester, or to Harry Heth at the Coal Pitts.
> March 2.   NICOLSON, HETH, & Co.[16]

An outstanding discussion of the Heth family's ownership and leasing of slaves belonging to others is found in Ronald Lewis's *Black Coal Miners of America*.[17] Also, in personally reviewing several years of Heth's manuscripts, numerous references to owning and hiring slaves were found.[18] However, one Heth document stood out during the research process. A Heth manuscript titled "Hands Purchased at my Father's Sale 181_" left open a ten-year span of possible dates, including the two explosion dates, 1810 and 1818. Over thirty male slaves were listed, and five of them had the word "dead" written next to their names in a different handwriting.[19] When the Chesterfield County Personal Property Tax records, the advertisement, and Heth's business and personal correspondence are all combined, the evidence in support of slave usage in his mines is strong.

Working in underground shafts with gases causing deadly conditions leads to the following deduction. As proven by the documentation, Chesterfield County had the first coal mine explosion deaths in the country.[20] In addition, the county appears to hold an even darker title. Like a phoenix rising out of the ashes, Chesterfield County appears to have another "first" in the country located on its soil based on the research. In my opinion, Chesterfield County contains in its community the location where the first slaves died in an underground explosion due to gas in a coal mine. By the written word from the past, "Heath's pits" appears to hold this claim. One or all of the slaves' names may have even been documented on the list referenced earlier titled "Hands Purchased at my Father's Sale."[21]

The death of slaves underground continued over the years until freedom became an option for those once shackled. On March 18, 1839, an explosion took place at Black Heath mine. Estimates of the number of deaths vary; however, at least forty lives were claimed, all but two of which were "colored men."[22] On March 16, 1839, just two days prior to the explosion, the Chesterfield County Personal Property Tax entry for the "Black Heath Company of Colliers" documented ownership of ninety-eight slaves over the age of sixteen.[23] What would the records show on the March 19? Unfortunately no official county death records exist for 1839, and the tax records did not include the names of the slaves.

An interesting lawsuit also provided evidence about the lethal quality of gas found in the county's coal mines. The lawsuit was initially heard in Chesterfield County Circuit Court prior to March 1836, and was appealed to the state court. In the Circuit Court, a jury awarded Mr. Hill, the plaintiff, restitution in the amount of $400 for his slave who was killed in a coal mine. Randolph was listed as the defendant who had hired Hill's slave. A portion of the Circuit Court case is provided below.

> The declaration alleged, that Hill hired a negro man slave to Randolph for one year, to work in Randolph's coal pits in Chesterfield; and that Randolph was bound to keep all his machinery, utensils and pits, in proper order and repair, to work his pits in a collier-like manner, and to use due diligence to prevent accident and hurt to the labourers employed therein, and to Hill's slave among the rest; yet Randolph, regardless of his duty in that behalf, and careless of the safety of Hill's slave, negligently suffered and directed him to descend into the pits when there was impure and noxious air therein, whereby the life of the slave was put in great jeopardy; and, well knowing the pits to be filled with impure and noxious air, caused and ordered

the slave to be kept at work in the pits, until by the impure and noxious air therein he was killed. Plea, not guilty. Trial, and verdict for Hill for 400 dollars.[24]

The Court of Appeals' documentation provided additional details regarding the morning that Hill's slave was killed. After the slaves had been in the pit for only thirty minutes, "they found that there was foul air in the pit, and became sick, some more and some less...." Only one bucket was provided by which the slaves could ascend from the darkness of the seventy-foot-deep mine shaft. With the delay caused by the slow extraction rate, it was too late for Hill's slave when the bucket became available again. The slave's body was removed from a pool of water "about eighteen inches deep." An additional description of the mine included, "That there were several apartments in the pit; ...and occasionally, foul air was found in one and not in the others. That such foul air would and could cause death."[25]

Although the defendant, Randolph, asked for a new jury trial as part of the appeal, the request was denied. As documented in Randolph v. Hill, the case ended with Mr. Hill being victorious in the state court as published in March 1836. "And *judgment affirmed*, by the equal division of this court."[26]

Even though the gas and other dangers in the mines were known concerns, the demand for coal grew and production continued. So, too, continued the explosions in the Chesterfield County mines. The explosions, whether by air combined with methane gas or the ignition of coal dust,[27] took place where the coal had been exposed in the shafts. The gas would even at times announce its presence, like a poisonous snake warning its potential victims. Henry Howe wrote about his July 14, 1843, visit into the shafts of the Midlothian mine. "I heard the gas escaping from the coal make a hissing noise...."[28]

Several publications listed dates and locations of the coal mine explosions in the county, which occurred over approximately seventy-five years.[29] Newspaper articles provided more information, including names not found on the county death records. Also the articles disclosed whether the victims could be removed from the underground shafts, or if they had to be left behind.

In some cases, the conditions in the mines were too dangerous for rescuers to retrieve the bodies immediately. An article printed by the *New-York Times* provided information about the fire resulting from the February 3, 1882, explosion.

> The search for the bodies of the other victims of the disaster had to be stopped, for the present at least. These mines caught on fire about a year ago and burned for weeks. In other mines of the same group the coal has been known to catch fire and burn for months. This new trouble has caused a great deal of trouble. It is, of course, impossible to tell how far the fire has extended or when it will exhaust itself.[30]

Conveying the personal side of the mining explosions and other fatal mine-related incidences was key when compiling the death list. As many names of the fatalities as could be located were included. However, with incomplete records for all the victims, an attempt was made to acknowledge as many of the losses as possible. Therefore, at the end of the death list an "Unknown" section was included.

While the death list proves slaves were a part of the mine fatalities, more probably perished than were recorded in the surviving documentation. Regardless of race or freedom status, their loved ones suffered from the loss. In total, an estimated 350 workers were killed as result of various mining disasters. Almost ninety percent of the deaths were due to explosions. Even though the gas risk was ominous, the workers continued on. Perhaps those who were free were not really free, as their families depended on them for survival.

The last documented large-scale explosion in the county took place at the Grove Shaft mine on February 3, 1882. Although snow fell soon afterwards, children who understood the consequences of the disaster lost their innocence. The following description of the event needs no explanation.

Women whose husbands had left their sides but a few hours before in robust health walked about the dark streets of the village wailing and crying for those they would never again see alive, while the sobs of scores of children of the doomed miners pierced the air throughout the long and weary night. Daybreak found the ground covered with snow to the depth of over six inches and snow still falling rapidly.[31]

One might wonder, "Where are the casualties that could be removed buried?" Although it would probably be impossible to locate the final resting place for all who perished, there may be a beam of light shining on some of those previously missing. On February 8, 1987, the *Richmond Times-Dispatch* printed an article discussing the disinterment of "226 souls" on land near the Midlothian Turnpike.[32] The existence of a small family cemetery was known, which the developer had conscientiously planned to preserve.[33] However, while clearing the land for development, a burial ground over four times larger was discovered.[34]

Neither the article nor the court case documented the number of family members buried at the original cemetery; however, "more than a hundred other people" were reported as unknowns.[35] The developer went through the appropriate legal procedures with the Chesterfield County Circuit Court.[36] "WHEREFORE, the plaintiff prays that it be allowed to remove the remains of such persons as might be buried in the grave sites on the land aforesaid and to re-inter them with due care and decency in another place acceptable to this Court and that the plaintiff be afforded such other and further relief as the Court may deem proper."[37] On June 16, 1986, the plaintiff received court approval to relocate the bodies.[38]

The location of the original cemetery was reviewed on the Chesterfield County court record's map[39] while compiling the death list. It became immediately apparent that the cemetery was very close to the Midlothian mines. Could it be possible the remains of many of those killed in the frequent mine explosions in the Midlothian area were laid to rest in this abandoned cemetery?

Consider the fact that the Midlothian Coal Mining Company Hospital was located just south of the cemetery. The hospital treated miners and provided long-term care for "those injured in the various mine explosions that occurred periodically in the nineteenth century."[40] At this juncture, it appears limited amounts of information have survived regarding the hospital. However, its existence is documented in O'Dell's *Chesterfield County Early Architecture and Historic Sites*, which indicates the two-story building was "demolished before ca. 1910."[41]

Unfortunately, the individuals moved were not identified. They were relocated from one unmarked grave area to another. According to the article, "the total number of graves moved was 226." They were moved to Maury Cemetery in the fall of 1986 and placed in forty vaults.[42] Since time had returned many of the "souls" to the earth's care, there was an indication that the remains of several individuals were placed in the same vault. The numbers would prove this as fact. Also, the newspaper article mentioned that the "top 6 inches of soil" was uncovered in an effort to carefully reveal what was left of the remains.[43]

A connection from the past exists with the discovery, and subsequent combining, of the 226 graves. Remember the number of years the mines operated "after the initial discovery" of coal in the area, mentioned in Chapter One? The number of years was the same as the graves, 226.[44]

Additional information regarding the transfer of the remains from Midlothian to Maury is documented on the City of Richmond Bureau of Cemeteries' interment card. The card states the unknowns were "moved from Chesterfield County (English Company Cemetery)." The date of the move was listed as the "week of 9-22-86," four and one-half months before the newspaper article was written.[45]

Is there a connection between the English Company and the cemetery? When reviewing the name list of those who perished, note the "English Coal Pits" location for the explosion on May 15, 1854. Also an 1855 article printed in the *New-York Daily Times* helps document the involvement of the English Company in the mining industry locally. "Another explosion occurred at the English Company's pits, in Chesterfield County, Va...."[46] The time frame for both explosions fits the *Richmond Times-Dispatch's* record that "the graves appeared to be very old," and the funeral home representative's statement, "At least 1860."[47]

The personal property tax documentation verified the use of black slaves in the mines. Therefore, slaves, just like the free blacks and white workers, would have perished in the mining explosions prior to 1860. Considering the slave population in the county in 1860 was over 4,300,[48] slaves could easily have been buried in the abandoned cemetery.

Minimal evidence apparently remained of those who were buried in the cemetery. The 1987 newspaper article indicated the funeral home representative felt "those buried there had been poor." The article further documented, "That might explain why no traces of metal were found."[49] Slaves would certainly have fit into the "poor" category. The cemetery was known to include white family members. However, the proximity to the coal mines and the documented use of slaves in the mines continue to provide strong evidence that black individuals could have been buried there as well.

Not sure if slaves and whites would have been buried next to each other? Review the evidence presented on this subject regarding the Perkinson (Watkins) Farm. A book published by the Chesterfield County Planning Department in 1983 documented a "Very large cem[etery]..." on the farm, which was located in another part of the county. The phrase "Slave cem. Adjoins that of whites" is particularly noteworthy.[50]

The complete history of the cemetery may remain a mystery. However, with the documented combining of the remains, it is possible that whites, slaves, and free blacks now share the same earthly home. Statistically, a myriad of combinations is possible, and may represent the diversity of us all.

At Maury Cemetery the earth is void of markers acknowledging the existence of the unknowns' graves at their small field of rest. Even the tombstones nearby have their backs turned to them. For the unknowns, whose names may be on the following list, this written word may be their only memorial. May the "memorialists" of this day bring hope to those who choose the path of healing. And may anyone who seeks knowledge from the past now have guidance where to search.

Basic Sources:

DR: Death Records – Chesterfield County Marriage
            Records and Vital Statistics, Register of Deaths,
            Lower and Upper Districts, 1853 – 1896 (records
            missing for 1854, 1857, 1859 and part of 1855)
NPA: Newspaper Articles

NOTE: Accurate interpretation of records and name spellings attempted, yet not guaranteed. Slave status is listed as documented, however the records and articles were incomplete. Therefore, it would be fair to deduct that additional individuals on the list and many of the "Unknowns" were slaves.

Mine Deaths

Adams, Bob (Robert) – Slave, Black Male, killed March 19, 1855 [incorrectly listed in DR as 1856], Midlothian Pits "Killed by an explosion," owned by Midlothian Co., "No information as to parents," information on death provided by Wm. B. Wooldridge, Superintendent (Listed in 1856 DR – page 39, No. 31, NPA – *Daily Dispatch,* March 21 and 22, 1855)

Ainsko, James – White Male, killed April 3, 1867, Bright Hope Mine, Clover Hill, "Explosion in pit," coal digger (NPA – *Daily Dispatch*, April 6, 1867)

Ainsko, John – White Male, killed April 3, 1867, Bright Hope Mine, Clover Hill, "Explosion in pit," 30, coal digger, parents J. &

Sarah Ainsko, born in Chesterfield (DR – page 80, No. 26, NPA – *Daily Dispatch,* April 6, 1867, *Petersburg Index* – April 6, 1867)

Ammonette, Beverley – See Amonette, Beverly

Amonette, Beverly – White Male, killed April 3, 1867, Bright Hope Mine, Clover Hill, "Explosion in pit," collier/coal digger, parents "unknown," born in Chesterfield (DR – page 82, No. 32, NPA – *Daily Dispatch*, April 6, 1867, *Petersburg Index*, April 6, 1867 listed as **Ammonette, Beverley**)

Anderson, Beverly – Black Male, killed April 3, 1867, Bright Hope Mine, Clover Hill, "Explosion in pit," mule driver (NPA – *Daily Dispatch*, April 6, 1867)

Anderson, Fred – Black Male, killed February 3, 1882, Chesterfield's Grove Shaft explosion, 23 (NPA – *Daily Dispatch* February 4 and 5, 1882)

Artis, John – Black Male, killed April 3, 1867, Chesterfield Bright Hope Mine, Clover Hill, "Explosion in pit," mule driver (NPA – *Daily Dispatch*, April 6, 1867)

Barham, Mr. – [White] Male, killed December 10, 1863, explosion in Chesterfield's Raccoon Pit, mine overseer (NPA – *Daily Dispatch,* December 15, 1863)

Bellman, Robert – Black Male, killed April 3, 1867, Bright Hope Mine, Clover Hill, "Explosion in pits," 23, collier/digger, parents W. & J. Bellman, born in Chesterfield, information on death provided by Jean [?] Bellman, mother (DR – page 80, No. 30, NPA – *Daily Dispatch*, April 6, 1867)

Bereford, Bob – See Binford, Bob

Berry, Thos. [Thomas] – White Male, killed December 1, 1856, "Killed in Pitts," 50, name of parents "Not Known," born in

Pennsylvania, information on death provided by Jno. [John] W. Jones, friend (DR – page 11, No. 44 – original ledger at Library of Virginia Record Center)

Binford, Bob – Black Male, killed February 3, 1882, Chesterfield's Grove Shaft explosion, 40 (NPA – *Daily Dispatch*, February 4 and 5, 1882, listed as **Bereford, Bob** in February 4th article)

Blankenship, Richard – White Male, killed April 13, 1859, Chesterfield's Bright Hope Pits, explosion, 20 (NPA – *Daily Express*, April 15, 1859)

Boisseau, Henry – Black Male, killed April 3, 1867, Bright Hope Mine, Clover Hill, "Explosion in pit" (NPA – *Daily Dispatch*, April 6, 1867)

Boisseau, Phil. – Black Male, killed April 3, 1867, Bright Hope Mine, Clover Hill, "Explosion in pit" (NPA – *Daily Dispatch*, April 6, 1867)

Booker, Robert – Black Male, killed February 3, 1882, Chesterfield's Grove Shaft explosion, 18, miner (NPA – *Daily Dispatch*, February 4, 5 and 7, 1882)

Bowman, Robert – White Male, killed April 3, 1867, Chesterfield Bright Hope Mine, Clover Hill, "Explosion in pits," 36, collier, parents H. & A. Bowman, born in Chesterfield, information on death provided by H. Bowman, father (DR – page 81, No. 7, NPA – *Daily Dispatch*, April 6, 1867 listed as John Bowman)

Branch, Albert – White Male, killed May 15, 1854, [incorrectly listed in DR as 1855] Chesterfield, "English Coal Pits," "Explosion at Pits," 34, miner, parent Flemming Branch, born in Chesterfield, information on death provided by John R. Vest, friend (1855 DR listed twice page 18 No. 5 and page 27 No. 5,

NPA – *Daily Dispatch*, May 16, 25, 1854, *Daily South-side Democrat*, May 17, 1854)

Branch, Andrew – Black Male, killed April 3, 1867, Chesterfield Bright Hope Mine, Clover Hill, "Explosion in pits," 21[?], collier, parents B. & P. Branch, born in Chesterfield, information on death provided by Billy Branch, father (DR – page 80, No. 28, NPA – *Daily Dispatch*, April 6, 1867)

Bright, Squire – Black Male, killed February 3, 1882, Chesterfield's Grove Shaft explosion, 55 (NPA – *Daily Dispatch*, February 4 and 5, 1882)

Brooks, Beverly – Black Male, killed February 3, 1882, Midlothian Dist., "Killed Grove Shaft," explosion, 36, information provided by Hannah Brooks, wife (DR – page [2], No. 43, NPA – *Daily Dispatch*, February 4 and 5, 1882)

Browder, John – Black Male, killed April 3, 1867, Chesterfield "Explosion in Pits," 16, parents G. & M. Browder, born in Chesterfield, collier, information provided by G. Browder, father (DR – page 80, No. 29)

Brown, James – White Male, killed February 3, 1882, Midlothian Dist., "Killed Grove Shaft," explosion, 31, miner, parents Thos. & Hannah, information on death provided by George Jewett (DR – page [2], No. 54, NPA – *Daily Dispatch*, February 4 and 5, 1882)

Brown, Thomas – White Male, killed May 15, 1854, Chesterfield's "English Coal Pits," "terrible explosion," (NPA – *Daily Dispatch*, May 16, 17, 25 1854, *Daily South-side Democrat*, May 17, 1854)

Burton, Joseph – White Male, involved in November 26, 1855 "dreadful explosion" at the Black Heath Coal Mines, initially "seriously burned and bruised," Chesterfield County, later article listed as died (NPA – *Daily Dispatch,* November 28, 1955, *Daily*

South-side Democrat, November 28, 1855, *New-York Daily Times*, November 30, 1855)

Burton, Bob – Slave, Black Male, killed March 19, 1855 [incorrectly listed in DR as 1856], Midlothian Pits, "Killed by an explosion," owned by Caroline Wooldridge, "No information as to parents," information on death provided by Wm. B. Wooldridge, Superintendent, insured in United States Life Insurance office (Listed in 1856 DR – page 39, No. 23, NPA – *Daily Dispatch*, March 21 and 22, 1855)

Burton, Stepney [Stephen]– Slave, Black Male, killed March 19, 1855 [incorrectly listed in DR as 1856], Midlothian Pits, "Killed by an explosion," owned by Caroline Wooldridge, "No information as to parents," information on death provided by Wm. B. Wooldridge, Superintendent, insured in United States Life Insurance office (Listed in 1856 DR – page 39, No. 22, NPA – *Daily Dispatch*, March 21 and 22, 1855)

Carrol, Thomas – White Male, killed May 20, 1876, explosion at Grove Shaft in Midlothian, no age listed, mine foreman (NPA – *The Rural Messenger*, May 27, 1876)

Carter, Edwin – Slave, Black Male, killed March 19, 1855 [incorrectly listed in DR as 1856], Midlothian Pits, "Killed by an explosion," owned by Midlothian Co., "No information as to parents," information on death provided by Wm. B. Wooldridge, Superintendent (Listed in 1856 DR – page 39, No. 33, NPA – *Daily Dispatch*, March 21 and 22, 1855)

Cheatham, Hobson – White Male, killed October 21, 1885, Chesterfield, Raccoon Pit, Clover Hill coal mines, "Killed by explosion of gas in coal pits," 30, miner, parents James R. & Mary H., information on death provided by James R. Cheatham, father, "member of the Masonic Lodge at Winterpock" (DR – page 1, No. 31, NPA – *New-York Times*, October 23, 1885, *Richmond Dispatch*, October 23, 1885)

Clark, Thompson – Black Male, killed March 1877, Chesterfield "scalded by explosion of boiler in pits," 64, born in Chesterfield, information on death provided by Lucy Clark, wife (DR - page 1, No. 35)

Clayton, Joseph – White Male, killed April 3, 1867, Chesterfield Bright Hope Mine, Clover Hill, "Explosion in pit," coal digger (NPA – *Daily Dispatch*, April 6, 1867, *Petersburg Index*, April 6, 1867)

Clayton, Oran – Slave, Black Male, killed March [19], 1855 [incorrectly listed in DR as 1856], Midlothian Pits, "Killed by an explosion," owned by Julia S. Wooldridge, "No information as to parents," information on death provided by Wm. B. Wooldridge, Superintendent, insured in the United States Life Insurance office (Listed in 1856 DR – page 39, No. 24, NPA – *Daily Dispatch*, March 21 and 22, 1855, also listed as **Lantern, Oran** and **Orange**)

Cogbill, Richard – White Male, killed February 3, 1882, Chesterfield's Grove Shaft explosion, 22 (NPA – *Daily Dispatch*, February 4 and 5, 1882)

Cole, Archer W. – White Male, killed April 3, 1867, Chesterfield "Explosion in pit," 16, collier/mule driver, Name of parent: William Cole, information on death provided by Joshua Cole, uncle (DR – page 82, No. 34, NPA – *Daily Dispatch*, April 6, 1867, *Petersburg Index*, April 6, 1867 listed as W. A. Cole)

Coleman, Asa – Black Male, killed April 3, 1867, Chesterfield Bright Hope Mine, Clover Hill, "Explosion in pit" (NPA – *Daily Dispatch*, April 6, 1867)

Coleman, Jeff – Black Male, killed February 3, 1882, Chesterfield's Grove Shaft explosion, 45 (NPA – *Daily Dispatch*, February 4 and 5, 1882)

Condrey, Artimas – White Male, killed October 1875, Clover Hill, "killed in pits," 21, parents Jeff & Martha Condrey, born in Chesterfield, information provided by Aaron Ferguson, friend (DR – page 4, No. 25)

Condry, Joseph – White Male, killed April 3, 1867, Chesterfield Bright Hope Mine, Clover Hill, explosion, coal digger (NPA – *Daily Dispatch*, April 6, 1867)

Corneau, James – White Male, killed May 20, 1876, "old Midlothian coal-pits" Grove Shaft, gas explosion, foreman, listed as member of Odd Fellows (NPA – *Daily Dispatch,* May 23, 1876, *Rural Messenger*, May 27, 1876)

Cosby, Thomas – White Male, killed April 3, 1867, Chesterfield Bright Hope Mine, Clover Hill, "Explosion in pit" (NPA – *Daily Dispatch*, April 6, 1867)

Cosby, William – See Cosley, William

Cosley, William – White Male, killed April 3, 1867, Bright Hope Mine, Clover Hill, "Explosion in Pits," 18, collier, parents J. & P. Cosley, information on death provided by Phebe Cosley, mother (DR – page 82, No. 36, NPA – *Daily Dispatch*, April 6, 1867 – lists name as **Cosby, William**)

Cournow, Joseph – White Male, killed February 3, 1882, Chesterfield's Grove Shaft explosion, 21, engineer, parent Thomas Cournow [deceased] (NPA – *Daily Dispatch*, February 4, 5 and 7, 1882, *New-York Tribune*, February 5 and 7, 1882)

Cournow, Thomas – White Male, killed May 20, 1876, Chesterfield Grove Shaft, explosion, pit boss (NPA – *Daily Dispatch*, February 5, 1882, *New-York Tribune*, February 5, 1882)

Cox, Curtis – Black Male, killed April 3, 1867, Bright Hope Mine explosion, Clover Hill, "Explosion in pit" (NPA – *Daily Dispatch*, April 6, 1867)

Cox, Gus. – Black Male, killed April 3, 1867, Bright Hope Mine explosion, Clover Hill, "Explosion in pit," mule driver (NPA – *Daily Dispatch*, April 6, 1867)

Cox, Sam – Black Male, killed February 3, 1882, Chesterfield's Grove Shaft explosion, 45 (NPA – *Daily Dispatch,* February 4 and 5, 1882)

Crostick, Robert – White Male, killed May 15, 1854 [incorrectly listed in DR as 1855], Chesterfield, "English Coal Pits," "Explosion at Pits," 30, miner, parents Josiah & Polly Crostick, born in Chesterfield, information on death provided by a friend (1855 DR listed twice page 18, No. 8 and page 27, No. 8, NPA – *Daily Dispatch*, May 16 and 25, 1854, *Daily South-side Democrat*, May 17, 1854)

Crump, Albert – White Male, killed April 13, 1859, Chesterfield's Bright Hope Pits, explosion, "about thirty-five," (NPA – *Daily Express*, April 15, 1859)

Cunluff, Joe – Black Male, killed February 3, 1882, Chesterfield's Grove Shaft, explosion, 60 (NPA – *Daily Dispatch*, February 4 and 5, 1882)

Cyra, Moses – White Male, killed May 15, 1854 [incorrectly listed in DR as 1855], Chesterfield, "English Coal Pits," "Explosion at Pits," 36, miner, parents Aaron & Nancy Cyra, born in Chesterfield, information on death provided by John R. Vest, friend (DR listed twice: page 18 No. 6 and page 27 No. 6, NPA – *Daily Dispatch*, May 16 and 25, 1855, *Daily South-side Democrat*, May 17, 1854, also listed as **Cyrie, Moses** and **Syrah, Moses)**

Cyrie, Moses – See **Cyra, Moses**

Dawson, Edward – White Male, killed December 12, 1856, Midlothian Coal Pits, drowned, caused "by the rush of water" (NPA – *Daily South-side Democrat*, December 16, 1856

Depp, David – Slave, Black Male, killed March [19] 1855 [incorrectly listed in DR as 1856], Midlothian Pits, "Killed by an explosion," owned by Gustavus Depp, "No information as to parents," information on death provided by Wm. B. Wooldridge, Superintendent, insured by owner in the United States Life Insurance office (Listed in 1856 DR – page 39, No. 19, NPA – *Daily Dispatch*, March 21 and 22, 1855, initially listed "in dying condition")

Depp, Dick – Slave, Black Male, killed March 19, 1855, [incorrectly listed in DR as 1856], Midlothian Pits, "Killed by an explosion," owned by Gustavus Depp, "No information as to parents," information on death provided by Wm. B. Wooldridge, Superintendent (Listed in 1856 DR – page 39, No. 20, NPA – *Daily Dispatch* March 21 and 22, 1855, also listed as **Dipp, Dick,** initially listed as "dangerously burned")

Dickenson, Henry – Slave, Black Male, killed December 12, 1856, Midlothian coal pits, drowned, caused 'by the rush of water," owned by Nicholas Mills, Esq. (NPA – *Daily South-side Democrat*, December 16, 1856)

Dipp, Dick – See Depp, Dick

Dixon, Henry – Slave, Black Male, killed October 1856, Midlothian Pits, "Drowned," owned by Nicholas Mills, "No information as to parents," information on death provided by Wm. B. Wooldridge, Superintendent (DR – page 39, No. 13)

Dobbins, Ezekiel – White Male, killed May 15, 1854, Chesterfield's "English Coal Pits," "terrible explosion," (NPA –

Daily Dispatch, May 16 and 25, 1854, *Daily South-side Democrat*, May 17, 1854)

Donahoe, Patrick – White Male, killed April 3, 1867, Bright Hope Mine, Clover Hill, "Explosion in pit," coal digger (NPA – *Daily Dispatch*, April 6, 1867, *Petersburg Index*, April 6, 1867 – listed as **Donnahue, Patrick**)

Donnahue, Patrick – See **Donahoe, Patrick**

Dorson, Wm. – White Male, killed March [19] 1855, Midlothian Pits, "Killed by an explosion," miner, parents "Not Known," born in England, information on death provided by W. B. Wooldridge, Superintendent (Listed at end of 1856 DR – page 40, No. 7)

Dunn, Thomas – White Male, killed March 19, 1855, Midlothian Mining Co. pits, explosion, 24 (NPA – *Daily Dispatch*, March 21 and 22, 1855, *New-York Daily Times*, March 22 and 23, 1855)

Dunn, William – White Male, killed December 12, 1856, Midlothian coal pits, drowned, caused "by the rush of water" (NPA – *Daily South-side Democrat*, December 16, 1856)

Dunn, Wm. – White Male, killed March [19] 1855, Midlothian Pits, "Killed by an Explosion," no age listed, miner, parents "Not Known," born in England, information on death provided by W. B. Wooldridge, Superintendent (Listed at end of 1856 DR – page 40, No. 6)

Ellett, John – White Male, killed May 15, 1854 [incorrectly listed in DR as 1855], Chesterfield, "English Coal Pits," "Explosion at Pits," 20, miner, parents Wm. & Phebe Ellett, born in Chesterfield, information on death provided by Wm. G. Flournoy, friend (1855 DR listed twice: page 18, No. 9 and page 27, No. 9, NPA – *Daily Dispatch* – May 16 and 25, 1854, *Daily South-side Democrat*, May 17, 1854, also listed as **Elliott, John**)

Ellett, William – White Male, killed May 15, 1854 [incorrectly listed in DR as 1855], Chesterfield, "English Coal Pits," "Explosion at Pits," 18, miner, parents Wm. & Phebe Ellett, born in Chesterfield, information on death provided by Wm. G. Flournoy, friend (1855 DR listed twice page 18, No. 10 and page 27, No. 10, NPA – *Daily Dispatch*, May 16, 17, 25, 1854, *Daily South-side Democrat*, May 17, 1854, also listed as **Elliott, William**)

Elliott, Phillip – Black Male, killed May 20, 1876, "old Midlothian coal-pits" Grove Shaft, gas explosion (NPA – *Daily Dispatch,* May 23, 1876, *Rural Messenger*, May 27, 1876)

Elliott, John – See Ellett, John

Elliott, William – See Ellett, William

Evans, John – White Male, killed March 19, 1855, Chesterfield Midlothian Coal pits, explosion, 29 (NPA – *Daily Dispatch*, March 21 and 22, 1855, *New-York Daily Times*, March 22 and 23, 1855)

Farley, James – White Male, killed December 12, 1856, Midlothian coal pits, drowned, caused "by the rush of water" (NPA – *Daily South-side Democrat*, December 16, 1856)

Farmer, Isaac – See Parmer, Isaac

Finn, Daniel – Black Male, killed October 30, 1895, Chesterfield "killed, a tumble in Cox shaft pits," 40, miner, parents James & Henrietta Finn, born in Chesterfield, information on death provided by Henrietta Finn, mother (DR – page 2, No. 46)

Finney, Henry – Black Male, killed April 3, 1867, Bright Hope Mine, Clover Hill, "Explosion in pit," deputy (NPA – *Daily Dispatch*, April 6, 1867)

Forsee, Jasper – Slave, Black Male, killed March 19, 1855, Midlothian Pits, "Killed by an Explosion," miner, DR listed owned by Thomas Forsee (newspaper article Forsee's estate), parents "Not Known," born "Not Known," information on death provided by W. B. Wooldridge, Superintendent (Listed at end of 1856 DR – page 40, No. 4, NPA – *Daily Dispatch*, March 21 and 22, 1855, also listed as **Forsey, Jasper**)

Forsee, Phill (Philip) – Slave, Black Male, killed March 19, 1855 [incorrectly listed in DR as 1856], Midlothian Pits, "Killed by an explosion," owned by Midlothian Co., "No information as to parents," information on death provided by Wm. B. Wooldridge, Superintendent (Listed at end of 1856 DR – page 39, No. 39, NPA – *Daily Dispatch*, March 21 and 22, 1855, also listed as **Foster, Phillip**)

Forsey, Jasper – See Forsee, Jasper

Foster, Phillip – See Forsee, Phill

Foulkes, Doctor – Black Male, killed April 3, 1867, Bright Hope Mine, Clover Hill, "Explosion in pit" (NPA – *Daily Dispatch*, April 6, 1867)

Fowler, Sam. – White Male, killed April 3, 1867, Bright Hope Mine explosion, Clover Hill, "Explosion in pit" (NPA – *Daily Dispatch*, April 6, 1867)

Furcron, James – White Male, killed September 1889, "Chesterfield pits," "burned in pit explosion," 28, miner, parents John & ___ , born in Chesterfield, information on death provided by J. W. Crostic, friend (DR – page 1, No. 30)

Gaines, Guo [?] – Black Male, killed April 3, 1867, Chesterfield "Explosion in pits," 18, collier, parents Ed & Nannie [?] Gaines, born in Chesterfield, information on death provided by Ed Gaines, father (DR – page 82, No. 44)

Galt, Isaac – See **Gault, Isaac**

Garland – Slave, Black Male, killed June 30, 1857, Chesterfield "explosion in the Black Heath Pits," (Source - Bickerton Lyle Winston)

Gates, Jordan – Black Male, killed April 3, 1867, Bright Hope Mine explosion, Clover Hill, "Explosion in pit," digger (NPA – *Daily Dispatch*, April 6, 1867)

Gault, Isaac – Slave, Black Male, killed March 19, 1855 [incorrectly listed in DR as 1856], Midlothian Pits, "Killed by an explosion," owned by Midlothian Co., "No information as to parents," information on death provided by Wm. B. Wooldridge, Superintendent (1856 DR – page 39, No. 37, NPA – *Daily Dispatch* March 21 and 22, 1855, also listed as **Galt, Isaac**)

Gibbs, Wiley – Black Male, killed April 3, 1867, Bright Hope Mine, Clover Hill, "Explosion in pit" (NPA – *Daily Dispatch*, April 6, 1867)

Giles, David – White Male, killed December 27, 1880, died in Chesterfield Poor House, "hurt in Coal mines," 60, miner, parents not listed, information on death provided by Wm. E. Gill, Supt. of Poor [House] (DR – No. 2, No. 52)

Godsey, Henry – White Male, killed May 15, 1854 [incorrectly listed in DR as 1855], Chesterfield, "English Coal Pits, "Explosion at Pits," 35, miner, parents Abram & Polly Godsey, born in Chesterfield, information on death provided by John R. Vest, friend (1855 DR listed twice page 18, No. 4 and page 27, No. 4, NPA – *Daily Dispatch*, May 16 and 25, 1854, *Daily South-side Democrat*, May 17, 1854)

Golden, Thomas M. – White Male, killed May 20, 1876, "old Midlothian coal-pits Grove Shaft, "explosion of gas," 26, miner, parents Saml. [Samuel] & Mary, born in Chesterfield, information on death provided by Mary Monroe [?], mother (DR – page 2 No. 48 [says "June 1876" - incorrect], NPA – *Daily Dispatch,* May 23, 1876, *Rural Messenger,* May 27, 1876)

Goode, Budd – Black Male, killed April 3, 1867, Chesterfield "Explosion in pits," 15, parents Thos. & Lilia Goode, information provided by Tom Goode, father (DR – page 82, No. 42)

Goode, John – Slave, Black Male, killed March 19, 1855, Midlothian Pits, "Killed by an Explosion," miner, owned by Wm. Goode, parents "Not Known," born "Not Known," information on death provided by W. B. Wooldridge, Superintendent, insured by owner in United States Life Insurance office (Listed at end of 1856 DR – page 40, No. 3, NPA – *Daily Dispatch,* March 21 and 22, 1855)

Goode, John – Slave, Black Male, killed October 1856, Midlothian Pits, "Drowned," owned by W.B. Gates, "No information as to parents," information on death provided by William B. Wooldridge, Superintendent (DR – page 39, No. 14)

Goode, John – Slave, Black Male, killed December 12, 1856, Midlothian coal pits, drowned, caused "by the rush of water," owned by Mr. Goode (NPA – *Daily South-side Democrat,* December 16, 1856)

Goode, Jordan – Slave, Black Male, killed March 19, 1855, Midlothian Pits, "Killed by an Explosion," miner, owned by Wm. Goode, parents "Not Known," born "Not Known," information on death provided by W. B. Wooldridge, Superintendent, insured by owner in United States Life Insurance office (Listed at end of 1856 DR – page 40, No. 2, NPA – *Daily Dispatch,* March 21 and 22, 1855)

Goode, William (D.) – White Male, killed April 3, 1867, Bright Hope Mine, Clover Hill, "Explosion in pit," (NPA – *Daily Dispatch*, April 6, 1867, *Petersburg Index*, April 6, 1867)

Gouldin, Samuel – White Male, killed March 19, 1855, Midlothian Mining Co., "Killed in the pits," explosion, 33, gas attendant, overseer in pits, born in Chesterfield, information on death provided by Mary Goulding, wife (DR – page 7, No. 17 – original ledger at Library of Virginia State Record Center, NPA – *Daily Dispatch* March 21 and 22, 1855, *New-York Daily Times*, March 22 and 23, 1855, also listed as **Goulen, Samuel**)

Goulen, Samuel – See Gouldin, Samuel

Graves, Isham – Black Male, killed February 3, 1882, Chesterfield's Grove Shaft explosion, 21 (NPA – *Daily Dispatch*, February 4, 5, 7 and 8, 1882)

Green, John – Black Male, killed February 3, 1882, Chesterfield's Grove Shaft explosion, 55 (NPA – *Daily Dispatch*, February 4 and 5, 1882)

Hackett, Mickie – White Male, killed April 3, 1867, Bright Hope Mine, Clover Hill, "Explosion in pits," 16, collier, parents M. & E. Hackett, born in Chesterfield, information on death provided by Elz. Hackett, mother (DR – page 81, No. 1, NPA – *Daily Dispatch*, April 6, 1867)

Hall, James E. – White Male, killed February 3, 1882, Midlothian Dist., "Killed Grove Shaft," explosion, 33, pit hand/deputy "boss," parents Thos. & Margarett, born in Chesterfield, information on death provided by Thos. Hall, parent (DR – page [2], No. 48, NPA – *Daily Dispatch*, February 4 and 5, 1882, *New-York Tribune*, February 5, 1882)

Hall, Robert – White Male, killed May 20, 1876, "old Midlothian coal-pits," Grove Shaft, gas explosion, listed as member of Odd

Fellows (NPA – *Daily Dispatch,* May 23, 1876, *Rural Messenger,* May 27, 1876)

Hall, Thomas M. – White Male, killed February 3, 1882, Midlothian Dist., "Killed Grove Shaft," explosion, 38, pit hand, parents Thos. & Margarett, information on death provided by Thos. Hall, parent (DR – page [2], No. 49, NPA – *Daily Dispatch,* February 4 and 5, 1882)

Ham, Nicholas – White Male, survived March 19, 1855 Midlothian Mining Co. pit explosion, died March 21, 1855, 25 (NPA – *Daily Dispatch,* March 21 and 22, 1855)

Hammond, Daniel – Black Male, killed February 3, 1882, Chesterfield's Grove Shaft explosion, 32 (NPA – *Daily Dispatch,* February 4 and 5, 1882)

Hancock, Dick (Richard) – Slave, Black Male, killed March 19, 1855 [incorrectly listed in DR as 1856], Midlothian Pits, "Killed by an explosion," owned by Dr. Jefferson Hancock, "No information as to parents," information on death provided by Wm. B. Wooldridge, Superintendent, insured in the United Stated Life Insurance office (Listed in 1856 DR – page 39, No. 41, NPA – *Daily Dispatch,* March 21 and 22, 1855)

Hancock, John – White Male, killed March 18, 1839, Black Heath Mine, explosion (NPA – *Gettysburg Republican Compiler,* April 9, 1839, *Richmond Enquirer,* March 23, 1839)

Harper, Jim (James) – White Male, killed April 3, 1867, Bright Hope Mine, Clover Hill, "Explosion in pit," digger (NPA – *Daily Dispatch,* April 6, 1867, *Petersburg Index,* April 6, 1867)

Harper, Peter – Black Male, killed February 3, 1882, Chesterfield's Grove Shaft explosion, 40 (NPA – *Daily Dispatch,* February 4 and 5, 1882 also listed as **Hoffer, Peter**)

Harris, Frederick – Slave, Black Male, killed March 19, 1855 [incorrectly listed in DR as 1856], Midlothian Pits, "Killed by an explosion," owned by Jno. [John] Harris, "No information as to parents," information on death provided by Wm. B. Wooldridge, Superintendent (Listed in 1856 DR – page 39, No. 42, NPA – *Daily Dispatch*, March 21 and 22, 1855)

Hendley, Joseph – Black Male, killed May 20, 1876, "old Midlothian coal-pits," Grove Shaft, gas explosion (NPA – *Daily Dispatch,* May 23, 1876, *Rural Messenger*, May 27, 1876)

Herrod, William (Billy) – Slave, Black Male, killed March 19, 1855, [incorrectly listed in DR as 1856], Midlothian Pits, "Killed by an explosion," owned by Nicholas Mills, "No information as to parents," information on death provided by Wm. B. Wooldridge, Superintendent (Listed in 1856 DR – page 39, No. 28, NPA – *Daily Dispatch*, March 21 and 22, 1855)

Hobbs, Lewis – White Male, killed February 3, 1882, Midlothian Dist., "Killed Grove Shaft," explosion, 50, parents Abram & Eliza, information on death provided by Mary Hobbs, wife (DR – page [2], No. 50, NPA – *Daily Dispatch*, February 4 and 5, 1882)

Hobson, Dick – Black Male, killed April 3, 1867, Bright Hope Mine, Clover Hill, "Explosion in pit" (NPA – *Daily Dispatch*, April 6, 1867)

Hoffer, Peter – See Harper, Peter

Holder, Charles – White Male, killed May 20, 1876, "old Midlothian coal-pits Grove Shaft, gas explosion, listed as member of Odd Fellows (NPA – *Daily Dispatch,* May 23, 1876, *Rural Messenger*, May 27, 1876)

Howard, Henry – Black Male, killed April 3, 1867, Bright Hope Mine, Clover Hill, "Explosion in pit," digger (NPA – *Daily Dispatch*, April 6, 1867)

Howe, Joseph – White Male, killed March 19, 1855, Midlothian Mining Coal Pits, explosion, parent John Howe (NPA – *Daily Dispatch*, March 21 and 22, 1855)

Hughes, Albert – Black Male, killed February 3, 1882, Chesterfield's Grove Shaft explosion, 30 (NPA – *Daily Dispatch*, February 4 and 5, 1882)

Hunt, Mr. – White Male, killed [December 1854], Midlothian Coal Pits, fell in the pits, father of Samuel Hunt (NPA – *Daily Dispatch*, March 21, 1855)

Hurt, Washington – Black Male, killed April 3, 1867, Bright Hope Mine, Clover Hill, "Explosion in pit" (NPA – *Daily Dispatch*, April 6, 1867)

Isaacs, Albert – White Male, killed April 3, 1867, Bright Hope mine, Clover Hill, "Explosion in pit" (NPA – *Daily Dispatch*, April 6, 1867)

Jackson, Louis (Lewis) – Slave, Black Male, killed March 19, 1855 [incorrectly listed in DR as 1856], Midlothian Pits, "Killed by an explosion," owned by the Midlothian Co., "No information as to parents," information on death provided by Wm. B. Wooldridge, Superintendent (Listed in 1856 DR – page 39, No. 38, NPA – *Daily Dispatch*, March 21and 22, 1855)

Jackson, Price – Black Male, killed April 3, 1867, Bright Hope Mine, Clover Hill, "Explosion in pit" (NPA – *Daily Dispatch*, April 6, 1867)

Jackson, Randall – Black Male, killed April 3, 1867, Bright Hope Mine, Clover Hill, "Explosion in pit" (NPA – *Daily Dispatch*, April 6, 1867)

Jackson, Thomas – Slave, Black Male, killed December 12, 1856, Midlothian coal pits, drowned, caused "by the rush of water," owned by the Midlothian Company (NPA – *Daily South-side Democrat*, December 16, 1856)

Jackson, Thos. – Slave, Black Male, killed October 1856, Midlothian Pits, "Drowned," owned by Midlothian Co., "No information as to parents*,*" information on death provided by William B. Wooldridge, Superintendent (DR – page 39, No. 9)

Jasper, James – Black Male, killed April 3, 1867, Chesterfield "Explosion in pits," 30, collier, parents J. & S. Jasper, born in Chesterfield, information on death provided by Joe Jasper, father (DR – page 82, No. 48)

Jefferson, Charles – Black Male, killed April 3, 1867, Bright Hope Mine, Clover Hill, "Explosion in pit" (NPA – *Daily Dispatch*, April 6, 1867)

Jefferson, Redd – Black Male, killed April 3, 1867, Bright Hope Mine, Clover Hill, "Explosion in pit" (NPA – *Daily Dispatch*, April 6, 1867)

Jewett, [?] – White Male, killed [June 14?], 1844, Black Heath coal mine explosion, father of John Jewett killed March 19, 1855 (NPA – *New-York Daily Times*, March 23, 1855)

Jewett, Anderson – White Male, killed February 3, 1882, Midlothian Dist., "Killed Grove Shaft," explosion, 31, miner, parents George & Martha, information on death provided by George Jewett (DR – page [2], No. 55, NPA – *Daily Dispatch*, February 4 and 5, 1882, lists an A. W. Jewett on 4th and A. A. Jewett on 5th)

Jewett, Andrew J. – White Male, killed February 3, 1882, Chesterfield Mid Lothian Pits, "killed by explosion of gas" [Grove Shaft], 30, miner, parents Geo. W. & Martha Jewett, born in Chesterfield, information on death provided by Elizabeth Clayton, mother-in-law (DR – page 3, No. 94, NPA – *Daily Dispatch*,

February 4 and 5, 1882, lists an A. W. Jewett on 4th and A. A. Jewett on 5th)

Jewett, George, Jr. – White Male, killed February 3, 1882, Midlothian Dist., "Killed Grove Shaft," explosion, 21, miner, parents George & Martha, born in Midlothian Dist. (DR – page [2], No. 53, NPA – *Daily Dispatch*, February 4 and 5, 1882)

Jewett, Jonathan – White Male, killed March 19, 1855, Midlothian Mining Co, explosion, 13 (NPA – *Daily Dispatch*, March 21 and 22, 1855, *New-York Daily Times*, March 23, 1855)

Johnson, Edmond – Black Male, killed April 3, 1867, Bright Hope Mine, Clover Hill, "Explosion in pit" (NPA – *Daily Dispatch*, April 6, 1867)

Johnson, Isaac – Slave, Black Male, killed March 19, 1855 [incorrectly listed in DR as 1856], Midlothian Pits, "Killed by an explosion," owned by Midlothian Co., "No information as to parents," information on death provided by Wm. B. Wooldridge, Superintendent (Listed in 1856 DR – page 39, No. 36, NPA – *Daily Dispatch*, March 21 and 21, 1855)

Johnson, Stephen – Black Male, killed May 6, 1887, Chesterfield pits, "piece of coal fell in [on] him in pits" 45, miner, parents Stephen & Sylvia, born in Chesterfield pits, information on death provided by Mary A. Johnson, mother (DR – page 3, No. 90)

Jones, Albert – Black Male, killed April 3, 1867, Bright Hope Mine, Clover Hill, "Explosion in pit" (NPA – *Daily Dispatch*, April 6, 1867)

Jones, Edmund – Black Male, killed April 3, 1867, Bright Hope Mine, Clover Hill, "Explosion in pit" (NPA – *Daily Dispatch*, April 6, 1867)

Jones, John – White Male, killed May 15, 1854, Chesterfield's "English Coal Pits," "terrible explosion," (NPA – *Daily Dispatch*, May 16 and 25, 1854, *Daily South-side Democrat*, May 17, 1854)

Kain, Jeremiah – See Kane, Jeremiah

Kane, Jeremiah – White Male, killed May 15, 1854, Chesterfield's "English Coal Pits," "terrible explosion," (NPA – *Daily Dispatch*, May 16 and 25, 1854, *Daily South-side Democrat*, May 17, 1854, also listed as **Kain, Jeremiah**)

Kelly, William – Black Male, killed April 3, 1867, Bright Hope Mine, Clover Hill, "Explosion in pit," digger (NPA – *Daily Dispatch*, April 6, 1867)

Kennedy, Thomas – White Male, was alive after March 19, 1855 explosion, however died either March 20 or March 21, 1855, Midlothian Mining Co. pits, explosion, "a lad of 14 years of age," (NPA – *Daily Dispatch*, March 21 and 22, 1855, *New-York Daily Times*, March 22, 1855)

Kenney, William – See Kinney, William

Kerner, John T. – White Male, killed April 3, 1867, Bright Hope Mine, Clover Hill, "Explosion in pits," (NPA – *Daily Dispatch*, April 6, 1867)

Kinney, William – Slave, Black Male, killed March 19, 1855 [incorrectly listed in DR as 1856], Midlothian Pits, "Killed by an explosion," owned by A. S. Wooldridge estate, "No information as to parents," information on death provided by Wm. B. Wooldridge, Superintendent (Listed in 1856 DR – page 39, No. 21, NPA – *Daily Dispatch*, March 21 and 22, 1855, also listed as **Kenney, William**)

Kiver, John – White Male, killed May 15, 1854, Chesterfield's "English Coal Pits," "terrible explosion," (NPA – *Daily Dispatch*,

May 16 and 25, 1854, *Daily South-side Democrat*, May 17, 1854, also listed as **Kyper, John**)

Kyper, John – See Kiver, John

Lane, Jeremiah – White Male, killed May 15, 1854 [incorrectly listed in DR as 1855], Chesterfield "Explosion at Pits," 25, miner, parents unknown, born in Ireland, information on death provided by John W. Jones, friend (1855 DR – Page 26, No. 42)

Langford, Daniel – Black Male, killed April 3, 1867, Bright Hope Mine, Clover Hill, "Explosion in pit," digger (NPA – *Daily Dispatch*, April 6, 1867)

Lantern, Oran – See Clayton, Oran

Lapraid, Isham – Slave, Black Male, died September 1856, Midlothian Pits, no cause of death given, owned by Midlothian Co., "No information as to parents," information on death provided by Wm. B. Wooldridge, Superintendent (DR – page 39, No. 8)

Layton, Thomas – White Male, killed April 3, 1867, Bright Hope Mine, Clover Hill, "Explosion in pit," 30, parents, "unknown," born "unknown," collier/coal digger (DR – page 82, No. 49, NPA – *Daily Dispatch*, April 6, 1867)

Leigers, A. L. – See Leigers, Benjamin Antoine [?]

Leigers, Benjamin Antoine [?] – White Male, killed October 21, 1885, Chesterfield pits, "Killed by explosion of gas in coal pits," 33, miner, parents Ben & Caroline, born in Richmond, information on death provided by Susan A. Leigers, widow, "member of the Masonic Lodge at Winterpock" (DR – page 4, No. 114, NPA – *New-York Times*, October 23, 1885, *Richmond Dispatch*, October 23, 1885 also listed as **Leigers, A. L.**)

Lester, John – See Lister, John

Lester, Thomas – White Male, killed December 12, 1856, Midlothian Coal Pits, drowned, caused "by the rush of water" (NPA – *Daily South-side Democrat*, December 16, 1856)

Lister, John – White Male, killed March 19, 1855, Midlothian Coal Pits, explosion, 25, "A Native of England" (NPA – *Daily Dispatch*, March 21 and 22, 1855, *New-York Daily Times*, March 22 and 23, 1855, also listed as **Lester, John**, and personal observation of tombstone in Midlothian)

Lockett, Jim (James) – White Male, killed April 3, 1867, Bright Hope Mine, Clover Hill, "Explosion in pit," coal digger (NPA – *Daily Dispatch*, April 6, 1867, *Petersburg Index*, April 6, 1867)

Logan, Alexander – Black Male, killed February 3, 1882, Chesterfield's Grove Shaft explosion, 40 (NPA – *Daily Dispatch*, February 4 and 5, 1882)

Logan, Peter – White Male, killed April 3, 1867, Bright Hope mine, Clover Hill, "Explosion in pit," digger (NPA – *Daily Dispatch*, April 6, 1867, *Petersburg Index*, April 6, 1867)

Luke, Nicholas – [White ?] Male, killed November 26, 1855, Chesterfield County "dreadful explosion at the Black Heath Coal Mines" (NPA – *Daily Dispatch*, November 28, 1855, *Daily South-side Democrat*, November 29, 1855, *New-York Daily Times*, November 30, 1855)

Magruder, Hiram – White Male, killed April 3, 1867, Bright Hope Mine, Clover Hill, "Explosion in pit," banksman (NPA – *Daily Dispatch*, April 6, 1867)

Mann, Dick – Black Male, killed April 3, 1867, Bright Hope Mine, Clover Hill, "Explosion in pit," (NPA – *Daily Dispatch*, April 6, 1867)

Marshall, John – White Male, killed May 20, 1876, "old Midlothian coal-pits," Grove Shaft, gas explosion, "only about eighteen or twenty years old" (NPA – *Daily Dispatch,* May 23, 1876, *Rural Messenger,* May 27, 1876)

Marshall, John – [White ?] Male, killed November 26, 1855, Chesterfield County "dreadful explosion at the Black Heath Coal Mines," (NPA – *Daily Dispatch,* November 28, 1855, *Daily South-side Democrat,* November 29, 1855, *New-York Daily Times,* November 30, 1855)

Marshall, William H. – White Male, killed February 3, 1882, Chesterfield's Grove Shaft explosion, foreman, 45 (NPA – *Daily Dispatch,* February 4 and 5, 1882, *New-York Tribune,* February 5, 1882)

Martin, Mark – Slave, Black Male, killed December 12, 1856, Midlothian coal pits, drowned, caused "by the rush of water," owned by William E. Martin (NPA – *Daily South-side Democrat,* December 16, 1856)

Martin, Mack – Slave, Black Male, killed October 1856, Midlothian Pits, "Drowned," owned by William E. Martin, "No information as to parents," information on death provided by William B. Wooldridge, Superintendent (DR – page 39, No. 15)

McTyre, Elijah – Black Male, killed April 3, 1867, Bright Hope Mine, Clover Hill, "Explosion in pit," digger (NPA – *Daily Dispatch,* April 6, 1867)

Miles, Frank – Black Male, killed April 3, 1867, Bright Hope Mine, Clover Hill, "Explosion in pit," (NPA – *Daily Dispatch,* April 6, 1867)

Millington, John – White Male, killed October 1874, Clover Hill "Accident in Mines," 20, miner, parents – "not known," born –

"not known," information on death provided by L.W. Wilkenson [?], Manager at Mines (DR – page [4], No. 31)

Mills, Edward – Slave, Black Male, killed December 12, 1856, Midlothian coal pits, drowned, caused "by the rush of water," owned by Nicholas Mills, Esq. (NPA – *Daily South-side Democrat*, December 16, 1856)

Mills, Frank (Francis) – Slave, Black Male, killed March [19] 1855 [incorrectly listed in DR as 1856], Midlothian Pits, "Killed by an explosion," no age listed, owned by Nicholas Mills, "No information as to parents," information on death provided by Wm. B. Wooldridge, Superintendent (Listed in 1856 DR – page 39, No. 27, NPA – *Daily Dispatch*, March 21 and 22, 1855)

Mills, James – Black Male, killed February 3, 1882, Chesterfield's Grove Shaft explosion, 30 (NPA – *Daily Dispatch*, February 4 and 5, 1882)

Mills, Ned – Slave, Black Male, killed October 1856, Midlothian Pits, "Drowned," owned by Nicholas Mills, "No information as to parents," information on death provided by William B. Wooldridge, Superintendent (DR – page 39, No. 12)

Mills, Patrick – Slave, Black Male, killed March 19, 1855 [incorrectly listed in DR as 1856], Midlothian Pits, "Killed by an explosion," owned by Nicholas Mills, "No information as to parents," information on death provided by Wm. B. Wooldridge, Superintendent (Listed in 1856 DR – page 39, No. 26, NPA – *Daily Dispatch*, March 21 and 22, 1855)

Mills, Willis (William) – Slave, Black Male, killed March 19, 1855 [incorrectly listed in DR as 1856], Midlothian Pits, "Killed by an explosion," owned by Nicholas Mills, "No information as to parents," information on death provided by William B. Wooldridge, Superintendent (Listed in 1856 DR – page 39, No.

25, NPA – *Daily Dispatch*, March 21 and 22, 1855, also listed as **Mills, Wilson**)

Mills, Wilson – See Mills, William

Moore, Geo. [George] W. – White Male, killed April 3, 1867, Bright Hope Mine, Clover Hill, "Explosion in pits," 39, collier/digger, parents "unknown," born in Chesterfield, information on death provided by Geo. [George] Moore, son (DR – page 81, No. 2, NPA – *Daily Dispatch*, April 6,1867, *Petersburg Index*, April 6, 1867)

Morgan, Richard – Black Male, killed February 3, 1882, Midlothian Dist., "Killed Grove Shaft," explosion, 39, miner, parents Jacob & Rebecca, information on death provided by Amy [?] Morgan, wife (DR – page [2], No. 57, NPA – *Daily Dispatch*, February 4 and 5, 1882)

Morris, John – White Male, killed February 3, 1882, Chesterfield's Grove Shaft explosion, 23 (NPA – *Daily Dispatch*, February 4 and 5, 1882, *New-York Tribune*, February 5, 1882)

Morris, William – Black Male, killed May 20, 1876, "old Midlothian coal-pits," Grove Shaft, gas explosion (NPA – *Daily Dispatch,* May 23, 1876, *Rural Messenger*, May 27, 1876)

Nunnally, C. E. – White Male, killed February 16 [?], 1874, Clover Hill, "Accident in Mines," 32, miner, born in Chesterfield, information provided by Harriet A. Nunnally, wife (DR – page [4], No. 32)

Nunnally, W. H. – White Male, killed February 16 [?], 1874, Clover Hill, "Accident in Mines," 25, miner, born in Chesterfield, information on death provided by Harriet A. Nunnally, sister-in-law (DR – page [4], No. 33)

Orange – See Clayton, Oran

Osborne, Daniel – Black Male, killed April 3, 1867, Bright Hope Mine, Clover Hill, "Explosion in pit," digger (NPA – *Daily Dispatch*, April 6, 1867)

Owens, Henry – Black Male, killed April 3, 1867, Bright Hope Mine, Clover Hill, "Explosion in pit," digger (NPA – *Daily Dispatch*, April 6, 1867)

Owens, John – Black Male, killed April 3, 1867, Bright Hope Mine, Clover Hill, "Explosion in pit," mule driver (NPA – *Daily Dispatch*, April 6, 1867)

Palmer, Isaac – White Male, killed April 13, 1859, Bright Hope Pits, explosion, 45, miner (NPA – *Daily Express*, April 15, 1859, *Petersburg Daily Intelligencer*, April 15, 1859, also listed as **Farmer, Isaac**)

Palmer, William – White Male, killed May 15, 1854, Chesterfield's "English Coal Pits," "terrible explosion," (NPA – *Daily Dispatch*, May 16 and 25, 1854, *Daily South-side Democrat*, May 17, 1854)

Parmer, Isaac – White Male, killed February 9, 1880, Chesterfield, Bright Hope Coal Pit explosion, "Killed in pits," 25, miner, parents Henry & Elizabeth Parmer, born in England, information on death provided by Eddie E. Parmer, widow (DR – page 3, No. 95

Patterson, Giles – Black Male, killed April 3, 1867, Bright Hope Mine, Clover Hill, "Explosion in pit" (NPA – *Daily Dispatch*, April 6, 1867)

Peacock, John (or Jabez) – White Male, killed May 15, 1854, Chesterfield's "English Coal Pits," "terrible explosion," "boy" (NPA – *Daily Dispatch*, May 16, and 25, 1854, *Daily South-side Democrat*, May 17, 1854)

Percell, William – See Purcell, William

Pickett, Henry – See Puckett, Henry

Pollard, Major – Black Male, killed February 3, 1882, Chesterfield's Grove Shaft explosion, 30 (NPA – *Daily Dispatch*, February 4 and 5, 1882)

Pope, Herrod [Herod] – Slave, Black Male, killed March 19, 1855, Midlothian Pits, "Killed by an explosion," owned by Charles Pope, miner, parents "Not Known," born "Not Known," information on death provided by W. B. Wooldridge, Superintendent, insured by owner in the United States Life Insurance office (Listed in original ledger at Library of Virginia State Record Center at end of 1856 DR – page 40, No. 1, NPA – *Daily Dispatch*, March 21 and 22, 1855)

Pringle, J. W. – White Male, killed December 12, 1856, Midlothian Coal Pits, drowned, caused "by the rush of water" (NPA – *Daily South-side Democrat*, December 16, 1856)

Pringle, Wm. – White Male, killed March [19] 1855, Midlothian Pits, "Killed by an explosion," miner, parents "Not Known," born in England, information provided by W. B. Wooldridge, Superintendent (Listed at end of 1856 DR – page 40, No. 8)

Puckett, George – White Male, killed April 3, 1867, Bright Hope Mine, Clover Hill, "Explosion in pits," 30, collier, parents J. & S. Puckett, born in Chesterfield, information on death provided by J. Puckett, father (DR – page 81, No. 4, NPA – *Daily Dispatch*, April 6, 1867)

Puckett, Henry – Slave, Black Male, killed March 19, 1855 [incorrectly listed in DR as 1856], Midlothian Pits, "Killed by an explosion," owned by Nicholas Mills, "No information as to parents," information on death provided by Wm. B. Wooldridge, Superintendent (Listed in 1856 DR – page 39, No. 29, NPA –

Daily Dispatch, March 21 and 22, 1855, also listed as **Pickett, Henry**)

Puckett, James (Jim) – White Male, killed April 3, 1867, Bright Hope Mine, Clover Hill, "Explosion in pits," 25[?], collier, parents J. & S. Puckett, born in Chesterfield, information on death provided by J. Puckett, father (DR – page 81, No. 5, NPA – *Daily Dispatch*, April 6, 1867)

Puckett, Thomas – White Male, killed April 3, 1867, Bright Hope Mine, Clover Hill, "Explosion in pits," 40, collier, parents J. & S. Puckett, born in Chesterfield, information on death provided by J. Puckett, father (DR – page 81, No. 6, NPA – *Daily Dispatch*, April 6, 1867)

Purcell, William – Slave, Black Male, killed March 19, 1855 [incorrectly listed in DR as 1856], Midlothian Pits, "Killed by an explosion," owned by Midlothian Co., "No information as to parents," information on death provided by Wm. B. Wooldridge, Superintendent (Listed in 1856 DR – page 39, No. 40, NPA – *Daily Dispatch*, March 21 and 22, 1855, also listed as **Percell, William**)

Railey, Fender – Slave, Black Male, killed March 19, 1855 [incorrectly listed in DR as 1856], Midlothian Pits, "Killed by an explosion," owned by Midlothian Co., "No information as to parents," information on death provided by Wm. B. Wooldridge, Superintendent (Listed in 1856 DR – page 39, No. 34, NPA – *Daily Dispatch*, March 21 and 22, 1855, also listed as **Riley, Fendall**)

Rightshaw, Joseph – See Shaw, Joseph

Riley, Fendall – See Raily, Fender

Ritchie, Armstead – Slave, Black Male, killed March 19, 1855 [incorrectly listed in DR as 1856], Midlothian Pits, "Killed by an explosion," owned by Midlothian Co., "No information as to parents," information on death provided by Wm. B. Wooldridge, Superintendent (Listed in 1856 DR – page 39, No. 30, NPA – *Daily Dispatch*, March 21 and 22, 1855)

Ritchie, Bristove – Slave, Black Male, killed October 1856, Midlothian Pits, "Drowned," owned by Midlothian Co., "No information as to parents", information on death provided by Wm. B. Wooldridge, Superintendent (DR – page 39, No. 10)

Roberts, N. P. (Nat.) – White Male, killed April 3, 1867, Bright Hope Mine, Clover Hill, "Explosion in Pits," 35, collier, parents "unknown," born in Dinwiddie, information provided by Geo. Garbett (DR – page 82, No. 43, NPA – *Daily Dispatch*, April 6, 1867, *Petersburg Index* – April 6, 1867)

Robertson, James Holt – White Male, killed February 1895, Chesterfield pits, "killed by a tumble in Cox shaft pits," 20, miner, parents William Z. & Cornettia [?] Ann, born in Chesterfield, information on death provided by William Z. Robertson, father (DR – page 3, No. 99)

Robertson, William B. – See Robinson, Wm. B.

Robinson, Bob – Slave, Black Male, killed March 25, 1860, Chesterfield, "Killed in pits," 58, owned by G. H. Robertson, information on death provided by G. H. Robertson, owner (DR – page 51, No. 24)

Robinson, James – Black Male, killed February 1878, Bermuda [district], "Killed in pitts," 68, miner, parents "Not known," information on death provided by Phebe Robinson, widow (DR – page [5], No. 37)

Robinson, Wm. B. – White Male, killed April 3, 1867, Bright Hope Mine, Clover Hill, "Explosion in pit," banksman (NPA – *Daily Dispatch*, April 6, 1867, *Petersburg Index*, April 6, 1867 listed as **Robertson, William B.**)

Ross, Edward (Ed) – Black Male, killed February 3, 1882, Chesterfield's Grove Shaft explosion, 55, miner (NPA – *Daily Dispatch*, February 4, 5, and 7, 1882, also listed as **Ross, Ned**)

Ross, Ned – See **Ross, Edward**

Rynard, John – White Male, killed March 18, 1839, Black Heath Mine, explosion, superintendent (NPA – *Richmond Enquirer*, March 23, 1839)

Selden, Jim – Black Male, killed April 3, 1867, Bright Hope Mine explosion, Clover Hill, "Explosion in pit," digger (NPA – *Daily Dispatch*, April 6, 1867)

Selden, Richard – Black Male, killed November 5, 1880, Mid Lothian, "Mine accident," 18, miner, parent Martha Reynolds, born in Chesterfield Co., information provided by Martha Reynolds, mother (DR – page [3], No. 23)

Shaw, Joseph – White Male, killed May 15, 1854, Chesterfield's "English Coal Pits," "terrible explosion," "boy" (NPA – *Daily Dispatch* – May 16 and 25, 1854, *Daily South-side Democrat*, May 17, 1854, also listed as **Rightshaw, Joseph**)

Shields, Joseph – White Male, killed February 3, 1882, Chesterfield's Grove Shaft explosion, 50 (NPA – *Daily Dispatch*, February 4 and 5, 1882)

Simeon – Slave, Black Male, date killed "not Rem." [listed in 1856 section], "Bever Pits," "Killed in the Pit," 60, owned by Jas. R. McTyre, information on death provided by Gustavus Robinson,

Manager (Listed in original ledger at Library of Virginia State Record Center in 1856 DR – page 11, No. 7)

Simms, William – Black Male, killed April 3, 1867, Bright Hope Mine, Clover Hill, "Explosion in pit," (NPA – *Daily Dispatch*, April 6, 1867)

Smith, George – White Male, killed April 13, 1859, Chesterfield's Bright Hope Coal Pit, explosion, 35 (NPA – *Daily Express*, April 15, 1859, *Petersburg Daily Intelligencer*, April 15, 1859)

Spears, Henry – Slave, Black Male, killed March 19, 1855 [incorrectly listed in DR as 1856], Midlothian Pits, "Killed by an explosion," no age listed, owned by Midlothian Co., *"No information as to parents,"* information on death provided by Wm. B. Wooldridge, Superintendent (Listed in 1856 DR – page 39, No. 35, NPA – *Daily Dispatch*, March 21 and 22, 1855)

Stewart, Pleasant – Black Male, killed February 3, 1882, Chesterfield's Grove Shaft explosion, 30 (NPA – *Daily Dispatch*, February 4 and 5, 1882)

Stokes, Simon – Black Male, killed April 3, 1867, Bright Hope Mine, Clover Hill, "Explosion in pit" (NPA – *Daily Dispatch*, April 6, 1867)

Summels, Robert – See Summels, Thomas

Summels, Thomas – Black Male, killed February 3, 1882, Chesterfield's Grove Shaft explosion, 40 (NPA – *Daily Dispatch* February 4, 5, and 7, 1882, *New-York Tribune*, February 6, 1882, also listed as **Summels, Robert**)

Syrah, Moses – See Cyra, Moses

Taylor, Richard – Black Male, killed October 1889, Chesterfield, "killed in pits by cars," 16, miner, parents Reuben & Emma, born in Chesterfield, information on death provided by Reuben Taylor, father (DR – page 4, No. 133)

Taylor, Solomon – Black Male, killed February 3, 1882, Chesterfield's Grove Shaft explosion, 40, miner (NPA – *Daily Dispatch*, February 4 and 5, 1882)

Thomas, William H. – White Male, killed April 3, 1867, Bright Hope Mine, Clover Hill, "Explosion in pits," 43, collier, coal digger, parents W. & J. Thomas, born in Chesterfield, information provided by wife (DR – page 81, No. 9, NPA – *Daily Dispatch*, April 6, 1867)

Thompson, Charles – [White ?] Male, killed November 26, 1855, Chesterfield County "dreadful explosion at the Black Heath Coal Mines," (NPA – *Daily Dispatch*, November 28, 1855, *Daily South-side Democrat*, November 29, 1855, *New-York Daily Times*, November 30, 1855)

Thurman, John B. – White Male, killed May 15, 1854 [incorrectly listed in DR as 1855], Chesterfield, "English Coal Pits," "Explosion at Pits," 29, parents "not known," born "not known," miner, information on death provided by John R. Vest, friend (1855 DR listed twice page 18 No. 7, page 27 No. 7, NPA – *Daily Dispatch*, May 16 and 25, 1854, *Daily South-side Democrat*, May 17, 1854)

Thweatt, William – Black Male, killed April 3, 1867, Bright Hope Mine, Clover Hill, "Explosion in pit" (NPA – *Daily Dispatch*, April 6, 1867)

Tompkins, Thomas – White Male, killed May 15, 1854, Chesterfield's "English Coal Pits," "terrible explosion," (NPA – *Daily Dispatch*, May 16, 1854, *Daily South-side Democrat*, May 17, 1854)

Traylor, Geo. [George] – White Male, killed April 3, 1867, Bright Hope Mine, Clover Hill, "Explosion in pit," mule driver (NPA – *Daily Dispatch*, April 6, 1867)

Trent, Ellet – Black Male, killed April 3, 1867, Bright Hope Mine, Clover Hill, "Explosion in pit" (NPA – *Daily Dispatch*, April 6, 1867)

Turpin, Joe – Black Male, killed April 3, 1867, Bright Hope Mine, Clover Hill, "Explosion in pit," "timberer" (NPA – *Daily Dispatch*, April 6, 1867)

Vest, George W. – White Male, killed July 1876, Chesterfield "Killed in pits," 50, born in Chesterfield, information on death provided by Geo. M. Wilson, clerk at pits (DR – page 3 No. 114)

Vest, Henry – See Vest, Patrick H.

Vest, Patrick H. – White Male, killed May 15, 1854, [incorrectly listed in DR as 1855], Chesterfield, "English Coal Pits," "Explosion at Pits," 26, miner, parents Ro. and Louisa Vest, born in Chesterfield information on death provided by John R. Vest, father (1855 DR listed twice page 18, No. 3, DR page 27, No. 3, NPA – *Daily Dispatch* May 16 and 25, 1854, *Daily South-side Democrat*, May 17, 1854, also listed as **Vest, Henry**)

Vest, Samuel – White Male, killed May 15, 1854, [incorrectly listed in DR as 1855], Chesterfield, "English Coal Pits," "Explosion at Pits," 21, miner, parents Ro. & Louisa Vest, born in Chesterfield, information on death provided by John R. Vest, father (1855 DR listed twice page 18, No. 2, DR page 27, No. 2; NPA – *Daily Dispatch*, May 16 and 25, 1854, *Daily South-side Democrat*, May 17, 1854)

Walker, Isaac – Slave, Black Male, killed March [19], 1855 [incorrectly listed in DR as 1856], Midlothian Pits, "Killed by an explosion," owned by A. S. Wooldridge, "No information as to parents," information on death provided by William B. Wooldridge, Superintendent (Listed in 1856 DR – page 39, No. 18, NPA – *Daily Dispatch*, March 21 and 22, 1855, initially listed as "badly burned" and "in a dying condition")

Washington, Daniel – Slave, Black Male, killed December 12, 1856, Midlothian coal pits, drowned, caused "by the rush of water," owned by the Midlothian Company (NPA – *Daily South-side Democrat*, December 16, 1856)

Washington, Daniel – Slave, Black Male, killed October 1856, Midlothian Pits, "Drowned," owned by Midlothian Co., "No information as to parents," information on death provided by William B. Wooldridge, Superintendent (DR – page 39, No. 11)

Weal, Jack – White Male, killed April 3, 1867, Bright Hope Mine, Clover Hill, "Explosion in pit," 30 [?], collier/gas man, parents "unknown," born in Chesterfield, information provided by Mrs. Weal, wife (DR – page 82, No. 33, NPA – *Daily Dispatch*, April 6, 1867, *Petersburg Index*, April 6, 1867)

White, Bristol – Slave, Black Male, killed December 12, 1856, Midlothian Coal Pits, drowned, caused "by the rush of water," owned by the Midlothian Company (NPA – *Daily South-side Democrat*, December 16, 1856)

Wilchilo, Patrick – Slave, Black Male, killed March 19, 1855, Midlothian Pits, "Killed by an Explosion," miner, owned by Wilchilo's estate, parents "Not Known," born "Not Known," information on death provided by W. B. Wooldridge, Superintendent, insured by the United States Life Insurance office (Listed at end of 1856 DR – page 40, No. 5, NPA – *Daily Dispatch*, March 21 and 22, 185, also listed as **Wincheloe, Patrick** and **Witchelow, Patrick**)

William – Slave, Black Male, killed February 13, 1858, Chesterfield "Killed at the pits," 23, parents [incorrectly listed as

Jno. & S. [?] A. Forloine], born in Chester[field?], owned by Jas.[?] C.[?] Gates, information on death provided by Jas.[?] C.[?] Gates, owner (DR – page 48, No. 34)

Williams, Charles – Slave, Black Male, killed March 19, 1855, Midlothian Pits, explosion, owned by Midlothian Co., (NPA – *Daily Dispatch*, March 22, 1855)

Williams, Robert – White Male, killed May 15, 1854, Chesterfield's "English Coal Pits," "terrible explosion," (NPA – *Daily Dispatch* – May 16, 17, 25 1854, *Daily Southside Democrat*, May 17, 1854)

Wilson, Charles – Slave, Black Male, killed March 19, 1855 [incorrectly listed in DR as 1856], Midlothian Pits, "Killed by an explosion," owned by Midlothian Co., "No information as to parents," information on death provided by Wm. B. Wooldridge, Superintendent (Listed in 1856 DR – page 39, No. 32, NPA – *Daily Dispatch*, March 21 and 22, 1855)

Wincheloe, Patrick – See Wilchilo, Patrick

Witchelow, Patrick – See Wilchilo, Patrick

Wood, Aaron – Black Male, killed April 3, 1867, Bright Hope Mine, Clover Hill, "Explosion in pit," digger (NPA – *Daily Dispatch*, April 6, 1867)

Wooldridge, Alfred – Slave, Black Male, killed March 19, 1855 [incorrectly listed in DR as 1856], Midlothian Pits, "Killed by an explosion," owned by A. S. Wooldridge, "No information as to parents," information on death provided by Wm. B. Wooldridge, Superintendent (Listed in 1856 DR – page 39, No. 16, NPA – *Daily Dispatch*, March 21 and 22, 1855)

Wooldridge, Archer – Slave, Black Male, killed March 19, 1855 incorrectly listed in DR as 1856], Midlothian Pits, "Killed by an explosion," owned by A. S. Wooldridge, "No information as to parents," information on death provided by Wm. B. Wooldridge, Superintendent (Listed in 1856 DR – page 39, No. 17, NPA – *Daily Dispatch*, March 21 and 22, 1855)

Wooldridge, Archer – Black Male, killed March 1874, Clover Hill "Accident in Mine," 70, born in Chesterfield, miner, information on death provided by Sarah Wooldridge, wife (DR – page 4, No. 48)

Wright, William – White Male, killed March 19, 1855, Midlothian Coal pits, explosion, "a boy" (NPA – *Daily Dispatch*, March 22, 1855, *New-York Daily Times*, March 23, 1855)

KILLED, NAMES UNKNOWN:

Unknowns – **"Some,"** killed approximately 1810, "Heath's pits" explosion (Humphrey, p. 7)

Unknowns – **"Some workman killed**," 1818, "Heath's pits," (Humphrey, p. 3)

Unknown – **1** Slave, Black Male killed, 1835 [?] – from "foul gas" in Randolph's Chesterfield coal mine (Leigh, Benjamin Watkins 1867.)

Unknowns – **51**, Black Males [Slaves?] killed March 18, 1839, explosion Chesterfield's Black Heath mine, "laborers were all colored men" (Humphrey, p. 6; NPA – *Richmond Enquirer*, March 23, 1839)

Unknowns – **"Some,"** killed 1840, Chesterfield's Will's pits, explosion, (Humphrey, p. 7)

Unknowns – **10**, killed June 14, 1844, Black Heath explosion (Humphrey, p. 6)

Unknowns – 7, killed 1850, Clover Hill Company's Cox Pits, explosion (Humphrey, p. 6)

Unknowns – 3, killed 1854, Bright Hope Company's Pits cave-in (Lutz, *Chesterfield*, p. 215)

Unknowns – 10, killed March 19, 1855, Midlothian's Grove Shaft explosion (Humphrey, p. 6; NPA – *Daily Dispatch*, March 21 and 22, 1855)

Unknowns – 5 Slaves, Black Males, killed April 13, 1859, Chesterfield's Bright Hope Coal Pit, gas explosion, two of the slaves were insured and owned by S. D. Wooldridge, two of the slaves were insured and owned by Mr. Chas. [Charles] Brewer, and the fifth slave was insured and owned by Mr. Absalom Martin. (NPA – *Daily Express*, April 13, 1859; Humphrey, p. 6)

Unknowns – 17, including 15 Slaves, Black Males, killed December 10, 1863, Chesterfield's Raccoon Slope explosion, "Most of the slaves were owned by the Chesterfield Coal Mine Company." (NPA – *Daily Dispatch*, December 15, 1863; Humphrey, p. 6)

Unknowns – 3, killed 1875, Chesterfield's Raccoon Co. mine – explosion (Humphrey, p. 7)

PRESUMED KILLED, RECORDS UNCLEAR:
(Not included in total count killed)

Berry, Richard – White Male, April 3, 1867, Bright Hope Mine, Clover Hill Pits, explosion (on part of list introduced as "most of whom must, of course, be put upon the dead list," in NPA – *Petersburg Index*, April 6, 1867)

Bertlam, George – White Male, April 3, 1867, Bright Hope Mine, Clover Hill Pits, explosion, "boy," driver (on part of list introduced as "most of whom must, of course, be put upon the dead list," in NPA – *Petersburg Index*, April 6, 1867)

Garbert, George – White Male, April 3, 1867, Bright Hope Mine, Clover Hill Pits, explosion, digger (on part of list introduced as "most of whom must, of course, be put upon the dead list," in NPA – *Petersburg Index*, April 6, 1867)

Garbert, John – White Male, April 3, 1867, Bright Hope Mine, Clover Hill Pits, explosion, digger (on part of list introduced as "most of whom must, of course, be put upon the dead list," in NPA – *Petersburg Index*, April 6, 1867)

Jordan, B. L. – White Male, April 3, 1867, Bright Hope Mine, Clover Hill Pits, explosion, digger (on part of list introduced as "most of whom must, of course, be put upon the dead list," in NPA – *Petersburg Index*, April 6, 1867)

Marshall, Thomas – White Male, April 3, 1867, Bright Hope Mine, Clover Hill Pits, explosion, gasman (on part of list introduced as "most of whom must, of course, be put upon the dead list," in NPA – *Petersburg Index*, April 6, 1867)

Palmer, Henry – White Male, April 3, 1867, Bright Hope Mine, Clover Hill Pits, explosion, digger (on part of list introduced as "most of whom must, of course, be put upon the dead list," in NPA – *Petersburg Index*, April 6, 1867)

Richards, William – White Male, April 3, 1867, Bright Hope Mine, Clover Hill Pits, explosion, digger (on part of list introduced as "most of whom must, of course, be put upon the dead list," in NPA – *Petersburg Index*, April 6, 1867)

Smith, Jack – White Male, April 3, 1867, Bright Hope Mine, Clover Hill Pits, explosion, overseer of trailers (on part of list introduced as "most of whom must, of course, be put upon the dead list," in NPA – *Petersburg Index*, April 6, 1867)

INJURED (per newspaper articles):

Cotton, George – White Male, November 26, 1855, "seriously burned and bruised," Chesterfield County "dreadful explosion at the Black Heath Coal Mines," 20 (NPA – *Daily Dispatch,* November 28, 1855, *Daily South-side Democrat,* November 29, 1855, *New York Daily Times,* November 30, 1855)

Gray, John – Slave, Black Male, March 19, 1855, "slightly" injured, Midlothian Coal pits, explosion, owned by A. S. Wooldridge (NPA – *Daily Dispatch,* March 21 and 22, 1855)

Hart, Samuel – See Hunt, Samuel

Howe, John – White Male, injured in March 19, 1855, "badly burned," Midlothian Coal Pits, explosion (NPA – *Daily Democrat,* March 21 and 22, 1855, *New-York Daily Times,* March 21, 1855)

Hunt, Samuel – White Male, injured in March 19, 1855, "dreadfully burned," Midlothian Coal Pits, explosion, 14 (NPA – *Daily Dispatch,* March 21 and 22, 1855, *New York Daily Times,* March 22, 1855, also listed as **Hart, Samuel**)

Johnson, Benjamin – Male, January 1882, Grove Shaft, "badly burned by the gas" (NPA – *Daily Democrat,* February 4, 1882)

Jones, Anthony – Slave, Black Male, March 19, 1855, "slightly" injured, Midlothian Coal Pits, explosion, owned by Nicholas Mills (NPA – *Daily Dispatch,* March 21 and 22, 1855)

Jones, Frederick – Slave, Black Male, March 19, 1855, "slightly" injured, Midlothian Coal Pits, explosion, owned by Midlothian Company (NPA – *Daily Dispatch,* March 21 and 22, 1855)

Lucas, David – Black Male, October 21, 1885, "was himself a little scorched," Clover Hill coal mine, explosion, (NPA – *New-York Times,* October 23, 1885; *Richmond Dispatch,* October 23, 1885)

Minor, Isaac – Slave, Black Male, March 19, 1855, "badly" injured, Midlothian Coal Pits, explosion, owned by Midlothian Company (NPA – *Daily Dispatch*, March 21 and 22, 1855)

Monroe, Lewis – Slave, Black Male, March 19, 1855, "slightly" injured, Midlothian Coal Pits, explosion, owned by Midlothian Company (NPA – *Daily Dispatch*, March 21 and 22, 1855)

Smith, Dick – Slave, Black Male, March 19, 1855, "slightly burned," Midlothian Coal pits, explosion, owned by Midlothian Company (NPA – *Daily Dispatch*, March 21 and 22, 1855)

Talbot, Henry – Slave, Black Male, March 19, 1855, "slightly" injured, Midlothian Coal Pits, explosion (NPA – *Daily Dispatch*, March 21, 1855)

Taliaferro, Henry – Slave, Black Male, March 19, 1855, "slightly injured, Midlothian Coal Pits, explosion, owned by Midlothian Company (NPA – *Daily Dispatch*, March 22, 1855)

White, Joel (Joe) – Slave, Black Male, March 19, 1855, "recovery doubtful," Midlothian Coal Pits, explosion, owned by Midlothian Company (NPA – *Daily Dispatch*, March 21 and 22, 1855)

Wright, William – Black Male, November 1855, "seriously burned and bruised," "dreadful explosion at the Black Heath Coal Mines," "and it was thought would die" (NPA – *Daily Dispatch*, November 28, 1855, *Daily South-side Democrat*, November 29, 1855, *New-York Daily Times*, November 30, 1855)

PROBABLE MINING DEATH:

Godfrey – Slave, Black Male, killed November 20, 1847, Midlothian, "Burned to death," 50, miner, owned by Nicholas Mills.[51]

The Slave Insurance Records, discussed in Chapter Three, show Godfrey was insured for two consecutive years by his owner, Nicholas Mills. The first policy dated March 31, 1846, lists Godfrey's occupation as "Miner at the Midlothian Mines." The second policy was taken out on Godfrey's life on March 30, 1847 and stated his occupation was a "miner" and the city of his death was Midlothian.[52] Although the record does not officially state the location of death specifically as a coal mine, the likelihood seemed plausible. Considering the numerous slaves Mr. Mills worked in the coal mines, and the nine that are listed as killed in the list, it appeared reasonable to include Godfrey as another one of the unfortunate victims.

Hopefully Godfrey found comfort in eternity, for his name means "peace of God."[53]

CHAPTER THREE

The Insurance Records

The Richmond Coal Basin, which includes Chesterfield County, was the site of the first commercial coal mining starting in 1748.[1] Earlier mine operations in the county are documented by the Virginia Historical Marker stating, "Coal was first mined here before 1730."[2] Considering the established practice in mining by the early 1800s, the county may have another title to add to its list. The county may hold the distinction of having the first coal-mining slaves in the country to be insured by their owners. Individual slave owners as well as corporations were beneficiaries of life insurance policies they purchased on their slaves.

Solid evidence exists to verify individual and corporate participation in the practice in Chesterfield County. In the nineteenth century, several insurance companies sold slave life insurance policies covering miners in the area. Apparently specific records for all of the companies involved in the business have not survived. However, enough company records exist to tell the story. The Slave Insurance List at the end of this chapter presents the compiled results.

The California Department of Insurance website proved to be a key initial source for policy information. In 2000 a state law was passed requiring insurance companies that conduct business in California to provide the slave insurance records of the company's predecessors. Companies had until October 2001, to provide the information to the state insurance office.[3] According to a newspaper article published in May 2002, "Some companies said they could not find such records, and others said the files had long since been destroyed or found only oblique references to slavery."[4]

Additional information was compiled from a variety of sources. The most significant primary documentation proved to be from the Nautilus Insurance Company, which insured many slaves in the Chesterfield County mines. Fortunately, Nautilus's successor, the New York Life Insurance Company, gifted its insurance policy ledgers to a public archive located in New York.

These valuable historical ledgers provided the majority of the names and data for the Slave Insurance List at the end of this chapter.

Not all companies that insured slaves conducted business in California, so continued research was necessary to locate additional slave insurers. That research revealed the Baltimore Life Insurance Company (BLIC) also insured slaves in Chesterfield County. Portions of the BLIC records, along with other insurance companies' records, have been compiled in the list for policies sold between 1846 and 1864.

Knowledge of the Baltimore Life Insurance Company's activities was first obtained by reviewing a book written by Mr. Jerry Hynson.[5] The book's introduction, written by Ms. Sharon Murphy, was also helpful.[6] As a result of guidance provided, a review of the BLIC records took place and a prolific amount of correspondence was discovered relating to Chesterfield County. The letters, written by company representatives, slave owners, and agents, led to critical discoveries about the insurance business. They communicated powerful messages and evoked images of the slave insurance business that the other records did not convey.

One significant letter was dated January 11, 1855. The correspondence from a Baltimore Life Insurance Company agent, Mr. Thomas Pollard, was addressed to the Secretary of the BLIC, Mr. Henry Thompson. The letter expounded upon the risks of insuring slaves in the coal mines in the area, thus providing valuable insight into the considerations surrounding the insurance transactions.[7]

The BLIC representative "conferred with several gentlemen who have experience on this subject." Major Wooldridge, President of the Mid Lothian Coal Mining Company, was one of the individuals questioned. Apparently he reported, "they have not lost any hands in his pits from gas since he has been connected with them...." Major Wooldridge referred to a twenty-year period of safety.[8]

Although Wooldridge's words were perhaps true, consider the wording a bit closer, and review the Records of Death again. Note that tragedies, including explosions, took place in the county's coal mines during that period. After all, the purpose of the inquiry by the BLIC was to determine if the mines in the area were safe. Since the guidelines for making that determination are unknown at this time, the risk parameters may have been very broad.

Mr. Pollard, the Richmond agent, mentioned the Black Heath pits specifically. "As at present advice I would not recommend insuring hands in these pits at any premium." He indicated which mines he felt were safer. "In the pits on the North side of the James River, lying in Henrico and Goochland, they have never had any accidents from gas."[9] All of the Chesterfield County coal mines, including the Black Heath pits, were south of the James River.

Since BLIC recommended denial only for Black Heath, the chain of insurance discussion continued. As evidenced by slave insurance rate schedules accompanying the letter, Mr. Pollard presented information from three area insurance companies to assess competitiveness. The Richmond Fire Insurance Company rates were directly quoted as part of the analysis. Also provided for review were the National Safety Life Insurance and Trust Company of Philadelphia and the National Loan Fund and Life Assurance Co. of London rates.[10]

It was determined that the competition's slave insurance pricing was lower than BLIC's rates, which was a concern. The company was advised to be aware of the possibility of losing business to its competitors. The following marketplace commentary was provided. "Insurance on negroes can only be made profitable by insuring a large number." A specific statement regarding the slave miner insurance pool was not made. However, in the same letter, the agent indicates the company would do well by insuring white persons. "We hope to get some insurance now on white persons. If we can once commence on this Species of insurance we should hope to do well with it."[11] Clearly, the BLIC agent did not appear comfortable with all of the Chesterfield County coal mines, with good reason. Two months after Mr. Pollard's letter was written, fifty-five men, both slave and white, were killed in an explosion in the Midlothian Coal Pit. There was no direct evidence that the BLIC was involved in insuring any of the slaves. However, the United States Life Insurance office issued policies for several of the slaves that were killed in the explosion.[12]

The BLIC's archival material illuminated another key fact about the importance of slave insurance and the mines. Although a specific county mine was not named, one letter captures the dangerous conditions without going into any discussion. "The parties who apply for insurance of the Coal Pit Hands are very anxious to get the Policies as they are keeping the hands above ground and idle till they get them insured."[13] Based on the letter's date of February 1857, and reviewing the insurance records at the end of the chapter, the slaves would be working at the Black Heath Pits.

As shown on the Slave Insurance List, fourteen slaves were insured in 1857 by BLIC in mining-related occupations in the county. However, policies were sold earlier by the company, as noted in "Securing Human Property." In July 1839, an owner asked for and received coverage from BLIC on his two slaves who were working in the Chesterfield coal mines. "BLIC initially complied with these requests, yet increasing numbers of steamboat and mining accidents…led to a temporary moratorium on such risks by mid-century."[14]

In addition to historic company records, newspaper articles also helped document this insurance practice. As referenced earlier, the *Daily Dispatch* reported on the March 1855 mining tragedy. Thirty-three slaves were included as either having been killed or listed as "in a dying condition." The article stated the United States Life Insurance office insured several of the slaves, and advised the owners that they "can get their money at once, by making proper application."[15] The reporter captured the practice quite clearly.

The *Daily Express* printed an article on April 15, 1859, describing the gas explosion at Bright Hope Pits several days earlier in Chesterfield County. The names of the four white miners killed were listed. Names of the five slaves who perished were not reported, however the names of their owners were provided. The reporter documented that, "All the negroes were insured."[16]

The exchange of money connected with the slave insurance policies did not stop with the company and slave owners. As documented in the BLIC records and referenced by the competition's slave rate sheets, slave insurance applications were accompanied by a doctor's medical examination form. Details such as the slave's number of respirations per minute, heartbeat, and any previous medical afflictions, were documented.

Chesterfield County Slave Census records, available for 1850 and 1860, clearly identified slave race. However, a review of over 8,000 slave listings did not reveal a single "W" indicating a White slave. Instead, the coding showed Black (letter "B") to be the overwhelming majority race, with "M" for Mulatto the next highest percentage.[17] It would be reasonable to believe that slaves from earlier and later periods had similar ethnic backgrounds.

Also, the non-white status of slaves was indicated in the plethora of advertisements published in newspapers during the mining period. In some cases, the same ad would run repeatedly. Although not specifically labeled as ads for coal miner policies, the National Safety Life Insurance and Trust Company proclaimed, "In Richmond, in Lisie's row, Pearl street, opposite the Penitentiary store, offers superior advantages to the public in regard to LIFE INSURANCE, either of white persons or slaves – the former insured upon the MUTUAL SYSTEM, the latter for one or more years."[18]

Regarding policy payouts, apparently no major explosions took place in the Midlothian area during the period 1846–1848, as indicated in the death list in the previous chapter. Evidence of this quieter period can also be found in the Nautilus Insurance Company death records, which showed only a few miner slaves died during that period.[19] Since the county did not begin keeping official death records until 1853, newspapers and publications were important forms of coal-mine fatality documentation. Based on the research, it appears that at least for a few years, the majority of the slaves avoided a violent death in the mines.

The following list does not include all the companies involved in writing slave insurance policies. However, the personalized list provides evidence that the practice appeared commonplace. The details are provided to help visualize the faces behind the names of the slaves. Perhaps reviewing the information on Clay, a 12-year-old black slave who was made to work in the Black Heath mine, will make the strongest impact of all.

NOTE: Accurate interpretation and listing of the policy and application information was attempted, yet is not guaranteed. For the Nautilus Insurance Company of New York slaves that were insured for two consecutive years, the age and policy information for the second policy only is listed. The Baltimore Life Insurance Company policy information includes excerpts from the Report of the Medical Examiner.

SOURCES:

CDOI: California Department of Insurance
LV: Library of Virginia
MHS: Maryland Historical Society – Baltimore Life Insurance Co. (policies noted as BLIC)[20]
NPA: Newspaper Article
SCRBC: Schomburg Center for Research in Black Culture, Manuscripts, Archives, and Rare Books Division – Nautilus Insurance Company of New York (policies noted as NIC)[21]
VHS: Virginia Historical Society Archives – The Virginia Life Insurance Company (policies noted as VLIC)

Slave Insurance List

Adam – NIC No. 483 – Male, Age: 37, Applicant: John Hobson, Policy Date: May 11, 1846, Slave Occupation: Miner, Residence: at the Mid Lothian Coal Mines, Insured for $450, Premium $8.59, Annual Payment: May 5, Expires: [Blank], Remarks: C. Clark (CDOI, SCRBC)

Alfred – VLIC No. 939 – Male, Age: [not known], Applicant: H. C. Cox, Policy Date: January 19, 1864, Slave

Occupation/Residence: Raccoon Pit of Clover Hill Coal Co., Chesterfield County, Virginia, Insured for $1,200, Annual Payment $69, Time of Payment January 19, 1864, Expires January 19, 1865 (VHS)

Ampy – NIC No. 391 – Male, Age: 40, Applicant: Mid Lothian Coal Mining Co., Policy Date: March 26, 1846, Slave Occupation: Miner, Residence: at the Mines, Insured for $375, Premium $8.21, Annual Payment March 21, Expires [March] 1847, Remarks: C. Clark (CDOI, SCRBC)

Anderson, Phill – NIC Nos. 411 and 1036 – Male, Age: 36, Applicant: Nicholas Mills, Insured for two consecutive years, Policy Date: March 30, 1847, Slave Occupation/Residence: Miner at the Mid Lothian Coal Mines, Chesterfield County, VA, Insured for $525, Premium $9.93, Time of Payment: March 25, Expires March 25, 1848, Remarks: H. Hancock, 150 (CDOI, SCRBC)

Barlett – NIC No. 312 – Male, Age: 24, Applicant: Chesterfield Mining Co., William Benton agent, Black Heath, Chesterfield County, VA, Policy Date: February 21 [1846], Slave Occupation: Miner, Slave Residence: at the Mines, Insured for $412, Premium $8.20, Annual Payment February 14, Expires February 14, 1847, Remarks: C. Clark (CDOI, SCRBC)

Barlette – NIC No. 482 – Male, Age: 21, Applicant: John Hobson, Policy Date: May 11 [1846], Slave Occupation: Miner, Slave Residence: Mid Lothian Coal Mines, Insured for $450, Premium $5.95, Annual Payment: May 5, Expires [blank], Remarks: C. Clarke (CDOI, SCRBC)

Burnette, Dabney – NIC No. 1217 – Male, Age: 31, Applicant: Elias Burnette, Policy Date: June 26 [1847], Slave Occupation: Employed at Mid Lothian Mines, Slave Residence: at mines Chesterfield County, VA, Insured for $525, Premium $9.55, Time of Payment: June 17, Expires June 17, 1848, Remarks: H. Hancock, 224 (CDOI, SCRBC)

Carter, Gilbert – BLIC No. 2807 – Black male, Age: 50, born near Winchester, VA, Insured by Tompkins & Co. for Michael Duval, Policy Date: [February 1847], Employment: Mining, Residence: Black Heath Pits Chesterfield Va., Family Physician: Dr. Ball, Chesterfield, Insured for $600, Premium $29.88, Expires [February 1848]
Partial Report of the Medical Examiner for the Baltimore Life Insurance Company, Dr. William Pollard – What are the number of respirations per minute? "80." What are the number of the heart's pulsations, and of those of the arteries? Are they natural in regard to their force, rhythm, volume, &c.? "About 16 – natural." After carefully reviewing the answers made by the applicant, and those made by the attending physician, and well weighing the result of your own examination, do you recommend the Company accept the risk? "I do."(MHS)

Charles – VLIC No. 938 – Male, Age: [not known], Applicant: W. H. Wilson, Policy Date: January 19, 1864, Slave Occupation/Residence: Raccoon Pit of Clover Hill Coal Co., Chesterfield County, VA, Insured for $1200, Annual Payment $69, Time of Payment January 19, 1864, Expires January 19, 1865 (VHS)

Cheatham, Patrick – NIC Nos. 420 and 1045 – Male, Age: 24, Applicant: Nicholas Mills, Insured for two consecutive years, Policy Date: March 30, 1847, Slave Occupation: Miner, Residence: Chesterfield County, VA, Insured for $525, Premium $7.83, Time of Payment: March 28, Expires March 28, 1848, Remarks: H. Hancock 150 (CDOI, SCRBC)

Clay – BLIC No. 2801 – Black male, Age: 12, born in Chesterfield, VA, Insured by Tompkins & Co. in behalf of Wm. E. Martin, Policy Date: [February 1857], Employment: Mining, Residence: Black Heath Coal Pits Chesterfield Virginia, Insured for $750, Premium $24.20, Expires February 1858

Partial Report of the Medical Examiner for the Baltimore Life Insurance Company, Dr. William Pollard – What are the number of respirations in a minute? "About 16." What are the number of the heart's pulsations, and of those of the arteries? Are they natural in regard to their force, rhythm, volume, &c.? "About 80 in the minute – natural." After carefully reviewing the answers made by the applicant, and those made by the attending physician, and well weighing the result of your own examination, do you recommend the Company accept the risk? "I do."(MHS)

Cole, Lewis – NIC Nos. 345 and 996 – Male, Age: 23, Applicant: Haley Cole, Insured for two consecutive years, Policy Date: March 12, 1847, Slave Occupation: Miner at Black Heath Pits, Residence: Chesterfield County, VA, Insured for $450, Premium $8.96, Annual Payment February 23, Expires February 28, 1848 (CDOI, SCRBC)

Congo – NIC No. 892 – Male, Age 33, Applicant: Daniel Wooldridge, Policy Date: February 3, 1847, Slave Occupation/Residence: Miner at the Clover Hill Pits, Chesterfield County, VA, Insured for $450, Premium $8.28, Time of Payment January 25, Expires January 25, 1848, Remarks: H. Hancock (CDOI, SCRBC)

Dabney, Davy – NIC No. 896 – Male, Age: 22, Applicant: John Darracott, Policy Date: February 3, 1847, Slave Occupation/Residence: Miner at Clover Hill Pits, Chesterfield County, VA, Insured for $450, Premium $6.48, Annual Payment January 28, Expires January 28, 1848, Remarks: H. Hancock (CDOI, SCRBC)

Dabney, London – NIC No. 895 – Male, Age: 24, Applicant: John Darracott, Policy Date: February 3, 1847, Slave Occupation/Residence: Miner at Clover Hill Pits, Chesterfield County, VA, Insured for $450, Premium $6.70, Annual Payment January 28, Expires January 28, 1848, Remarks: H. Hancock (CDOI, SCRBC)

David – NIC No. 894 – Male, Age: 25, Applicant: Daniel Wooldridge, Policy Date: February 3, 1847, Slave Occupation/Residence: Miner in the Clover Hill Pits, Chesterfield County, VA, Insured for $450, Premium $6.75, Annual Payment January 28, Expires January 28, 1848, Remarks: H. Hancock (CDOI, SCRBC)

Dickenson, Henry – NIC Nos. 425 and 1050 – Male, Age: 24, Applicant: Nicholas Mills, Insured for two consecutive years, Policy Date: March 30, 1847, Slave Occupation: Miner, Residence: Chesterfield County, VA, Insured for $450, Premium $6.71, Time of Payment March 28, Expires March 28, 1848, Remarks: H. Hancock, 150 (CDOI, SCRBC)

Edward – BLIC No. 2798 – Black male, Age: 22, born in Chesterfield, Va., insured by Tompkins & Co. for Wm. E. Martin, Policy Date: [February 1857], Employment: Mining, Residence: Chesterfield Co. Black Heath Pits, Family Physician: Dr. Hancock, Chesterfield, Insured for $950, Premium $30.60, Expires February 1858
Partial Report of the Medical Examiner for the Baltimore Life Insurance Company, Dr. William Pollard – What are the umber of respirations per minute? "80." What are the number of the heart's pulsations, and of those of the arteries? Are they natural in regard to their force, rhythm, volume, &c.? "16 in the minute." After carefully reviewing the answers made by the applicant, and those made by the attending physician, and well weighing the result of your own examination, do you recommend the Company accept the risk? "I do."(MHS)

Ellis, Peter – NIC Nos. 343 and 899 – Male, Age: 26, Applicant: Joseph A. Ellis, Insured for two consecutive years, Policy Date: February 8, 1847, Slave Occupation/Residence: Miner at the Mid Lothian Mines, Insured for $506 [?], Premium $7.94, Annual Payment January 23, Expires February 23, 1848, Remarks: H. Hancock (CDOI, SCRBC)

Finley, Nelson – NIC No. 449 – Male, Age: 36, Applicant: Charles Mills, Policy Date: April 16, 1846, Slave Occupation: Miner Residence: at Mid Lothian mines, Insured for $450, Premium $8.50, Annual Payment March 28, Expires March 28, 1847, Remarks: C. Clarke (CDOI, SCRBC)

Flournoy, Anderson – NIC Nos. 413 and 1038 – Male, Age: 37, Applicant: Nicholas Mills, Insured for two consecutive years, Policy Date: March 30, 1847, Slave Occupation/Residence: Miner at the Mid Lothian Coal Mines, Chesterfield County, VA, Insured for $337, Premium $6.50, Time of Payment March 28, Expires March 25, 1848, Remarks: H. Hancock, 150 (CDOI, SCRBC)

George – BLIC No. 2804 – Black male, Age: 13, born in Goochland County, Insured by Tompkins & Co. for Wm. E. Martin, Policy Date: [February 1847], Employment: Mining (works above ground), Residence: Black Heath Coal Pits Chesterfield Co. Va., Family Physician: Dr. Hancock, Chesterfield, Insured for $750, Premium $24.20, Expires February 1858
Partial Report of the Medical Examiner for the Baltimore Life Insurance Company, Dr. William Pollard – What are the number of respirations per minute? "80." What are the number of the heart's pulsations, and of those of the arteries? Are they natural in regard to their force, rhythm, volume, &c.? "About 16 in the minute – natural." After carefully reviewing the answers made by the applicant, and those made by the attending physician, and well weighing the result of your own examination, do you recommend the Company accept the risk? "I do." (MHS)

Giles, Dick – NIC No. 834 – Male, Age: 24, Applicant: Jefferson Hancock, Policy Date: January 23, 1847, Slave Occupation: Chesterfield County Clover Hill Coal Pits, Slave Residence: Chesterfield County, VA, Insured for $487, Premium $7.15, Annual Payment January 19, Expires January 19, 1848, Remarks: H. Hancock (CDOI, SCRBC)

Godfrey – NIC Nos. 427 and 1052 – Male, Age: 51, Applicant: Nicholas Mills, Insured for two consecutive years, Policy Date: March 30, 1847, Slave Occupation: Miner, Slave Residence: Chesterfield County, VA, Insured for $337, Premium $8.39, Time of Payment March 28, Expires March 28, 1848, Remarks: H. Hancock, 150
Dead – loss paid February 1, 1847, Date of Death: November 20, 1847, Cause of Death: Burned to Death, Place of Death: Midlothian, VA (CDOI, SCRBC)

Griffin – NIC No. 344 – Male, Age: 25, Applicant: Nelson Tumly, Policy Date: March 8, 1846, Slave Occupation: Miner, Residence: Black Heath Mines, Insured for $300, Premium $6.00, Annual Payment July 25, Expires July 25, 1847 (CDOI, SCRBC)

Hall, Bob – NIC No. 392 – Male, Age: 22, Applicant: Mid Lothian Mining Co., Policy Date: March 26 [1846], Slave Occupation: Miner, Slave Residence: at the Mines, Insured for $412, Premium $5.95, Annual Payment March 17, Expires [Blank], Remarks: C. Clark (CDOI, SCRBC)

Hall, Bob – NIC No. 973 – Male, Age: 34, Applicant: Richard Hall, Policy Date: March 5, 1847, Slave Occupation: Miner, Slave Residence: Chesterfield County Mid Lothian Mines, Insured for $412, Premium $6.38, Annual Payment March 17, Expires March 17, 1848, Remarks: H. Hancock, 150
Dead – loss paid [not known] , Date of Death: March 22, 1847, Cause of Death: Killed in a Coal mine, Place of Death: Coal Mines, KY (CDOI, SCRBC)

Hall, Charles – NIC No. 313 – Male, Age: 52, Applicant: Chesterfield Mining Co., William Benton agent, at Black Heath Mines, Policy Date: February 21, 1846, Slave Occupation: Miner, Slave Residence: at the Mines, Insured for $300, Premium $9.06, Annual Payment February 14, Expires February 14, 1847, Remarks: C. Clark (CDOI, SCRBC)

Hall, Daniel – NIC No. 311 – Male, Age: 48, Applicant: Chesterfield Mining Co., William Benton agent, at Black Heath, Chesterfield County, VA, Policy Date: February 21, 1846, Slave Occupation: Miner, Slave Residence: at the Mines, Insured for $412, Premium $12.12, Annual Payment February 14, Expires February 14, 1847, Remarks: C. Clark (CDOI, SCRBC)

Hancock, Jordan – NIC No. 309 – Male, Age: 35, Applicant: Woodson W. Hancock, Policy Date: February 21 [1846], Slave Occupation: Miner, Residence: at the Mid Lothian Mines, Insured for $412, Premium $7.66, Annual Payment: February 16, Expires: February 16, 1847, Remarks: C. Clark (CDOI, SCRBC)

Hanes, Henry (also known as Hanes, Harris) – NIC Nos. 422 and 1047 – Male, Age: 24, Applicant: Nicholas Mills, Insured for two consecutive years, Policy Date: March 30, 1847, Slave Occupation: Miner, Slave Residence: Chesterfield County, VA, Insured for $525, Premium $7.83, Time of Payment March 28, Expires March 28, 1848, Remarks: H. Hancock, 150 (CDOI, SCRBC)

Hanes, Harris – See Hanes, Henry

Harrod, Billy – NIC Nos. 410 and 1035 – Male, Age: 34, Applicant: Nicholas Mills, Insured for two consecutive years, Policy Date: March 30, 1847, Slave Occupation/Residence: Miner at the Mid Lothian Coal Mines, Chesterfield County, VA, Insured for $412, Premium $7.68, Time of Payment March 28, Expires March 28, 1847, Remarks: H. Hancock, 150 (CDOI, SCRBC)

Henry – NIC No. 893 – Male, Age: 37, Applicant: Daniel Wooldridge, Insured for two consecutive years, Policy Date: February 3, 1847, Slave Occupation/Residence: Miner in the Clover Hill Pits, Chesterfield County, VA, Insured for $375, Premium $7.24, Annual Payment January 28, Expires January 28, 1848, Remarks: H. Hancock (CDOI, SCRBC)

Henry – BLIC No. 2812 – Black male, Age: 14, born in Chesterfield, Insured by Tompkins & Co. "in behalf" of Wm. E. Martin, Employment: Mining, Residence: Black Heath Coal Pits Chesterfield, Family Physician: Dr. Hancock, Chesterfield, Insured for $750, Per Cent $3.28, Premium $24.60, Expires February 1858

Partial Report of the Medical Examiner for the Baltimore Life Insurance Company, Dr. William Pollard – What are the number of respirations per minute? "About 80." What are the number of the heart's pulsations, and of those of the arteries? Are they natural in regard to their force, rhythm, volume, &c.? "About 15 – natural." After carefully reviewing the answers made by the applicant, and those made by the attending physician, and well weighing the result of your own examination, do you recommend the Company accept the risk? "I do."(MHS)

Henry – BLIC No. 2819 – Black male, Age: 40, Insured by James L. Porter, Policy Date: [February 1857], Employment: Mining, Residence: Black Heath Coal Pits Chesterfield Co. Va., Family Physician: Dr. Hancock of Chesterfield, Insured for $800, Premium $31.60, Expires February 1858

Partial Report of the Medical Examiner for the Baltimore Life Insurance Company, Dr. Hancock for Dr. Thomas Pollard – What are the number of respirations per minute? "His respirations are normal." What are the number of the heart's pulsations, and of those of the arteries? Are they natural in regard to their force, rhythm, volume, &c.? "Pulse beats 72 per minute – soft and very good." After carefully reviewing the answers made by the applicant, and those made by the attending physician, and well weighing the result of your own examination, do you recommend the Company accept the risk? "I should [?] judge he was sound & healthy and advise risk."

On the *"Application For Life Insurance on the Life of Another"* the answers completed by James L. Porter were important to add. *What has been the condition of his health, during his past life, and with what diseases has suffered? "His health has been perfect so far as I know. I have owned him ten years upwards." Have you ever made application to any other Insurance Company and what answer did you receive? "The Valleys Insurance Co. agreed this day to insure him but in ascertaining that their extra Rates were higher by ½[p/c?] than those of the Balt. L. I. Co. I came to the latter."* (MHS)

Hewlett – NIC No. 974 – Male, Age: 34, Applicant: Higginson Hancock, Policy Date: March 5, 1847, Slave Occupation/Residence: Miner at Coal Mines Mid Lothian, Chesterfield County, VA, Insured for $450, Premium $8.33, Annual Payment February 23, Expires February 23, 1848, Remarks: H. Hancock (CDOI, SCRBC)

Horace – BLIC No. 2805 – Black male, Age: 25, born in Essex County, Va., Insured by Tompkins & Co. "in behalf" of Jos. T. Tompkins, Policy Date: [February 1847], Employment: Mining, Residence: Black Heath Coal Pits Chesterfield, Family Physician: Dr. Ball, Chesterfield, Insured for $825, Premium $28.46, Expires February 1858
Partial Report of the Medical Examiner for the Baltimore Life Insurance Company, Dr. William Pollard – What are the number of respirations per minute? "About 78." What are the number of the heart's pulsations, and of those of the arteries? Are they natural in regard to their force, rhythm, volume, &c.? "About 16 – in the minute – natural." After carefully reviewing the answers made by the applicant, and those made by the attending physician, and well weighing the result of your own examination, do you recommend the Company accept the risk? "I do."(MHS)

Hunt, John – NIC Nos. 423 and 1048 – Male, Age: 34, Applicant: Nicholas Mills, Insured for two consecutive years, Policy Date: March 30, 1847, Slave Occupation: Miner, Residence: Chesterfield County, VA, Insured for $450, Premium $8.33, Time of Payment March 28, Expires March 28, 1848, Remarks: H. Hancock, 150 (CDOI, SCRBC)

Isaac – NIC No. 898 – Male, Age: 35, Applicant: Jefferson Cosby, Policy Date: February 8, 1847, Slave Occupation/Residence: Miner at Clover Hill Pits, Chesterfield County, VA, Insured for $375, Premium $6.98, Time of Payment February 2, Expires February 2, 1848 *Dead – Loss Paid: October 1847, Date of Death: October 1847, Cause of Death: Typhoid Fever, Place of Death: Chesterfield County, VA* (CDOI, SCRBC)

Jacob – NIC No. 1108 – Male, Age: 30, Applicant: Richard Archer, Policy Date: April 28, 1847, Slave Occupation/Residence: Miner at the Mid Lothian Coal Mines, Chesterfield County, VA, Insured for $525, Premium $9.50, Time of Payment April 21, Expires April 21, 1848, Remarks: H. Hancock, 193 (CDOI, SCRBC)

James, Madison – NIC Nos. 416 and 1041 – Male, Age: 33, Applicant: Nicholas Mills, Insured for two consecutive years, Policy Date: March 30, 1847, Slave Occupation: Miner, Residence: Chesterfield County, VA, Insured for $525, Premium $9.67, Time of Payment March 28, Expires March 28, 1848, Remarks: H. Hancock, 150 (CDOI, SCRBC)

Jefferson – BLIC No. 2796 – Black male, Age: 22, born in Chesterfield, Insured by Tompkins & Co. for Wm. E. Martin, Policy Date: [February 1857], Employment: Mining, Residence: Black Heath Coal Pits Chesterfield Va., Family Physician: Dr. Hancock, Chesterfield, Insured for $950, Premium $30.60, Expires February 1858 *Partial Report of the Medical Examiner for the Baltimore Life Insurance Company, Dr. William Pollard – What are the number of respirations per minute? "about 15." What are the number of the heart's pulsations, and of those of the arteries? Are they natural in regard to their force, rhythm, volume, &c.? "About 70." After carefully reviewing the answers made by the applicant, and those made by the attending physician, and well weighing the* *result of your own examination, do you recommend the Company accept the risk? "I do."*(MHS)

Johnson, Richard – NIC No. 307 – Male, Age: 25, Applicant: Mid Lothian Coal Mines, Policy Date: February 21, 1846, Slave Occupation: Miner, Residence: at the Mines, Insured for $487, Premium $7.30, Annual Payment February 10, Expires February 10, 1847 (CDOI, SCRBC)

Jones, Anthony – NIC Nos. 421 and 1046 – Male, Age: 33, Applicant: Nicholas Mills, Insured for two consecutive years, Policy Date: March 30, 1847, Slave Occupation: Miner, Residence: Chesterfield County, VA, Insured for $525, Premium $9.67, Time of Payment March 28, Expires March 28, 1848, Remarks: H. Hancock, 150 (CDOI, SCRBC)

Jones, Sam – NIC Nos. 270 and 920 – Male, Age: 41, Applicant: James Moody, Policy Date: February 16, 1847, Slave Occupation/Residence: Miner at the Clover Hill Pits, Insured for $375, Premium $8.56, Annual Payment January 26, Expires January 26, 1848, Remarks: H. Hancock (CDOI, SCRBC)

Kiner, Sam – NIC Nos. 424 and 1049 – Male, Age: 37, Applicant: Nicholas Mills, Insured for two consecutive years, Policy Date: March 30, 1847, Slave Occupation: Miner, Residence: Chesterfield County, VA, Insured for $525, Premium $10.13, Time of Payment March 28, Expires March 28,1848, Remarks: H. Hancock, 150 (CDOI, SCRBC)

Ligou, Jack (also listed as Sigon, Jack) – NIC No. 1078 – Male, Age: 25, Applicant: Joseph Mayo, Policy Date: April 12, 1847, Slave Occupation: Miner, Residence: Mid Lothian Coal Mines, Chesterfield County, VA, Insured for $450, Premium $6.75, Time of Payment April 8, Expires April 8, 1848, Remarks: H. Hancock, 165 (CDOI, SCRBC)

Lockett, Henry – NIC No. 1101 – Male, Age: 18, Applicant: Edmund A. Lockett, Zachariah H. Brooks executor, Policy Date: April 26, 1847, Slave Occupation/Residence: Miner at the Coal Mines Mid Lothian, Chesterfield County, VA, Insured for $450, Premium $6.35, Time of Payment April 13, Expires April 13, 1848, Remarks: H. Hancock, 193 (CDOI, SCRBC)

Lockett, Jim – NIC No. 1099 – Male, Age: 21, Applicant: Edmund A. Lockett, Zachariah H. Brooks executor, Policy Date: April 26, 1847, Slave Occupation/Residence: Miner at the Mid Lothian Coal Mines, Chesterfield County, VA, Insured for $450, Premium $6.39, Time of Payment April 13, Expires April 13, 1848, Remarks: H. Hancock, 193 (CDOI, SCRBC)

Lockett, Joe – NIC No. 1098 – Male, Age: 55, Applicant: Edmund A. Lockett, Zachariah H. Brooks executor, Policy Date: April 26, 1847, Slave Occupation/Residence: at the Mid Lothian Coal Mines, Chesterfield County, VA, Insured for $275, Premium $7.75, Time of Payment April 13, Expires April 13, 1848, Remarks: H. Hancock, 193 (CDOI, SCRBC)

Lockett, Jordan – NIC No. 1102 – Male, Age: 26, Applicant: Edmund A. Lockett, Zachariah H. Brooks executor, Policy Date: April 26, 1947, Slave Occupation/Residence: Miner at the Mid Lothian Coal Mines, Chesterfield County, VA, Insured for $525, Premium $8.24, Time of Payment April 13, Expires April 13, 1848, Remarks: H. Hancock, 193 (CDOI, SCRBC)

Lockett, Ned – NIC No. 1100 – Male, Age: 23, Applicant: Edmund A. Lockett, Zachariah H. Brooks executor, Policy Date: April 26, 1847, Slave Occupation/Residence: Miner at the Mid Lothian Coal Mines, Chesterfield County, VA, Amount $450, Premium $6.62, Time of Payment April 13, Expires April 13, 1848, Remarks: H. Hancock, 193 (CDOI, SCRBC)

Maston, William – NIC Nos. 304 and 877 – Male, Age: 25, Applicant: A. S. Wooldridge - Pres. [Mid Lothian Coal Mining

Co.], Insured for two consecutive years, Policy Date: February 3, 1847, Slave Occupation/Residence: Miner at the Mid Lothian Coal Mines, Insured for $487, Premium $7.36, Annual Payment February 10, Expires February 18, 1848, Remarks: H. Hancock (CDOI, SCRBC)

McTyre, Thomas – BLIC No. 2806 – Black male, Age: 36, born in Chesterfield County, Va., Insured by Tompkins "in behalf" of James R. McTyre, Policy Date: [February 1847], Employment: Mining, Residence: Black Heath Pits Chesterfield Co. Va., Family Physician: Dr. Hancock, Chesterfield, Insured for $712, Premium $26.91, Expires February 1858
Partial Report of the Medical Examiner for the Baltimore Life Insurance Company, Dr. William Pollard – What are the number of respirations per minute? "About 78." What are the number of the heart's pulsations, and of those of the arteries? Are they natural in regard to their force, rhythm, volume, &c.? "About 16." After carefully reviewing the answers made by the applicant, and those made by the attending physician, and well weighing the result of your own examination, do you recommend the Company accept the risk? "I do."(MHS)

Mills, Cyrus – NIC Nos. 428 and 1053 – Male, Age: 38, Applicant: Nicholas Mills, Insured for two consecutive years, Policy Date: March 30, 1847, Slave Occupation: Miner, Residence: Chesterfield County, VA, Insured for $487, Premium $9.64, Time of Payment March 28, Expires March 28, 1848, Remarks: H. Hancock, 150 (CDOI, SCRBC)

Mills, George – NIC Nos. 418 and 1043 – Male, Age: 43, Applicant: Nicholas Mills, Insured for two consecutive years, Policy Date: March 30, 1847, Slave Occupation: Miner, Residence: Chesterfield County, VA, Insured for $450, Premium $10.75, Time of Payment March 28, Expires March 28, 1848, Remarks: H. Hancock, 150 (CDOI, SCRBC)

Mills, Harry – NIC Nos. 414 and 1039 – Male, Age: 34, Applicant: Nicholas Mills, Insured for two consecutive years, Policy Date: March 30, 1847, Slave Occupation: Miner, Residence: Chesterfield County, VA, Insured for $525, Premium $9.72, Time of Payment March 28, Expires March 28, 1848 (CDOI, SCRBC)

Mills, Jim – NIC Nos. 412 and 1037 – Male, Age: 24, Applicant: Nicholas Mills, Insured for two consecutive years, Policy Date: March 30, 1847, Slave Occupation/Residence: Miner at the Mid Lothian Coal Mines, Chesterfield County, VA, Insured for $525, Premium $7.83, Time of Payment March 28, Expires March 28, 1848, Remarks: H. Hancock, 150 (CDOI, SCRBC)

Mills, Lewis – NIC Nos. 415 and 1040 – Male, Age: 24, Applicant: Nicholas Mills, Insured for two consecutive years, Policy Date: March 30, 1847, Slave Occupation: Miner, Residence: Chesterfield County, VA, Insured for $450, Premium $6.70, Time of Payment March 28, Expires March 28, 1848, Remarks: H. Hancock, 150 (CDOI, SCRBC)

Mills, Ned (a/k/a Miller) – NIC Nos. 408 and 1034 – Male, Age: 47, Applicant: Nicholas Mills, Insured for two consecutive years, Policy Date: March 30, 1847, Slave Occupation: Miner at the Mid Lothian Coal Mines, Residence: Chesterfield County, VA, Insured for $300, Premium: $7.29, Time of Payment: March 25, Expires: March 25, 1848, Remarks: H. Hancock, 150 (CDOI, SCRBC)

Montague, Harry (Henry)– NIC Nos. 271 and 922 – Male, Age: 26, Applicant: James Moody, guardian, Insured for two consecutive years, Policy Date: February 16, 1847, Slave Occupation/Residence: Miner at Clover Hill Coal Pits, Insured for $412, Premium $6.46, Annual Payment January 26, Expires January 26, 1848, Remarks: H. Hancock (CDOI, SCRBC)

Moody, Henry – NIC Nos. 249 and 921 – Male, Age: 17, Applicant: David Moody, Insured for two consecutive years,

Policy Date: February 16, 1847, Slave Occupation/Residence: Miner at Clover Hill Pits, Insured for $394, Premium $5.66, Annual Payment January 26, Expires January 26, 1848, Remarks: H. Hancock (CDOI, SCRBC)

Moody, Joe – NIC Nos. 272 and 923 – Male, Age: 36, Applicant: James Moody, guardian, Insured for two consecutive years, Policy Date: February 16, 1847, Slave Occupation/Residence: Miner at the Clover Hill Pits, Insured for $525, Premium $9.93, Annual Payment January 26, Expires January 26, 1848, Remarks: H. Hancock (CDOI, SCRBC)

Moody, Phill – NIC Nos. 248 and 919 – Male, Age: 51, Applicant: David Moody, Insured for two consecutive years, Policy Date: February 11, 1847, Slave Occupation/Residence: Miner at the Clover Hill Pits, Insured for $206, Premium $5.08, Annual Payment January 26, Expires January 26, 1848, Remarks: H. Hancock (CDOI, SCRBC)

Moody, Robert – NIC No. 925 – Male, Age: 20, Applicant: James Moody, guardian for Sarah E. Moody, Policy Date: February 16, 1847, Slave Occupation: Miner at the Clover Hill Pits, Residence: Chesterfield County, VA, Insured for $412, Premium $5.81, Time of Payment February 10, 1847, Expires February 10, 1848, Remarks: H. Hancock (CDOI, LV, SCRBC)

Nork, Nathan – See York, Nathan

Peter – BLIC No. 2803 – Black male, Age: 15, born in Chesterfield County, Va., Insured by Tompkins & Co. "in behalf" of Wm. E. Martin, Policy Date: [February 1857], Employment: Mining, Residence: Black Heath Coal Pits Chesterfield Co. Va., Family Physician: Dr. Hancock, Chesterfield, Insured for $750, Premium $24.20, Expires February 1858
Partial Report of the Medical Examiner for the Baltimore Life Insurance Company, Dr. William Pollard – What are the number of respirations per minute? "About 80." What are the number of

the heart's pulsations, and of those of the arteries? Are they
natural in regard to their force, rhythm, volume, &c.? "About 16 –
natural." After carefully reviewing the answers made by the
applicant, and those made by the attending physician, and well
weighing the result of your own examination, do you recommend
the Company accept the risk? "I do."(MHS)

Peter – NIC No. 481 – Male, Age: 37, Applicant: John Hobson,
Policy Date: May 11, 1846, Slave Occupation: Miner, Residence:
Mid Lothian Coal Mines, Insured for $300, Premium $5.79,
Annual Payment May 5, Expires [blank], Remarks: C. Clarke
(CDOI, SCRBC)

Picket, Henry – NIC Nos. 417 and 1042 – Male, Age: 28,
Applicant: Nicholas Mills, Insured for two consecutive years,
Policy Date: March 30, 1847, Slave Occupation: Miner,
Residence: Chesterfield County, VA, Insured for $525, Premium
$8.93, Time of Payment March 28, Expires March 28, 1848,
Remarks: H. Hancock, 150 (CDOI, SCRBC)

Pollard, Tom – NIC No. 835 – Male, Age: 35, Applicant:
Higginson Hancock, Policy Date: January 23 [?], 1847, Slave
Occupation: Miner, Residence: Chesterfield County, VA, Insured
for $450, Premium $8.37, Annual Payment January 18, Expires
January 18, 1848, Remarks: H. Hancock (CDOI, SCRBC)

Porter, Edgar – NIC No. 308 – Male, Age: 15, Applicant: Mid
Lothian Mining Co., Policy Date: February 21, [1846], Slave
Occupation: Miner, Residence: at the Mines, Insured for $375,
Premium $5.24, Annual Payment February 10, Expires February
10, 1847, Remarks: C. Clarke (CDOI, SCRBC)

Porter, Frank – NIC No. 1226 – Male, Age: 27, Applicant: James
L. Porter, Policy Date: June 30, [1847], Slave Occupation: at work
at Clover Hill "Pitts," Residence: Chesterfield County, VA,
Insured for $450, Premium $9.00, Time of Payment June 19,

Expires June 19, 1848, Remarks: H. Hancock, 224 (CDOI, SCRBC)

Porter, Henry – NIC No. 1227 – Male, Age: 32, Applicant: James L. Porter, Policy Date: June 30 [1847], Slave Occupation: at work at Clover Hill "Pitts," Residence: Chesterfield County, VA, Insured for $450, Premium $10.13, Time of Payment June 19, Expires June 19, 1848, Remarks: H. Hancock, 224 (CDOI, SCRBC)

Porter, Jordan – NIC No. 1228 – Male, Age: 40, Applicant: Alexander Martin, Policy Date: June 30 [1847], Slave Occupation: at work at Clover Hill "Pitts," Residence: Chesterfield County, VA, Insured for $300, Premium $8.25, Time of Payment June 19, Expires June 19, 1847 [Incorrect year listed, actually 1848], Remarks: H. Hancock, 224 (CDOI, SCRBC)

Red, Sam – See Rid, Sam

Reuben (a/k/a Dutch) – NIC Nos. 426 and 1051 – Male, Age: 33, Applicant: Nicholas Mills, Insured for two consecutive years, Policy Date: March 30,1847, Slave Occupation: Miner, Residence: Chesterfield County, VA, Insured for $300, Premium $5.52, Time of Payment March 28, Expires March 28, 1848, Remarks: H. Hancock , 150 (CDOI, SCRBC)

Reuben – NIC No. 1107 – Male, Age: 19, Applicant: Richard Archer, Policy Date: April 28, 1847, Slave Occupation/Residence: Miner at the Mid Lothian Coal Mines, Chesterfield County, VA, Insured for $450, Premium $6.30, Time of Payment April 21, Expires April 21, 1848, Remarks: H. Hancock, 193 (CDOI, SCRBC)

Richard – BLIC No. 2797 – Black male, Age: 24, born in Chesterfield Co. Va., Policy Date: [February 1847], Insured by Tompkins & Co. "in behalf" of Wm. E. Martin, Employment: Mining, Residence: Black Heath Coal Pits Chesterfield Co. Va.,

Family Physician: Dr. Hancock, Chesterfield, Insured for $950, Premium $30.96, Expires February 1858

Partial Report of the Medical Examiner for the Baltimore Life Insurance Company, Dr. William Pollard – What are the number of respirations per minute? "about 14." *What are the number of the heart's pulsations, and of those of the arteries? Are they natural in regard to their force, rhythm, volume, &c.?* "About 70 – natural." *After carefully reviewing the answers made by the applicant, and those made by the attending physician, and well weighing the result of your own examination, do you recommend the Company accept the risk?* "I do."(MHS)

Rid, Sam (also listed as Red, Sam) – NIC Nos. 419 and 1044 – Male, Age: 39, Applicant: Nicholas Mills, Insured for two consecutive years, Policy Date: March 30, 1847, Slave Occupation: Miner, Residence: Chesterfield County, VA, Insured for $450, Premium $9.31, Time of Payment March 28, Expires March 28, 1848, Remarks: H. Hancock, 150 (CDOI, SCRBC)

Robert – BLIC No. 2800 – Black male, Age: 41, born in Prince Edward County, insured by Tompkins & Co. "in behalf" of Wm. E. Martin, Policy Date: [February 1857], Employment: Mining, Residence: Black Heath Coal Pits Chesterfield Co., Family Physician: Dr. Hancock, Chesterfield, Insured for $850, Premium $33.83, Expires February 1858

Partial Report of the Medical Examiner for the Baltimore Life Insurance Company, Dr. William Pollard – What are the number of respirations in a minute? "About 60." *What are the number of the heart's pulsations, and of those of the arteries? Are they natural in regard to their force, rhythm, volume, &c.?* "About 18 – natural." *After carefully reviewing the answers made by the applicant, and those made by the attending physician, and well weighing the result of your own examination, do you recommend the Company accept the risk?* "I do."(MHS)

Sigon, Jack – See Ligou, Jack

Smith, Charles – NIC No. 310 – Male, Age: 42, Applicant: Thomas Marshalls, Policy Date: February 21 [1846], Slave Occupation: Miner, Residence: at the Mines, Insured for $262, Premium $11.15[?], Time of Payment February 9, Expires February 9, 1847, Remarks: C. Clark (CDOI, SCRBC)

Stephen – VLIC No. 945 – Male, Age: [not known], Applicant: J. R. Gates, Policy Date: January 19, 1864, Slave Occupation/Residence: Beaver Pit of Clover Hill Coal Co., Chesterfield County, VA, Amount $1,500, Annual Payment $86.25, Time of Payment January 19, 1864, Expires January 19, 1865 (VHS)

Stokes – BLIC No. 2802 – Black male, Age: 33, born in Chesterfield County, insured by Tompkins & Co. "in behalf" of Wm. E. Martin, Policy Date: [February 1857], Employment: Mining, Residence: Black Heath Coals Pits Chesterfield, Family Physician: Dr. Hancock, Chesterfield, Insured for $900, Premium $33.12, Expires February 1858
Partial Report of the Medical Examiner for the Baltimore Life Insurance Company, Dr. William Pollard – What are the number of respirations in a minute? "About 14." What are the number of the heart's pulsations, and of those of the arteries? Are they natural in regard to their force, rhythm, volume, &c.? "About 70 in the minute." After carefully reviewing the answers made by the applicant, and those made by the attending physician, and well weighing the result of your own examination, do you recommend the Company accept the risk? "I do."(MHS)

Swann, Philip – NIC No. 228 – Male, Age: 45, Applicant: F.A. Clarke, Policy February 2, 1846, Slave Occupation: Miner, Residence: Mid Lothian Coal Mines, Amount $225, Premium $5.43, Annual Payment [blank], Expires January 25, 1847, Remarks: C. Clarke
Died – loss paid November 1846, Date of Death: August 28, 1846, Place of Death: Coal Mines (CDOI, SCRBC)

Walker, Israel – NIC Nos. 215 and 862 – Male, Age: 29, Applicant: A. S. Wooldridge – Pres., Insured for two consecutive years, Policy Date: February 3, 1847, Slave Occupation: Miner, Residence: Mid Lothian Mines, Chesterfield County, VA, Insured for $525, Premium $9.34, Annual Payment January 23, Expires January 23, 1848, Remarks: II. Hancock (CDOI, SCRBC)

Watkins, Lewis – NIC No. 340 – Male, Age: 25, Applicant: William M. Watkins, Policy Date: March 5, 1846, Slave Occupation: Miner, Residence: Mid Lothian "Pitts," Insured for $525, Premium $7.88, Annual Payment February 23, Expires February 23, 1847, Remarks: C. Clarke (CDOI, SCRBC)

Watkins, William – NIC No. 342 – Male, Age: 30, Applicant: William M. Watkins, Policy Date: March 5, [1846], Slave Occupation: Miner, Residence: Mid Lothian Mines, Insured for $487, Premium $8.82, Annual Payment February 25, Expires February 25, 1847, Remarks: C. Clarke (CDOI, SCRBC)

Watkins, William Henry – NIC No. 341 – Male, Age: 20, Applicant: William Watkins, Policy Date: March 5, 1846, Slave Occupation: Miner, Residence: Mid Lothian "Pitts," Insured for $506, Premium $7.13, Annual Payment February 25, Expires February 25, 1847, Remarks: C. Clarke (CDOI, SCRBC)

Watson – BLIC No. 2799 – Black male, Age: 24, born in North Carolina, Insured by Tompkins & Co. for Wm. E. Martin, Policy Date: [February 1857], Employment: Mining, Residence: Black Heath Coal Pits Chesterfield Va., Family Physician: Dr. Hancock, Chesterfield, Insured for $900, Premium: $30.96, Expires February 1858
Partial Report of the Medical Examiner for the Baltimore Life Insurance Company, Dr. William Pollard – What are the number of respirations in a minute? "about 78." What are the number of the heart's pulsations, and of those of the arteries? Are they natural in regard to their force, rhythm, volume, &c.? "About 15 in the minute – natural." After carefully reviewing the answers

made by the applicant, and those made by the attending physician, and well weighing the result of your own examination, do you recommend the Company accept the risk? "I do."(MHS)

Wills, Jim – NIC Nos. 306 and 870 – Male, Age: 30 Applicant: A. S. Wooldridge – Pres. Mid Lothian Coal Mine Co., Policy Date: February 3, 1847, Slave Occupation/Residence: Miner at the Mid Lothian Coal Mines, Insured for $525, Premium $9.50, Annual Payment February 10, Expires February 10, 1848, Remarks: H. Hancock (CDOI, SCRBC)

Wilson – NIC Nos. 407 and 1033 – Male, Age: 43, Applicant: Nicholas Mills, Insured for two consecutive years, Policy Date: March 30, 1847, Slave Occupation: Miner at the Mid Lothian Coal Mines, Residence: Chesterfield County, VA, Insured for $262, Premium $6.26, Time of Payment March 28, Expires March 28, 1848, Remarks: H. Hancock, 150 (CDOI, SCRBC)

Winfred, Jim – NIC No. 1103 – Male, Age: 28, Applicant: William Winfred, Jr., Policy Date: April 26, 1847, Slave Occupation/Residence: Miner at the Mid Lothian Coal Mines, Chesterfield County, VA, Insured for $525, Premium $8.93, Time of Payment April 13, Expires April 13, 1848, Remarks: H. Hancock, 193 (CDOI, SCRBC)

Wright, Harry – NIC No. 384 – Male, Age: 29, Applicant: Mid Lothian Coal Mining Co. for the benefit of Elizabeth Wright estate, Policy Date: March 20, [1846], Slave Occupation: Miner, Residence: at the Mines, Insured for $525, Premium $9.34, Annual Payment: March 14, Expires [blank], Remarks: C. Clarke (CDOI, SCRBC)

Wright, Henry – NIC No. 382 – Male, Age: 22, Applicant: Mid Lothian Coal Mining Co. for the benefit of Elizabeth Wright estate, Policy Date: March 20, Slave Occupation: Miner, Residence: at the Mines, Insured for $487, Premium $7.00,

Annual Payment March 14, Expires [Blank], Remarks: C. Clark (CDOI, SCRBC)

Wright, Joe – NIC No. 383 – Male, Age: 35, Applicant: Mid Lothian Coal Mining Co. for the benefit of Elizabeth Wright estate, Policy Date: March 20, 1846, Slave Occupation: Miner, Residence: at the mines, Insured for $412, Premium: $7.66, Annual Payment March 14, Expires [Blank], Remarks: C. Clark (CDOI, SCRBC)

Wright, Randolph – NIC No. 381 – Male, Age: 25, Applicant: Mid Lothian Coal Mining Co. for the benefit of Elizabeth Wright estate, Policy Date: March 20, 1846, Slave Occupation: Miner, Residence: Black Heath mines, Insured for $487, Premium: $7.31, Annual Payment: March 14, Expires [Blank], Remarks: C. Clark (CDOI, SCRBC)

York, Ben – NIC Nos. 429 and 1054 – Male, Age: 35, Applicant: Nicholas Mills, Insured for two consecutive years, Policy Date: March 30, 1847, Slave Occupation: Miner, Residence: Chesterfield County, VA, Insured for $600, Premium $11.16, Time of Payment March 28, Expires March 28, 1848, Remarks: H. Hancock, 150 (CDOI, SCRBC)

York, Nathan (also listed as Nork, Nathan) – NIC Nos. 447 and 1055 – Male, Age: 37, Applicant: Nicholas Mills, Insured for two consecutive years, Policy Date: March 30, 1847, Slave Occupation: Miner, Residence: Chesterfield County, VA, Insured for $600, Premium $11.58, Time of Payment March 28, Expires March 28, 1848, Remarks: H. Hancock, 150 (CDOI, SCRBC)

UNKNOWNS – SLAVE NAME NOT PROVIDED:

Life insurance company not listed, black male, age not listed, owned by Mr. Chas. [Charles] Brewer

Dead – Date of Death: April 13, 1859, Cause of Death: Killed in
coal mine explosion, Place of Death: Chesterfield County (NPA –
Daily Express, April 15, 1859)

Life insurance company not listed, black male, age not listed,
owned by Mr. Chas. [Charles] Brewer
Dead – Date of Death: April 13, 1859, Cause of Death: Killed in
coal mine explosion, Place of Death: Chesterfield County (NPA –
Daily Express, April 15, 1859)

Life insurance company not listed, black male, age not listed,
owned by Mr. Absolom Martin
Dead – Date of Death: April 13, 1859, Cause of Death: Killed in
coal mine explosion, Place of Death: Chesterfield County (NPA –
Daily Express, April 15, 1859)

Life insurance company not listed, black male, age not listed,
owned by S.D. Wooldridge
Dead – Date of Death: April 13, 1859, Cause of Death: Killed in
coal mine explosion, Place of Death: Chesterfield County (NPA –
Daily Express, April 15, 1859)

Life insurance company not listed, black male, age not listed,
owned by S.D. Wooldridge
Dead – Date of Death: April 13, 1859, Cause of Death: Killed in
coal mine explosion, Place of Death: Chesterfield County (NPA –
Daily Express, April 15, 1859)

NOTES

CHAPTER ONE

[1] Salmon and Peters, *Guidebook to Virginia's Historical Markers*, 148.

[2] Salmon and Peters, 119.

[3] Wilkes, *Mining History*, 1.

[4] Wilkes, 1.

[5] Wilkes, 51.

[6] Wilkes, 36–42.

[7] Wooldridge, A. & A., *Proposals*.

[8] Wooldridge, 4.

[9] Virginia Auditor, Chesterfield County Personal Property tax records, 1826–1838.

[10] Wooldridge, 29.

[11] Wooldridge, 23–25.

[12] Virginia Auditor, CC PP tax records, 1837–1843.

[13] Virginia General Assembly, petition, 1836.

[14] Virginia Auditor, Powhatan County Personal Property tax records, 1837–1843.

[15] Virginia Auditor, CC PP tax records, 1826–1838.

[16] Virginia Auditor, CC PP tax records, 1833.

[17] Wooldridge, 4.

[18] Wooldridge, 4.

[19] Mid-Lothian Coal Mining Company, *Charter, Scheme,* 1835.

[20] Lutz, *Chesterfield,* 192.

[21] Wooldridge, 3.

[22] Lewis, *Coal, Iron and Slaves,* 4, 52.

[23] Virginia Auditor, CC PP tax records, 1801, 1812.

[24] Wooldridge, 12.

[25] Wooldridge, 101–102.

[26] Virginia Auditor, CC PP tax records, 1833.

[27] Virginia Auditor, CC PP tax records, 1837.

[28] Valentine Museum, *Richmond Portraits*, 132–133.

[29] Wooldridge, 5.

[30] Wooldridge, 5.

[31] Wooldridge, 14, 15.

[32] Mid-Lothian Coal Mining Company, *Charter, scheme,* 1835.

[33] Mid-Lothian Coal Mining Company, *Charter, scheme,* 1835, 3.

[34] Mid-Lothian Coal Mining Company, *Charter, scheme,* 1835, 5.

[35] Mid-Lothian Coal Mining Company, *Charter, scheme,* 1835, 2.

[36] Mid-Lothian Coal Mining Company, *Charter, scheme,* 1835, 7.
[37] Virginia Auditor, CC PP tax records, 1837.
[38] Virginia Auditor, CC PP tax records, 1837–1848.
[39] Wooldridge, 28.
[40] Humphrey, *Historical Summary,* 6; *Richmond Enquirer,* "The Black Heath Coal Mine," 3-23-1839.
[41] *Richmond Enquirer,* 3-23-1839.
[42] Virginia Auditor, CC PP tax records, 1839.
[43] *Richmond Enquirer,* 3-23-1839.
[44] *Richmond Enquirer,* 3-23-1839.
[45] *Niles National Register,* October 14, 1843.
[46] Heinrich, "The Midlothian, Virginia, Colliery in 1876," *Transactions,* Am. Inst. of Mining Engineers Vol. IV, 1875-1876.
[47] *Rural Messenger,* "Terrible Explosion," May 27, 1876.

CHAPTER TWO

[1] Virginia General Assembly, Legislative Petition, January 1851, 2.
[2] Virginia General Assembly, Legislative Petition, January 1851, 1.
[3] Virginia General Assembly, Legislative Petition, January 1851, 4.
[4] Humphrey, *Historical Summary,* 1.
[5] Humphrey, 7.
[6] Humphrey, 3.
[7] *The American Heritage Dictionary of the English Language,* Fourth Edition.
[8] Humphrey, 3.
[9] Ulery, *Explosion Hazards,* 1.
[10] Ulery, 2.
[11] *Rural Messenger,* "Terrible Explosion," May 27, 1876.
[12] Humphrey, 7.
[13] Virginia Auditor, CC PP tax records, 1810.
[14] Virginia Auditor, CC PP tax records, 1811.
[15] Virginia Auditor, CC PP tax records, 1818.
[16] *Richmond Enquirer,* Want ad, March 2, 1810.
[17] Lewis, *Black Coal Miners.*
[18] Papers of Henry Heth, "Hands Purchased at my Father's sale," Accession #38-114, Special Collections, University of Virginia Library, Charlottesville, Va.
[19] Papers of Henry Heth, "Hands Purchased."

[20] Humphrey, 1, 5, 7.

[21] Papers of Henry Heth, "Hands Purchased."

[22] *Richmond Enquirer,* "The Black Heath Coal Mine," 3-23-1839.

[23] Virginia Auditor, CC PP tax records, 1839.

[24] Leigh, Benjamin Watkins, *Court of Appeals,* 383-384.

[25] Leigh, Benjamin Watkins, *Court of Appeals,* 385.

[26] Leigh, Benjamin Watkins, *Court of Appeals,* 383.

[27] Wilkes, *Mining History,* 1.

[28] Howe, *Historical Collections,* 231.

[29] Humphrey, Lutz, Wilkes.

[30] *New-York Times,* "Thirty-two Men Killed; the Terrible Explosion in the Midlothian Mine. No Hope of Rescuing Any of the Imprisoned Miners Alive –Heartrending Scenes at the Mouth of the Pit – One Body Recovered." New York, N.Y. February 5, 1882. http://www.nytimes.com/ (accessed April 18, 2008).

[31] *New-York Tribune* , Feb. 5, 1882.

[32] *Richmond Times Dispatch,* 2-8-97.

[33] *Virginia Associates v. Irving H. Cosby,* case 4362-86, page 3.

[34] *Richmond Times Dispatch,* 2-8-97.

[35] *Richmond Times Dispatch,* 2-8-97.

[36] *Virginia Associates v. Irving H. Cosby,* case 4362-86.

[37] *Virginia Associates v. Irving H. Cosby,* case 4362-86, page 5.

[38] *Virginia Associates v. Irving H. Cosby,* case 4362-86, ORDER pages 2–3.

[39] *Virginia Associates v. Irving H. Cosby, case* 4362-86.

[40] O'Dell, *Chesterfield County,* 91.

[41] O'Dell, *Chesterfield County,* 91.

[42] *Richmond Times Dispatch,* 2-8-97.

[43] *Richmond Times Dispatch,* 2-8-97.

[44] *Richmond Times Dispatch,* 2-8-97; Wilkes, *Mining History,* 1.

[45] City of Richmond, Maury interment card.

[46] *New-York Daily Times,* "Another Explosion," Nov. 30, 1855.

[47] *Richmond Times Dispatch,* 2-8-97.

[48] United States, *Population schedules,* 1860.

[49] *Richmond Times Dispatch,* 2-8-97.

[50] O'Dell, *Chesterfield County,* 494.

[51] Nautilus Insurance Company Slavery Era Ledgers, Death Claim Book, Page 1, No. 13, Sc MG 715, SCRBC.

[52] Nautilus Insurance Company Slavery Era Ledgers, Box 1, Vol. 1 1845 – 1847 Policy # 427 and Box 2, Vol. 2, 1847, Policy # 1052, Sc MG 715, SCRBC.

[53] http://www.behindthename.com/name/godfrey (Accessed October 26, 2007)

CHAPTER THREE

[1] Bird, *Virginia's Coal Ages.*

[2] Salmon and Peters, *Guidebook*, 119, Marker O-35.

[3] http://www.insurance.ca.gov [accessed 11-10-2007].

[4] *San Francisco Chronicle,* "Thousands Online," May 2, 2002.

[5] Hynson, *Baltimore Life.*

[6] Hynson, *Baltimore Life*, III–X.

[7] The BLIC January 11, 1855, letter.

[8] The BLIC January 11, 1855, letter.

[9] The BLIC January 11, 1855, letter.

[10] The BLIC January 11, 1855, letter.

[11] The BLIC January 11, 1855, letter.

[12] *Daily Dispatch*, "Latest" from March 22, 1855.

[13] The BLIC February 1857, letter.

[14] Murphy, "Securing Human Property," 630.

[15] *Daily Dispatch*,"Latest" from March 22, 1855.

[16] *Daily Express*, "The Explosion," April 15, 1859.

[17] United States, *Population schedules of the seventh census,* 1850; *Population schedules,* 1860.

[18] *Daily Dispatch* – January 21, 1854.

[19] Nautilus Insurance Company of New York, Sc MG 715, SCRBC.

[20] The Baltimore Life Insurance Company Papers, MS 175, H. Furlong Baldwin Library, Maryland Historical Society.

[21] Nautilus Insurance Company Slavery Era Ledger, Slavery Era Insurance Policies, Box 1, Vol. 1 Policy Register 5-1000, 1845–1847; Slavery Era Insurance Policies, Box 2, Vol. 2 Policy Register 1001-1590, 1847, Nautilus Insurance Company Slavery Era Ledger, Sc MG 715, SCRBC.

APPENDIX ONE

BEN LOMOND COAL COMPANY DOCUMENTATION[1]

The manuscripts are presented in their entirety, including misspellings.

PROPOSALS FOR INCORPORATING THE BEN LOMOND COAL COMPANY

T.W. WHITE PRINTER, OPPOSITE BELL TAVERN, RICHMOND

1837

SCHEME OF THE BEN LOMOND COAL COMPANY.

In the year 1825, A. S. Wooldridge and A. L. Wooldridge, commenced a coal business at the Stone Henge Pits, in the County of Chesterfield, Virginia, under the firm of A. & A. Wooldridge. They then held those Pits, by a lease from the heirs of Martin Railey, dec'd, at a very exorbitant price, which had been extensively wrought by the late Maj. Harry Heth, and at the period named, had been abandoned, and were filled with water. The Lessees were, at that time, very much embarrassed in their pecuniary affairs; yet they persevered, under these adverse circumstances, to draw off the water, at a heavy expenditure, and to re-open the mines, which proved to contain no coal undeveloped. The prospect of success, from further exploration, was considered not only extremely doubtful, but the evident outlay of a large amount was established beyond all doubt. And at this period also, it is proper to state, that the Lessees and their agents, possessed a very limited stock of knowledge in the science of conducting this intricate business; their operations, therefore were conducted on a very limited scale, under great embarrassments, till the year 1828 – when a partner was solicited to take an interest in the business, chiefly for the purpose of increasing the means to carry on the business. This acquisition to the capital was a limited one; still it had the desired effect, and gave a degree of confidence, which enabled the concern, (then A. & A. Wooldridge & Co.,) to prosecute it with success – which has been conducted under the same style to this time, – although one of the parties parted with his interest, in the year 1832.

The foregoing statement, is made only to give a historical sketch of the origin of a business, the termination of which, is the foundation of another on different principles, attended by all the facilities and advantages, gained by years of toil and experience – which, we confidently believe, will heir all these advantages, and afford a rich reward to those who may hereafter prosecute the business. A. & A. Wooldridge & Co., therefore, take this mode of laying before the public, a proposal to embrace all of their property, *real* and *personal*, connected with the coal trade, under an act of incorporation, styled the *Ben*

Lomond Coal Company, passed by the Legislature of Virginia, on the 27th day of February last. They also think it proper to state, that they are induced to pursue this course, for the plain and obvious reason, that the concern of A. & A. Wooldridge & Co., is about to terminate by limitation; and as it is not in the power of any member, or portion of the concern, to carry on the business, they think it best to adopt this mode of disposing of such portion of the stock, as may be required to meet their engagements, – and divide the residue of the stock, &c., between the partners, in proportion to their several interests. In pursuing which course, they will be enabled to keep this diversified property in a body, which has taken years of care and labor to bring together, and which is rendered doubly valuable as a whole, inasmuch as the possession of one portion of the property, adds strength and increased value to the other portions – which we think will be evident, by a reference to the lists of property embraced in the general schedule, herewith submitted. We are fully aware of the difficulty to be apprehended, at this peculiar time of financial embarrassments, to meet with success in such an enterprise; but with a fixed determination to remove every doubt and difficulty, we do cherish the confident belief, that the advantages here offered will be readily embraced, when it is seen that the owners of the property have not valued it themselves, but have called upon disinterested gentlemen, of the greatest experience, judgment and integrity, in the country, to make the valuation on a scale suitable to the times. Maj. Jesse Snead, Messrs. Geo. E. Wills, and Thos. R. Potts, were selected on account of their intimate knowledge with the coal business generally, and particularly their knowledge of the value of the different pieces and parcels of property contained in the several lists, which were examined personally, and specifically valued in detail, agreeable to the lists herewith attached. As the coal property was not included in the valuations made by them, it is proper to state, that they thought it advisable not to make the valuation on this portion of property – alleging, that in all the valuations they had made, they had been governed by unerring principles, in putting a specific and undoubted value upon the property included in the lists made by them; but as the value of the coal property was, from its nature, of a speculative character, they thought best not to value it in the same schedule, but unite with others in the expression of their opinions on the subject.

We think it unnecessary to say much upon this subject, since the public are already well informed of the general character of the resources and advantages now offered. Suffice it to say, that we offer the coal-fields and pits, in operation, with the negroes, mules, machines, engines, rail roads, buildings, and fixtures of every description whatever – as well, also, as the coal-yard and farm, with the labor and stock thereon, – affording the facilities for foraging and feeding the necessary force required in the mining operations, – which renders the Company or Corporation, independent for supplies, labor and means of almost every kind, and affords a profit nearly nett except the transit of coal upon the rail road. The farm contains over 900 acres, and was a portion of the original Falls plantation, and is situated on the south side of James river, opposite to the lower part of the city of Richmond, – bounded on the north and west by the property of Joseph Marx, on the east by James river, and on the south by the property of William Hancock. The Coal-yard Island, with buildings, &c,. – originally a part of this tract, upon which our coal-yards are situated, – is bounded on the east by James river, on the north by the property of Joseph Marx, and on the south and west by Mill creek; acknowledged to be most advantageously improved and arranged for an extensive trade, – possessing many eligible, unoccupied sites for new coal-yards, glass-houses, furnaces, forges, &c. &c. The rents and income from the produce of this property, in its present condition, would amount to more, annually, than the interest on the amount of the valuation; and if occupied, as it shortly must be, the revenue will be greatly increased. On this property, is situation an extensive building, now used as a receptacle for rough food, or forage, intended to be used at the mines, with a rail road thereto, as well as to the lumber house, which affords the facility of receiving and delivering, direct from both, the articles daily required for the pits.

The Chester Lodge Lot at Warwick, contains about nine acres, and was selected as a shipping yard. Should the coal trade ever be carried to that place, the advantages to the Virginia coal trade would be incalculably great, by avoiding the bar in James river, between Warwick and the present shipping yards. The height of the banks at this point, offer great advantages for the erection of coal yards and staiths, at such elevations, as to afford the facility of selecting the various quantities of coal, by a process of screening, without additional labor, which would greatly add to the character and value of the Virginia coal. The improvements on this property are, a dwelling-house of old fashion, but very roomy and convenient, and although somewhat out of repair, is built of first rate materials, and may be put in good repair at a small expense; the kitchen is built of brick, and contains four rooms. There is an excellent wharf, also, on this property, and ships of a large class may lay so near the shore to the ship. It is bounded on the east by James River, on the south by the property of John Turpin, and on the west and north by the property of Christopher Roberts.

The East Lothian tract contains about 300 acres, occupied by Dr. A. L. Wooldridge – had lately been improved at great expense, and is in every respect in good order, and is a very desirable residence. About half of this tract is in wood and timber, chiefly pine of second growth, which is of the most valuable kind, for curbing, propping and geering of coal mines; the open land is enclosed, and has been manured and improved – a large portion is excellent meadow land, and by proper cultivation, would form a valuable auxiliary to the feeding department. The situation is very healthy and beautiful, and its location is immediately at the pits, though not estimated as cold [coal] land, in consequence of its being on the eastern side of the out crop of the Stone Henge seam of coal. A portion of this tract, called the Dower land, containing 98 acres, was held by different owners, a portion of whom sold their separate interests to A. & A. Wooldridge & Co., and *they* own 10/20ths of this particular portion, and will convey the title to so much only; which said tract is bounded on the north by the lands of ---- Sowell, dec'd; on east by the lands of Haley Cole; on the south by the land of Thomas M. Burfoot; and on the west by the Union pit, Creek pits, and Stone Henge pit tracts.

The Rosewood tract of land contains about 200 acres, and is in the direct range of both the great coal stratas on Falling creek, which has excited universal admiration, so far as the great thickness and purity of these seams of coal have been known. The mines of England, Scotland, and Wales, though acknowledged to be the most extensive and valuable known to exist in Europe, do not present such thick coal formations, as those of Falling creek. The outcrop of the Stone Henge coal formation, passes through the eastern and southern portion of the Rosewood tract, and forms the coal-field rise and dip to a central line through the tract, running nearly north and south; and at or near the same point, the out crop of the Railey Hill and Midlothian seams pass through the tract, dipping to the west, and forming the coal-field on its northern and western division. By reference to a geological survey of the whole range of coal-fields in this section of the mineral region, the most unerring evidences of the mineral ranges prove, beyond all speculation, the existence of coal formations throughout this tract, with the small exception, of the ordinary *trouble* at the junction of the two seams, forming the extreme dip of the Stone Henge seam, and the out crop of the Midlothian seams. This tract is in its virgin state: and if the coal formation continues of its usual thickness and purity, of which there cannot be a reasonable doubt, the area of the mineral deposite upon this tract will afford unlimited supplies for an incalculable length of time. To illustrate the truth of this opinion, we beg leave to mention one or two examples of the correctness of our views, viz: A piece of property, called the Green Hole pit, containing three acres only, was wrought by the late Wm. Robertson, father of John Robertson, Esq., now our worthy representative in Congress, between thirty and forty years ago, since which time this property has been successively wrought by Cornelius Buck, Orris Paine, Nelson Cary, and others; and within the last two or three years, A. & A. Wooldridge & Co. became the owners of it – then generally believed to be in an exhausted state; and during the last year they re-opened these mines, and their explorations have developed further and large deposites of coal, from which they obtained, during the last and present year, their principal supplies of coal; and by recent developments in the adjoining mines of Mills, Reid & Co., a body of coal, belonging to this tract, is found to exist on a level with *their* present workings, from which the coal may be wrought to very great advantage, as it may be done by them, without the expense of a new pit; and they have become the purchasers of this portion of the Green Hole coal, at the price of two cents per bushel, to be estimated as the coal stands in the field; and *we* think this portion of the coal-field will contain from one to two millions of bushels of merchantable coal, independent of the coal-field from which we are now receiving our daily supplies.

We would also remark, that at the time of Mr. Mills' purchase of Railey Hill pits, they had been abandoned by the late Maj. H. Heth, and had filled with water – since which they have been re-opened, and further developments prove that they were far more valuable than had ever been estimated, and although not more than five acres of this land has been wrought, the wealth which it has yielded to its present proprietor is acknowledged on all hands to be very great, and yet the value of this property is not held in higher estimation than at any former period.

It is proper to say, that these are various qualities of coal on Falling creek, each suited to particular purposes; and in consequence of our having had the command of all the qualities, by means of working both the Stone Henge and Midlothian pits, we enjoyed great advantages in filling the various orders, – and as the Rosewood land is possessed of both of those seams, the Ben Lomond Company must enjoy all the advantages of the trade in each. We would further remark that A. & A. Wooldridge & Co. would not have offered their interest alone in this property, (say 2/3ds,) if the other interest could have been obtained upon the same terms they have priced theirs at in the following schedule; they have offered to purchase the other interest, and make the payments in stock or money at the same rate, which was refused – consequently the Ben Lomond Company can only be subjected to a charge of reasonable rent on this portion, (say 1/3,) but with the right of working the whole at pleasure.

With reference to the interest in the Road pits, the Union pits, and Cunliffe's old pits, the prices put on them are so extremely low as not to require a passing remark, and we will only say that we have taken from the Road pit about thirty thousand bushels of coals in the last few weeks, and are not receiving regular supplies therefrom; and we have reason to believe that a basin of coal exists to the west of the old works on the Union pit tract, very similar to the present workings of Mills, Reid & Co. at their Green Hole pit – and as the Union coal formation is the same, and adjoins their Green Hole pits, it is not at all improbable that they possess a similar value.

The tract, called Cunliffe's old pits, contains about 160 acres, and was formerly estimated as one of the most valuable coal-fields in the neighborhood, and adjoins the Old Black Heth pits, Murchie's pits, and Blount's pits, and although abandoned for the supposed want of coal, like many other mines in the neighborhood which have been neglected and abandoned for the same cause, – which have been re-opened, and by new explorations, developed greater value than was ever before attached to them; we confidently believe that the prospect is fair for such a result in this case. This tract is well enclosed, and has a commodious dwelling house and other buildings, now in the occupancy of Mr. Charles Cunliffe.

(Page 11)

GENERAL SCHEDULE.

_____

NO. 1

A List of Coal Property belonging to A. & A. Wooldridge & Co. and embraced in the Ben Lomond Coal Charter, estimated viz:.

Two undivided third parts of the Rosewood Tract,
   containing about 200 acres, bounded on the north
   by the property of the Midlothian Coal Mining
   Company, on the south and east by James McTyre's
   property, and on the west by the lands of ---- Roberts,
   dccd. Value of the whole tract is estimated at $75,000.
   The interest of A. & A. Wooldridge & Co. being
   two-thirds, is $50,000 00

Cunliffe's Old Pits, contains about 160 acres,
   bounded on the south by the Manchester
   Turnpike, on the east by the lands of ---- Sowell,
   decd., on the north by the Old Black Heth Pits,
   and on the west by the lands of John Murchie,
   decd., Blount's Pits, and also by Ross & Currie's,
   now owned and occupied by the Black Heth
   Company of colliers. A. & A. Wooldridge
   & Co. will convey a title to one-fourth of this
   tract, valued at $22,000, their proportion being   5,500 00
Our Green Hole (or Laurel) Pits contain 3 acres,
   and is bounded on the west by the Pits. of N.
   Mills, now occupied by Mills, Reid & Co.; and
   on the north, east, and south by the Union Pits.
   We are now working this property, and value it
   at - - - - - -   8,000 00

                    $63,500 00

(Page 12)

Amount brought forward, - - -   63,500 00

The Union Pits 33 ½ acres, and is bounded
   on the west by the coal lands of N. Mills, by
   A. & A. Wooldridge & Co.'s Green Hole or
   Laurel Pits, and the lands of the Creek Coal
   Company; on the north by the lands of — Sowell,
   Decd., and on the east and south by the East
   Lothian Tract. The Road Tract, commonly called
   Wooldridge's Old Pits, contains about
   13 acres, and is bounded on the south and east
   by N. Mills' Railey Hill Pits, on the north by
   the Buckingham road, and on the west by
   the Maidenhead Pits. We own three-eighths
   of the Road Pits, and one-fourth of nine-twentieths
   in the Union Pits described above, and value both
   of these interests at the sum of - -   2,500 00

                    $66,000 00

NO. II.

Valuation by Mssrs. Snead, Wills & Potts, of the
   Falls Farm, Coal Yard Island, Chester Lodge,
   ad East Lothian Tract, as may be seen in detail,
   by reference to List No. 2, - - -   60,000 00

NO. III.

Valuation by Mssrs. Snead, Wills & Potts, of 73 Slaves at Pits and on the Farm, which will also be seen in detail, *by reference to List No. 3*, -	48,250 00

NO. IV.

Valuation, by the same, of Personal Property at the Pits, at the Farm, and Coal Yard, which will be set forth in detail, *by reference to List No. 4,*	30,906 50
To which add this amount, as a cash capital, to be retained by the Company, - - -	20,000 00

$225,156 50

(Page 13)

DETAILED SCHEDULE.

NO. 1
LIST OF COAL LANDS,
AND THEIR ESTIMATED VALUE.

Two-thirds Rosewood (or Cobbs') containing 200 acres, embracing the Stone Henge and Midlothian seams of coal, - - - -	$50,000 00	
Laurel Pit, (now in operation) -	8,000 00	
Three-eights Road Pits, containing about 13 acres, (now in operation,) and one-fourth of nine-twentieths of Union Pits, containing 33 ½ acres, -	2,500 00	
One-fourth Buck & Cunliffe's Pits, -	5,500 00	
		$66,000 00

NO. 2
LIST OF REAL ESTATE,

Valued by Mssrs. Snead, Wills & Potts, belonging to Messrs. A. & A. Wooldridge & Co., situated in the County of Chesterfield, 30th June, 1837.

The Falls Farm (except Coal Yard Island) containing about nine hundred acres, with all the improvements thereon, - - - -	$30,000 00

Coal Yard Island, containing about
twenty acres, with all the buildings,
wharves, staiths, stages, shipping bar-
rows, rail roads, and improvements
thereon, - - - -   25,000 00

                     $55,000 00 $66,000 00

(Page 14)

Amounts brought forward,	$55,000 00	$66,000 00

Chester Lodge Lot, at Warwick, containing eight or nine acres, -   1,000 00
East Lothian Tract, containing about
300 acres, well timbered, with a comfortable dwelling house, all the neces-
saray out-houses, enclosures, &c.; embraced in this tract, is a portion called
the Dower land, containing 98 acres,
of which A. & A. W. & Co. will
convey 10/20ths, - - -   4,000 00

                                    $60,000 00

(Signed)   JESSE SNEAD,
                     GEO. E. WILLS,
                     THOMAS. R. POTTS.
     A true copy.

NO. 3
LIST OF SLAVES,

Valued by the same, belonging to Mssrs. A. & A.
Wooldridge & Co., at their Pits, on the 28th of June,
1837.

1. Abram Moseley, age about 27 years	$850 00
2. Billy Cole,	" 46 "	200 00
3. Bob Sheppard,	" 30 "	600 00
4. Bob Anderson,	" 27 "	850 00
5. Ben Hare,	" 45 "	650 00
6. Billy Quaker,	" 28 "	300 00
7. Barlett Abbott,	" 30 "	800 00
8. Charles Hall,	" 35 "	1000 00
9. Daniel Hall,	" 27 "	1000 00
10. Dick Truly,	" 40 "	600 00
11. Davy Woolroy,	" 23 "	800 00
12. Dick Brooks,	" 25 "	850 00

13. Frank Hall,   " 24 "   850 00

                                                            $9,350 00 $126,000 00

                                      (Page 15)

        Amounts brought forward, $9,350 00 $126,000 00

14. Frank May, age about 45 years,   200 00
15. Flemming,   " 11 "   450 00
16. George Tompkins,   " 27 "   850 00
17. George Allen,   " 40 "   300 00
18. Henry Hare,   " 12 "   500 00
19. Harry Burton,   " 35 "   550 00
20. Harry Jacobs,   " 40 "   300 00
21. Jim Dutch,   " 25 "   900 00
22. Joe Anderson,   " 20 "   900 00
23. Jim Barrett,   " 21 "   1000 00
24. John Goode,   " 25 "   1000 00
25. Jesse,   " 35 "   850 00
26. Isaac Sublett,   " 25 "   1000 00
27. Jerman,   " 33 "   375 00
28. Lewis Barclay,   " 22 "   900 00
29. John and Lucy Sheppard,   100 00
30. Major Dudley,   " 26 "   900 00
31. Matt Fendley,   " 45 "   850 00
32. Moses Ragland,   " 24 "   800 00
33. Ned Fendley,   " 27 "   750 00
34. Nathan Branch,   " 38 "   650 00
35. Peter Lumpkin,   " 60 "   150 00
36. Sie Branch,   " 22 "   1000 00
37. Sam Clarke,   " 16 "   600 00
38. Selden,   " 11 "   450 00
39. Tom Straghan,   " 26 "   900 00
40. Surry Winfree,   " 35 "   450 00
41. Vivian Sheppard,   " 36 "   150 00
42. Warner,   " 26 "   1200 00
43. Winston Barclay,   " 24 "   1000 00
44. Watkins,   " 16 "   750 00
45. Archer,   " 26 "   800 00

Total value of Negros at Pits, $30,925 00 $126,000 00

                                      (Page 16)

        Amount brought forward, $126,000 00

LIST OF SLAVES,

Valued by the undersigned, belonging to Mssrs. A. & A.
Wooldridge & Co., at their Falls Farm and Coal
Yard, 30th June, 1837.

1. Anthony, age about 38 years,		$850 00
2. Davy,	" 35 "	850 00
3. Sawney,	" 38 "	850 00
4. Solomon,	" 25 "	900 00
5. Clinton,	" 20 "	900 00
6. Anderson,	" 25 "	900 00
7. Washington,	" 23 "	800 00
8. John,	" 19 "	900 00
9. William,	" 17 "	900 00
10. Moses,	" 17 "	850 00
11. Ned,	" 23 "	900 00
12. Joe,	" 25 "	900 00
13. Sam,	" 16 "	850 00
14. George,	" 16 "	800 00
15. Ben,	" 42 "	625 00
16. Rueben,	" 36 "	800 00
17. Taliaferro,	" 36 "	200 00
18. Billy Lighter,	" 23 "	200 00
19. George,	" 50 "	50 00
20. Bartlette,	" 25 "	400 00
21. Stephen,	" 45 "	500 00
22. Nelson,	" 27 "	800 00
23. Leantha,	" 30 "	400 00
24. Nelson, (her son,)	" 4 "	200 00
25. Fanny,	" 25 "	400 00
26. Warner, (her son,)	" 5 "	200 00

$16,925 00 $126,000 00

(Page 17)

Amounts brought forward, $16,925 00 $126,000 00

27. Maria, age about 50 years,   200 00
28. Rose,   " 50 "   200 00

Total value of Negroes on Farm, $17,325 00
Total value of Negroes at Pits,   30,925 00

Total Value of Slaves, $48,250 00

(Signed)   JESSE SNEAD,
                     GEO. E. WILLS,
                     THOMAS. R. POTTS.
A true copy.

NO. 4

LIST OF PROPERTY,

Valued by the same, belonging to Mssrs. A. & A.
Wooldridge & Co., at their Pits, on the 28th of June,
1837.

One thirty-horse power Engine, with
   pumping and winding apparatus, with
   extra brass buckets, clacks, cranes,
   ropes and extra pipes, $10,000 00
Buildings, Rail Roads, &c. at Midlo-
   thian Pit,   1,000 00
One 8 Horse Winding Engine complete   2,400 00
Buildings, Rail Roads, &c. at Stone
   Henge,   2,000 00
Thirty-two Mules at Pits,   3,200 00
Four Coal Machines, Pit Heads,
   Pullies, &c.,   800 00
Four cast-iron hand Pumps, with Brass
   Buckets, Clacks and Pipes,   200 00
Two Rail Road Cars – 1 with hay body,   300 00
Two Wagons and one Cart, with Gear,   100 00

                    $20,000 00 $174,250 00

(Page 18)

Amounts brought forward, $20,000 00 $174,250 00

One Slate Car,   50 00
One Coal Screen and five Wheelbarrows,   25 00
Three Straw Cutters, and three patent
   balances,   125 00
One steel Homony Mill,   35 00
Two tons assorted Bar Iron   220 00

One set Blacksmith's Tools, Drill

Braces, &c.	75 00
One set Carpenter's Tool's, 2 x Cut, 3 Pit Saws, Axes, &c.	100 00
Turning Lathe, and Tools for turning wood and iron,	125 00
Ten Bogies, Iron Axles and Wheels,	200 00
Twelve Water Buckets, and 50 Corves complete	120 00
Two sets Sinking Tools, Boring Rods, &c.,	50 00
Baskets, Basket Bales and Fire Pans,	50 00
One set Iron and one set Wood Blocks and Ropes,	125 00
Two Grindstones, Pit Tools, Drills, Mauls, Wedges, Pecks, &c.,	150 00
One Surveyor's Chain, Compass and Plotting Instruments,	50 00
Buildings, Rail Roads, &c. at Laurel Pit,	550 00
Castings for Coal Drop,	750 00

Total Am't of per. property at the Pits, $22,800 00

(Signed)   JESSE SNEAD,
                    GEO. E. WILLS,
                    THOMAS. R. POTTS.

A true copy.

$174,250 00

(Page 19)

Amount brought forward, $174,250 00

LIST OF PERSONAL PROPERTY,

Valued by the undersigned belonging to Mssrs. A. & A. Wooldridge & Co., at their Falls Farm and Coal Yard, 30th June, 1837.

Twenty Mules,	$2,000 00
Thirty Head of Cattle,	700 00
Forty-five head of Hogs	140 00
Three Four-Horse Wagons,	240 00
One Two-Horse do.	80 00

Four Tumbling Carts and Gears	120 00	
Two Ox Carts,	120 00	
Five Three-Horse Ploughs,	60 00	
Nine Two-Horse do.	35 00	
Eight One-Horse do.	25 00	
Four Cultivators,	12 00	
Seven Coulters,	8 00	
Five Iron-tooth Harrows or Drags,	20 00	
Two Wheat Fans,	50 00	
One Straw Cutter,	20 00	
One Corn Sheller,	20 00	
One set Blacksmith's Tools,	30 00	
Two Rollers,	8 00	
Eighteen sets Mule Gears,	20 00	
Ten Wheat Cradles,	25 00	
Nine Grass Scythes,	9 00	
Nine Reap Hooks,	4 00	
Five Narrow Axes,	3 00	
Seven Grubbing Hoes,	4 00	
Twelve Weeding Hoes,	4 00	
One set of Carpenter's Tools	20 00	
Two pair Mauling Wedges	2 50	
	$3,740 50	$174,250 00

(Page 20)

Amounts brought forward,	$3,740 00	$174,250 00
Six Shovels and three Spades,	4 50	
Six Forked Hoes,	3 00	
Three Iron Pitchforks,	1 50	
Two large Iron Pots,	2 00	
Office fixtures and kitchen Furniture at yard,	55 00	
Twenty thousand German Stock Bricks, at $15 per 1000,	300 00	
Growing Crops on the Falls Farm (wheat excepted,)	4,000 00	
Total value of per. property at Farm,	$8,106 50	
Do. do. at Pits,	22,000 00	

Total value of personal property, negroes excepted,	$30,906 50

To which add this amount, as a cash capital, to be

retained by the Company,   20,000 00

$225,156 50

(Signed,)   JESSE SNEAD,
                   GEO. E. WILLS,
                   THOMAS. R. POTTS.
A true copy.

(Page 21)

Manchester, July 2d, 1837.

Dear Sir, – Your note of the 1st was handed to me an hour or so past, and I with pleasure comply with your several requests. As to the territorial extent of the Rosewood tract of land, my knowledge is only from common report, which is that it contains about two hundred acres, and was so estimate by my father during the period he was part owner.

In answer to your second and third inquiries, I do think from its peculiar locality, the Stone Henge seam of coal probably passes through the eastern and southern division of this tract, and equally probably that the Midlothian seam of coal passes through in the northern and western division.

In reply to your last inquiry, I think no land could be more directly in the range of the coal-field; and I will add, I know of no tract of unexplored land of the same number of acres that I consider of more value for its mineral deposit than it.

Yours most respectfully,
A. MICHAELS

Mr. F. Clarke.

Midlothian, 10th July, 1837.

Dr. Wooldridge, – In compliance with your and Mr. Fred Clarke's request, that I should give my opinion of the extent and location of the Rosewood tract of land, better known as Cobb's tract, in reference to its position in the coal-field of Chesterfield, it may be proper for me to premise, in giving the opinion I entertain, that I was born and raised very near this land, and that it immediately adjoins the Grove tract, formerly owned by me and conveyed to the Midlothian Coal Mining Company, – that my attention has often been drawn to its position, and much reflection necessarily bestowed upon it in connection with my interest in the adjoining land. I therefore feel no hesitation in coming to, and expressing the opinion, that this tract contains both the Midlothian and Stone Henge strata of coal, and is of great value as coal land. The interest owned by your concern in the tract, which contains about 200 acres, is 2/3ds in fee simple.

A.S. WOOLDRIDGE.

I know all the coal property owned by A. & A. Wooldridge & Co., and think the value put on each piece is lower than I should have estimated it.

JOHN HETH.

Gentlemen, – In reply to your note respecting your coal property, I have to say – I have been about thirty years engaged in coal operations in Europe and this country – I have lived at several coal mines in this neighborhood, and am at present the manager of the Black Heath Company's Mines, and fully concur with Maj. Wooldridge and Capt. Heth as to the value of your coal property, – and as to both seams of coal passing through Cobb's land, and think the estimate you put into them reasonable and low.

JOHN REYNARD.

Having been requested to state how long I have been engaged in the coal mining business, and to give my opinion of the tract of land known by the name of Cobb's, as regards its value as coal property,– in reply, I state that I have been engaged for the last eight years as an assistance and superintendent at the coal mines in the immediate neighborhood of Cobb's, – that I am now the superintendent for the Midlothian Coal Mining Company, and engaged in sinking two shafts for said Company on the Grove tract immediately adjoining Cobb's; and thus knowing the position of Cobb's, as being favorable situated in the coalfield of Chesterfield, I fully concur with Maj. Wooldridge in the opinions he has expressed, that the Midlothian and Stone Henge strata of coal bed extend through Cobb's tract, and that it is of great value as coal land.

Z. McGRUDER, Jr.

Coal Mine, 16th July, 1837.

Mr. F. Clarke,

Dear Sir, – Your letter dated 4th July, in which you ask my opinion as to the extent and value of the Rosewood tract of land, as connected with the coal formation in this neighborhood – has been received. So far as I am enabled, by having directed my time and attention almost exclusively to the various mining operations in the great coal-field of this county, my opinion is given with pleasure. So much has been developed as regards the geological position of the coal-fields adjoining to, and in the direct line of, the coal strata already explored, as to leave no doubt that the Rosewood tract, from its position, is directly intersected by three of the most extensive and valuable bodies of coal, (Stone Henge, the Creek coal, 60 to 70 feet thick, and the Midlothian.) I have no hesitation in saying that such is my opinion, the valuation ($50,000) is sufficiently low.

As regards the valuation of all the balance of the property embraced in the Ben Lomond Scheme, (made by the three gentlemen named in your letter,) I have

only to say that my confidence in their superior judgment in such matters, leaves
no doubt, that it is fair and reasonable.

Yours very respectfully,
CHARLES CUNLIFFE

Chesterfield Coal Mines, July 23d, 1837.

Gentlemen, – Having been requested to give my opinion of the value placed
upon your coal lands, but more particularly the Rosewood tract, it is with
pleasure that I can state that I am unacquainted with and land of the *same extent,
that I value so highly.* From geological surveys made of it, and its contiguity to
lands where coal has been found, I cannot doubt the existence of the Stone Henge
and Midlothian seams of coal passing through it, in as extensive formations as
any place where explored.

The Midlothian Company have struck the Top Stone Henge seam at the
depth of 270 feet, and will get a working seam at less than 100 feet deeper. This
pit is sunk from 2 to 300 yards (in a direct line with the coal strata) from the
northern boundary of the Rosewood land. The other coal lands I consider you
have estimated at a fair and reasonable price.

It may be necessary to state here, that I was brought up in the north of
England to the coal business from early life, and have continued in said business.
For the last four years I have had the management of different mines in this
country and have given much attention to the course and dip of the metals in the
Falling Creek region.

Yours respectfully,
THOMAS R. POTTS.

Messrs. A. & A. Wooldridge & Co.
Manchester.

Richmond, July 27, 1837.

Messrs. A. & A. Wooldridge & Co.

Gentlemen, – My opinion has been asked as to your coal property, &c. I am
unable to speak understandably upon the subject, not knowing its relative locality
to the coal region contiguous thereto, further than the plat exhibited a few days
since. I will premise that I have been several years engaged in coal operations,
and have paid some attention to the surface evidences, as well as to the
lineaments of coal fields, and feel persuaded in my own mind that I hazard but
little in saying, that with great certainty the several strata of coal found on the
adjoining tracts of land, will be found also embodied in yours.

Very respectfully,
EDWARD ANDERSON.

Richmond, July 31st, 1837.

Mr. F. Clarke,

Dear Sir, – Your request for my opinion of the value of the coal lands, which Messrs A. & A. Wooldridge & Co. propose to convey to the Ben Lomond Coal Company is before me, and I reply by saying, that I consider the price at which you offer the coal lands, (sixty-six thousand dollars,) very low – forming this opinion from a slight personal knowledge of the situation of these lands, and a careful examination of the geological survey of the coal minerals of the neighborhood.

Yours most respectfully,
JESSE SNEAD.

Black Heth, July 31st, 1837.

Messrs. A. & A. Wooldridge & Co.,

Gentlemen, – I received your note of the 26th inst., in which you request an expression of my opinion with regard to the value of certain coal lands therein named.

The Rosewood (or Cobb's) tract, from the fact of its being in a direct line with the Midlothian and Stone Henge workings, and its proximity thereto, in my opinion warrants the belief, that it does contain both those valuable seams of coal. Indeed, I know of no other property in the neighborhood (that is not already being worked,) that offers so great inducements for enterprise as this.

I have examined the estimates put upon your other coal property also – and have no hesitation in saying, that compared with the price at which property, similarly situated in the neighborhood, has generally been sold, your estimates are moderate, fair and reasonable.

With my best wishes for your prosperity, and the success of the Virginia coal trade, I remain, gentleman,

Yours sincere friend, &c.
GEO. E. WILLS.

We beg leave to say, that among the slaves contained in the list of valuation, will be found, in requisite proportions, the most valuable artizans in every branch of the coal business, viz: carpenters, blacksmiths, engineers, sinkers, diggers, trailers, banksmen, drivers, corve makers, &c. &c. These qualifications are not only essential, but indispensable, and when proclaimed at the public annual hireings, produce an increase price of hire from one third to one-half more than for raw or unskilled hands; and taking the range of prices for such hands during the last two years, we entertain no doubt they would have commanded, and will now command in a body, the average price of $150 each.

Say 60 hands at $150,	$9,000 00
To which let us add, as the annual product of the farm,	10,000 00
For rent of coal yard and produce of the island,	1,500 00

$20,500 00

Thus it will be seen, from the foregoing statement, that a portion only of this property would produce a dividend of not less than ten per cent on the whole amount of the property embraced in the Ben Lomond Scheme, without bringing into use the coal property, and the produce of a large and valuable portion of the real and personal property, as will be seen by reference to the foregoing lists; and which under this aspect, secures to the proprietors of this stock, a certain and satisfactory interest on the whole investment, in its most unproductive situation.

Now let us estimate the yield of this property *embarked in the coal trade* – having to prepare the Rosewood coal-field for extensive operations, viz: 13 hands, with the necessary number of mules, machines, tools &c., are sufficient for the sinking of one pit; and as two new shafts will be necessary to catch both the Stone Henge and Midlothian coal stratas, 26 hands, &c. will be required for the sinking of two new pits, one of which is already begun, and both may be finished during the first year, – while the residue of the hands and other fixtures contained in the schedule, may produce from the other mines, now open and in operation, as much coal as will defray all the expenses the Company would be subjected to, over and above the resources of the farm and other property; and the Company may reasonably calculate on accomplishing the object of putting this varied and valuable property in full and successful operation, with but little if any other resources than the produce of the property herein enumerated. But if a different course should prove to be desirable on the part of the Company, so as to hasten the consummation of the objects in view, and to derive a larger revenue from the produce of the other coal property contained in the list, while they are prosecuting their sinking operations of the Rosewood tract, they may do so, at a very small additional expense, by hireing a few additional hands to operate with their surplus force in the pits now open and in operation – by which course, it is believed that the Company will not only sustain the expenses of their sinking operations, but in the first year may calculate on a handsome dividend.

After Rosewood coal field shall have been fully explored, and the developments of such coal formations, as we have the very best reasons to believe do exist there, then we may most reasonably estimate the results of operations thereon as follows:

The annual produce of two shafts on the Rosewood tract, say 1,000,000 bushels coals, estimated at 10 cents per bushel of 5 pecks, is	$100,000 00
From which deduct the rents on 1,000,000 bushels of coal at 1 cent per bushel, will be $10,000 – and one-third being the proportion of John Cobbs and Thomas Cobbs in the Rosewood	

tract, will be	$3,333 33	
For hire of 100 raw hands, including clothes and part feeding, at $150, is	15,000 00	
For wages to overseers and agents, oil, candles, ropes, iron, powder, and contingents,	11,666 67	30,000 00

Yielding more than 30 per cent. nett, $70,000 00

While we trust these calculations will be found to have been made on the most reasonable basis, and founded strictly in fact and it truth, we also feel the utmost confidence, that under prudent and judicious management, the results will be more permanent and more productive, than we have given reasons in the foregoing statements to expect.

We purpose to dispose of at least 500 shares of 100 dollars each in the Ben Lomond Charter, to be paid for by approved negotiable notes, at 4, 8, 12 and 15 and 18 months date from the time the Company shall be organized. Certificates of stock will be issued when the notes are paid. And from the proceeds of the sale of this portion of the stock, $20,000 shall be held by the directors as a cash capital, for the use and benefit of said Company, and the residue to be paid over to A. & A. Wooldridge & Co., or their Trustees, who shall first convey good and sufficient titles to the property, agreeable to the foregoing statement.

In conclusion, we would say that the operations in coal mines are precarious, and liable to many casualties, perhaps to a greater degree than some other pursuits; but it is believed, that when the works are fairly explored, judiciously laid out, and properly wrought, that they are as susceptible of calculation, and that their results may be as truly estimated as those of any other species of property depending on the future; and the undersigned have labored to avoid such errors as are calculated to mislead those who may wish to become interested in this enterprise; and in all statements, calculations, and estimates, they have been influenced solely by the results of their own experience and honest opinions.

A. L. WOOLDRIDGE,
G. V. CLARKE,
HENRY CLARKE.

Chesterfield Co., Va.
August 1st, 1837.

AN ACT
TO INCORPORATE THE

BEN LOMOND COAL COMPANY.

Passed February 27, 1837.

---

1. *Be it enacted by the General Assembly,* That Henry Clarke, Gustavus V. Clarke, and Frederick Clarke, and such other persons as may hereafter be associated with them, shall be, and are hereby incorporated and made a body politic and corporate, under the name and style of *"The Ben Lomond Coal Company,"* for the purpose of digging, mining, raising and transporting coal within the counties of Chesterfield and Powhatan, and are hereby invested with all the rights, privileges and powers conferred upon such bodies politic and corporate, by an act "prescribing general regulations for the incorporation of manufacturing and mining companies," passed February the thirteenth, eighteen hundred and thirty seven, and are made subject to the restrictions and regulations prescribed by said act.

2. *Be it further enacted,* That the capital stock of said company shall not be less than fifty thousand dollars, nor more than five hundred thousand dollars, to be divided into shares of one hundred dollars each; and that said company shall have the right to purchase and hold land not exceeding three thousand acres in the aforesaid counties.

3.   This act shall be in force from the passing thereof.

AN ACT

Prescribing General Regulations for the Incorporation of Manufacturing and Mining Companies.

Passed February 13th, 1837.

---

1. *Be it enacted by the General Assembly of Virginia,* That whensoever hereafter any joint stock company shall be incorporated for the purposes of manufacturing, or for the purposes of exploring and mining for gold, coal, copper, iron or other mineral substances, such company shall be established with the rights and privileges, and under the rules, regulations, and restrictions hereinafter provided.

2. Said company shall have power, under the name and style set forth in the act of incorporation, to sue and be sued, contract and be contracted with, to have and use a common seal, and change the same at pleasure; and may hold real estate, the number of acres, and the county or counties, corporation or corporations in which said real estate is situate, to be specified in the said act of incorporation; and personal property for the purpose of conducting the business of manufacturing, exploring or mining, for which said company shall be incorporated; and shall have power to make such by-laws, rules and regulations, not contrary to the laws of the United States, or of this commonwealth, as may be deemed expedient and proper for the government of said corporation; but they shall not be authorized in any manner to divert the capital of said company from the specific purposes for which they are incorporated: *Provided*, nothing herein contained shall be construed as to prevent any corporation from tilling any lands held by them, or from selling any timber, wood or other material upon their lands.

3. The amount of the capital stock of such company shall be specified in said act of incorporation, fixing a minimum and maximum sum, to be raised by subscription, in shares to be specified; for which purpose, books of subscription may be opened by the corporators or commissioners named in said act, as the case may be, at such times and places as the said corporators or commissioners may designate, who, as soon as the minimum sum specified as the capital stock of said company shall have been subscribed for, shall call a meeting of the subscribers by advertisement, for two weeks, in some newspaper published in the neighborhood, or by some other convenient mode of notification.

4. And whensoever the mining or manufacturing operations of the company to be incorporated, are proposed to be located and carried on upon the lands of property of any person or persons who may be willing to sell the said lands or property, with the privileges and appurtenances necessary for said operations, to said company, or to convert the same into stock of the said company, and convey to them the said lands or property at a fair valuation, the said owner or owners shall, in the books of subscription, to be opened as aforesaid, fairly set forth and specify the quantity of land, with a precise description of the metes and bounds thereof, and a full statement of the other property, rights, privileges and appurtenances, which he or they propose to cede, sell or convey to, or to convert into stock of the said company, and the price affixed to and demanded by said owner or owners for said lands and other property; or if said owner or owners propose to sell a part to said company, and to subscribe the residue of said lands and property, he or they shall enter on the said books, a full description of the part which he or they propose to sell, and the part which he or they propose to subscribe as stock of the said company, with the prices and terms of payment required therefor; and the said lands, property, &c., so subscribed by said owner or owners, shall be taken in full payment of his or their said subscriptions, and shall thereafter be and constitute a part of the capital stock of said company, subject to be disposed of in like manner with the residue of their stock and property; and the lands, property, &c., which said owner or owners shall propose to sell to the said company, and which shall have been entered on the books of subscription, with the price and terms of payment affixed thereto, shall, if subscriptions be made in said books, and if the company shall thereupon proceed

to organize itself, by calling a general meeting of the subscribers and electing a board of directors, as hereinafter to be provided, be considered and held as property of said company, and the price of said lands, property, rights, privileges and appurtenances so entered in the books of subscription, shall be a lawful debt of the said company, and it shall be lawful for the said owner or owners to sue for and recover the same in any court having competent jurisdiction. And unless the said owner or owners of the said lands, property, privileges and appurtenances shall at the first meeting and organization of said company or so soon thereafter as may be required of him or them convey and assure to the said company a valid and perfect title in fee simple to the said lands, property &c., according to the specification and description thereof, entered on the books as aforesaid, and also deliver possession of the same when demanded, the said company may, on such failure, either enforce a specific performance of the contract on the part of the said owner or owners, or at the election of the said company, may regard the subscription or sale of the said lands and property as forfeited and void.

5. For managing the affairs of such mining or manufacturing company, there shall be chosen at the first meeting of the stockholders, to be called as aforesaid, and on the first Monday of the month of May of every year thereafter, a convenient number of directors, not less than five, nor more than ten, who shall be stockholders of the said company; in which elections, and in all other meetings, the stockholders shall be entitled to one vote for every share owned by them respectively, up to the number of fifteen inclusive, and to one additional vote for every five shares from fifteen to one hundred, and to one additional vote for every twenty shares over and above one hundred, and may vote in person or by proxy, in such manner as may from time to time be prescribed in general meeting. The said directors, or a majority of them may choose from their own body a president, and in his absence, a president *pro tempore*. They shall have power to call general meetings of the stockholders; to supply vacancies in their own body – to appoint such officers, agents and clerks as the stockholders in general meeting shall authorize – to take bonds with sufficient surety for the good conduct, fidelity and attention of such officers, agents and clerks, and to do all other acts and things touching the affairs of the company, not otherwise specially provided for.

6. The presence of stockholders entitled to a majority of the whole number of votes, in person or by proxy, shall be necessary to the transaction of business at any general meeting of the stockholders; and such meetings shall be organized by the appointment of a chairman and secretary, but a smaller number may adjourn from time to time. And if there should be no election of directors then in office shall continue until the next annual election by the stockholders in general meeting, in which the major part of the stock shall be represented.

7. If the whole amount of capital stock authorized to be raised by any act of incorporation shall not have been subscribed for before the company incorporated by said act shall have commenced its operations, it shall in such case be lawful for the president and directors of said company, whensoever they may deem it expedient, to cause books of subscription to be opened from time to time unitl the whole amount of the capital stock authorized to be raised by said act shall have been subscribed for; and also, if so to them is shall seem proper, to fix the price

of the additional stock at such a premium as they may from time to time direct – which premium shall be the common property of all the stockholders of said company, in proportion to the capital stock owned by them respectively.

8. So much of the price of each share subscribed, whether before or after the company shall have been organized, as shall remain unpaid at the time when the subscriber shall become a member of the company, shall be afterwards paid by the subscriber, his executors, administrators or assigns, in such instalments and at such times as the president and directors shall from time to time require; and if any subscriber, his executers, administrators or assigns, shall fail to make payment of any sum so required of him, after thirty days notice of such requisition shall have been given in some newspaper published in the neighborhood, or by some other convenient mode of notification, it shall be lawful for the company to recover the same, or such part thereof as shall not have been paid, with lawful interest from the time when due, and costs, on ten days previous notice, in any county or corporation within whose jurisdiction the defendant may be found; or, if he be not found within the commonwealth, then upon motion in any superior court for any county or corporation in this commonwealth within which the cause of action may have originated, on three weeks previous notice in some newspaper published within said county or corporation, or contiguous thereto. And the company shall moreover have full power, in such manner as their by-laws may prescribe, to sell at public auction the stock of such delinquent to satisfy any judgment recovered against him, or to satishy the amount, with interest, due from him in arrear as aforesaid, though no judgment may have been recovered, and to transfer upon their books to the purchaser, his executors, administrators or assigns, the stock so sold; and if the nett proceeds of such sale, after defraying the costs and charges thereof, shall be more than sufficient to satisfy what is due from the delinquent, they shall pay over the balance to him or his order.

9. If any stockholder shall sell and transfer the stock held by him, before the payment of the full amount subscribed for, he shall be liable for the payment of the residuum of the amount due thereafter upon his subscription of stock, in case the person to whom said stockholder shall have sold and transferred his stock, shall fail to pay the same.

10. The stock and all other property of such company as may be incorporated as aforesaid, shall be deemed personal estate, and as such shall pass to the executors, administrators or assigns of the stockholders. It shall be transferable only upon the books of the company, in such manner as the by-laws shall prescribe; and, until so transferred, the company shall be under no obligation to recognize the right of any assignee, and in the meantime may lawfully pay over the dividends to him who shall appear upon their books to be the stockholder, his executors or administrators, without being in any manner held liable to any other claimant. But real estate purchased by the company shall be conveyed to them, and, when sold by them, shall be conveyed to the purchaser by deed, as real estate, and as such shall be held liable to the payment of the debts of the company, and to sale under execution of *fieri facias*, in like manner as the lands of public debtors are sold.

11. Certificates of stock, signed by the president and counter-signed by the secretary of the board of directors, and authenticated under the seal of the company, shall be delivered by the president and directors to each stockholder, in such manner and form as the stockholders in general meeting may direct.

12. The president and directors shall keep a regular journal of their proceedings, recorded in well bound books, and the proceedings of each day shall be verified by the signature of the president. The vote of each member, on every question decided by them when a division shall have been called for, shall be entered on the journal, if such entry shall be demanded by any member of the said board, which shall be laid before the stockholders at their general meetings.

13. The president and directors shall cause regular books of account to be kept, and balanced at least once in every year. And they shall cause dividends of the nett profits of the company, or so much thereof as they may deem it prudent to divide, to be declared and paid to the stockholders at such time and in such manner as the by-laws may prescribe. And should any portion of the capital stock of the company be included in any dividend so declared and paid, the directors by whom such dividend is declared shall be liable, respectively, to all persons holding claims or demands against said company at the period of declaring such dividend; and moreover, each stockholder who shall participate in the dividend of such capital stock shall be liable to such creditors to the extent of the capital stock so received by him under such dividend. But such dividends of the capital stock may be made, when there shall exist no claims or demands against said company, and such dividend shall have been ordered by the stockholders in general meeting, and after three months previous notice in some newspaper in the neighborhood, or by some other convenient mode of notification.

14. Whenever four-fifths of the capital stock of such company shall become concentrated by purchase or otherwise in the hands of less than five persons, or more than one half of the same shall be and remain in the hands of one person for more than six months, all the corporate powers and privileges granted by the act of incorporating such company shall cease and determine.

15. If the company should not be organized by the appointment of a president and directors within two years form the passage of the act of incorporation, then all its provisions shall be null and void. And if at any time the company shall suspend their operations for the space of two years, then their rights and privileges shall cease and their charter shall be forfeited. But whensoever the said corporation shall be dissolved, whether by lapse of time or any other cause, their previous contracts, paying the debts due by them, and satisfying all liabilities which they may have incurred, and for the distributions of the property of the corporation among those entitled to the same.

16. That all acts for the incorporation of manufacturing or mining companies passed after the passage of this act shall continue in force for the period of thirty years and no longer, and shall at all times after the lapse of fifteen years from the organization of the company be liable to be amended or repealed at the pleasure of the legislature, in the same manner as if an express provision to that effect were therein contained, unless there shall have been inserted in such act of incorporation an express provision to the contrary.

17. *Be it further enacted*, That the president and directors of said company shall exhibit its books and property, condition, &c., to the inspection of such agent or agents as the general assembly may from time to time for that purpose appoint.

18. *Be it further enacted*, That no company claiming the benefit of this act shall by deed of trust, mortgage or otherwise, incumber their property for the purpose of giving preference to one creditor over another; and that whenever any such deed or mortgage shall be given to any one or more creditors, it shall endure to the benefit of all the creditors of such company existing at the time of such conveyance, and all such creditors shall be entitled to rateable satisfaction out of the property embraced by such conveyance.

19. This act shall commence and in be in force from and after the passage thereof.

The Legislative Petition provided below was submitted to the Virginia General Assembly in December 1836, requesting the granting of a charter to set up the "Benlomond Coal Company." The company was officially incorporated in February 1837 as the "Ben Lomond Coal Company."[2]

[Accurate interpretation of script attempted, yet not guaranteed.]

To The Honorable Senate and House of Delegates of the Legislature of Virginia

December 15, 1836

The memorial of the undersigned, Citizens of Virginia, humbly represent unto your Honorable bodies, that a portion of the undersigned have been engaged in Coal mining operations in the vicinity of Richmond for several years past, while a portion of them have been extensive consumers of this valuable and indisposable article of fuel, and that they have witnessed with deep regret the fatal consequences resulting from the insufficiency of supplies of Coals to meet the great and increasing demand, not only for Manufacturing purposes, but for domestic use and comfort. They also respectfully beg leave to represent that the mines heretofore operated, have mostly been on or near the outcrop of the coal strata and consequently much nearer the surface of the earth, and less liable to fill with water & have been wrought at comparatively small expense, but as these mines, generally have been exhausted, it becomes necessary therefore to sink deeper Pits, the expense of which, as well as the working of mines at such increased enterprise and we deem it unnecessary to speak of the loss which our community sustains in the products of her mineral resources or its influence on the domestic exchanges of the country. Since it must be evident that the total amount of these exports brings to our community a currency even better than gold by giving life and confidence to the proper currency of our Banks.

Your memorialists have witnessed the liberality manifested by your Honorable bodies on many occasions in the encouragement of laudable enterprises of this character, and are induced to hope that they will not be denied a participation in the enjoyment of these privileges. They therefore pray that your Honorable bodies will grant to them and such as may be associated with them, a charter to obtain the necessary capital by means of a joint stock company to be stated the Benlomond Coal Company with corporate powers for the purpose of conducting general coal mining operations in the counties of Chesterfield and Powhatan with such regulations, limitations and restrictions as to your Honorable bodies may seem just and proper. And your [illegible] as in duty bound, will ever pray to.

[Signed by:] Henry Clarke, E. [?] Clarke, Jas. Govan [?] James Allen, A. Pleasants, Archibald [?] Govan, Isaac [?] Davenport [?], H___ Fry, Tho. B. Bigg__, Samuel [illegible], [illegible], [illegible], W. Dunlop, [illegible], [illegible], James [illegible], [?] Mead

Accompanying the Petition was a separate single-page document. Excerpts are provided below:

"Amount paid by A. & A. Wooldridge & Co. to the Chesterfield Rail Road Co. for the transportation of coals upon said Road within the year 1835 [illegible]."

The document lists thirteen months of payment starting with January 24, 1835, and ending with January 1836:

"Making the amount paid for transit of within the year 1835 thirty three thousand nine hundred dollars and ninety cents – as appears of the Books of A. & A. W. & Co.

William H. Shields
14th December 1836"

---

[1] A. & A. Wooldridge and Company, *Proposals for Incorporating the Ben Lomond Coal Company.* Richmond: T.W. White, 1837. Special Collections, University of Virginia Library, Charlottesville, Va., Virginia Historical Society, Richmond.

[2] Virginia General Assembly. Legislative Petitions of the General Assembly, Chesterfield County, 1836. Reel 40, Box 56 Folder 29; Accession # 36121.

APPENDIX TWO

CHARTER, SCHEME AND CONDITIONS OF SUBSCRIPTIONS OF THE MIDLOTHIAN COAL MINING COMPANY.[1]

This corporate information was published in 1835. The manuscript is presented in its entirety, including misspellings.

SCHEME.

The proprietors of the lands chartered under the title of the Midlothian Coal Mining Company, deem it proper to offer a concise statement of the reasons which induced them to apply for a charter, and of the probable advantages and profits, likely to accrue from the purchase of stock in said company.

The Midlothian tract of land and coal mines is the larger of the two tracts embraced in the charter, and contains 283 acres, being under a lease until the 31st of December, 1837, by which time, it is believed that all or most of the coal that can be conveniently and profitably hoisted, will have been raised from the only shaft that has been sunk on that tract; and it will be necessary to sink another shaft on the dip of the present workings from six to seven hundred feet deep.

The Grove tract of land, the other embraced in the charter, contains 121½ acres, and adjoins the Midlothian on the south, and through which the Midlothian stratum of coal is confidently believed to pass. This tract extends considerably to the south east of the Midlothian, and adjoins the Stone Henge coal mines, and is known to contain the Stone Henge strata of coal, and as it will be necessary to sink on this tract also a shaft from four to five hundred feet deep, a union of these two tracts, containing distinct strata of coal of different qualities, all superior for particular purposes, appeared essential in the prosecution of a large and profitable coal concern.

The sinking and working of these shafts advantageously will require a large capital, which the proprietors do not possess. To adventure in the business of sinking and mining without ample funds, is in opposition to their positive conviction, that a large and profitable business can only be carried on with sufficient capital, would demonstrate at least, that some of the proprietors had profited but little from a long and hard-earned experience. They therefore concluded, that by chartering their property, and creating a capital of $100,000, from the sale of (Page 4) one half of their lands and mines, a sum sufficient in their opinion, if judiciously invested in slaves, engines and shafts, to place their property, by the period at which the lease on the Midlothian will expire, in a condition to be as productive to the purchasers of the one half, and as productive to themselves, as to the other half, as the whole property would be rendered by any resources they might individually command.

This view of the subject is not merely a conjectural one. The proprietors were born and raised in sight of the Chesterfield coal mines, and have been close and anxious observers of the whole course of the coal business from early life, and some of them have been long engaged in the coal business, and know practically the disadvantages attending the want of capital, and they risqué nothing in advancing the opinion, that most of the failures to acquire wealth in the prosecution of the coal business hitherto have been attributable to that cause. With sufficient capital judiciously employed upon a coal field as extensive and promising as that embraced in their charter, it is conveniently believed no failure to realize in profits, a product equal to the prudent wishes of the most sanguine adventurer will occur.

To demonstrate the correctness of this opinion, it is considered necessary only to exhibit a few simple facts:

The Midlothian tract lies immediately adjoining the coal mines of Nicholas Mills, esquire, and those of the Black Heath company of colliers. The coal from these mines passes into the Midlothian land as its extreme north east corner, (certainly the most desirable point of the land for it to enter) and running in its usual course, say about 12 degrees west of south, and dipping to the west, renders it extremely probable that the whole tract may contain coal, the spaces occupied by the troubles incident to the coal fields of Virginia excepted. In any event, it will be seen that this stratum of coal, believed to be the thickest and largest discovered in this county, and in quality surpassed by none for the general purposes, in passing through this tract will have a range exceeding a half mile to the south, and the mean distance to the west of nearly the same extent, being equal to a half mile square, and in passing from the Midlothian tract in its usual course, and from the surface signs and other indications, considered by colliers as almost unerring, this stratum must enter the Grove tract, and extend there to the south nearly a half mile, and to the west about a quarter of a mile. That the Grove tract then extending to the south-east, takes in the Stone Henge strata of coal, (Page 5) which enters that tract also at the extreme north-east corner, passing to the south, bearing about 12 degrees west, as is usual, (and as may be seen by the outrunning of the coal to the surface) nearly a half mile, and dipping to the west to the centre of the land, and time may prove, extending under the Midlothian strata.

Thus it will be seen, that the space fairly presumed to contain coal in these two tracts is about equal to three quarters of a square mile.

The Midlothian coal may be rated over twenty feet thick; and at Stone Henge there are three strata that have been worked; the first stratum over nine feet thick, the second two and a half feet, and the third four and a half feet thick, with another stratum beneath, the thickness of which has not been ascertained. These several strata, although of the same kind, are different in quality, each superior, and answers well for all the various purposes to which bituminous coal is applied.

One well located shaft on the Grove tract in the Stone Henge strata – another on the same tract in the Midlothian stratum, and a dip shaft on the works of the Midlothian tract, all finding coal in regular condition, and which it is believed will be the case, whenever these shafts shall be sunk, would enable the company to put into market from one to three millions of bushels of coal annually; and with additional shafts, the product may be extended to a much larger quantity.

With this prospect, judging from the extent of the lands, the thickness of the coal, its variety of strata and richness of quality, and the indications and belief, that it may traverse the whole extent of the lands embraced in the charter, except the space occupied by the usual difficulties of the coal fields of this country, all tending to produce the most decided belief, that ages will pass by before the coal will be exhausted – and where the lands, hands, engines and fixtures are all owned by the company, it must be evident that a permanent business may be established with the prospect of immense profits.

Thus, a million of bushels of coal at the pits, at the present price, is worth, $90,000; and when nothing but feeding and clothing of the hands employed, the wages of superintendents, the cost of oil, ropes, iron, powder, timber, &c. are to be deducted, it will occur to persons conversant with the expenses of coal mines, or to any person who will investigate the subject, that $20,000 will defray the whole necessary annual expense of a force greatly more than necessary to hoist a million of bushels of coal, to wit:

(Page 6)

For clothing and feeding 140 hands at $50 each,	$7,000
For 2 superintendents (1 at the yard, and 1 at the pits),	3,000
For 2 overseers and 2 clerks,	2,500
For powder $1,000, iron $1,000, oil $1,000, ropes $1,000,	4,000
For timber $1,000, contingencies $2,500,	3,500
	$20,000

Leaving of the $90,000, under this view of the case, in profits, $70,000; now add to this sum the gain between the receiving account and the shipping account, of at least 25 per cent which is gained since the coal has been transported by the rail-road to James river; the rail-road transporting the coal at 5 pecks to the bushel. And it is sold at 4 pecks to the bushel. The quantity thus gained will be 250,000 bushels; and as this gain takes place at the yard, where the coal is worth 15 cents per bushel. The profits from this source will amount to $37,500, a sum greatly more than sufficient to defray the whole expense, leaving the original $90,000 as the profits per annum to a company carrying on business to this extent: and it must be borne in mind that the force above stated, may exceed largely a million of bushels, in new and well arranged mines; and that for every additional thousand bushels the company will receive $112 50 [$112.50] in profits.

These profits may seem startling at the first view, but they are nevertheless the result of well-founded calculations, and it is confidently believed will be realized, if this scheme shall be put in operation, upon the principals herein stated.

It will be perceived that the foregoing calculations are founded upon the value of the coal at the pits, and assumes 9 cents as that value, per bushel. This was done to render the statement more simple. Coal at the yard may be rated as worth 15 cents per bushel; the difference between 9 and 15 cents is the toll of 6 cents charged by the rail-road company for transportation of the coal. The gross sum in money made by a company annually raising and selling a million of bushels of coal, with the force before estimated, will be,

For 1,000,000 bushels received and shipped at 15 cents,	$150,000
For the gain on the 1-5 peck, say 250,000 bushels,	37,500
	$187,500

(Page 7)

From the foregoing amount should be deducted the charge of the railroad company for the transportation of a million of bushels of coal,	$ 60,000
To which add this sum, being the annual expenses of the company,	20,000
	$ 80,000

This sum of $80,000 being the whole amount for expenses and transportation, leaves the sum of $107,500 as the annual profits, and exceeds the former estimate by $17,500, and which should be set apart as forming an accumulating fund for the purpose (with the hires of unemployed hands herein after named) of purchasing additional slaves, engines, or sinking shafts, as occasion may require.

A few items of the expenses of carrying on the coal business heretofore, in many cases without capital, will account for the profits of the coal business being so precarious, and the losses by it so common, hand hires, rents, horse-power, high prices for the purchase of supplies on credit, discount of drafts and commissions on sales (independent of the forced sales of coal for less than value, as must often take place without capital when the demand for coal is dull), have hitherto, in many cases, exhausted all the profits, and in some instances, done more; indeed it is evident that the coal business heretofore, must, under good management, have been very productive, or it never could have sustained itself under the disadvantageous circumstances in which it has generally been prosecuted.

The great secret in coal mining, is in the quantity raised; up to a certain quantity, all is absorbed in expenses; beyond that, all is profit.

Thus to meet an expenditure of $20,000, the quantity raised and sold must be about 160,000 bushels, which at 9 cents per bushel, is $14,400; add to this sum the profits on the 1-5 peck, say 40,000 bushels, at 15 cents per bushel, is $6,000, making the sum of $20,400. This statement is founded in the capital system. Now add to it the extra expenses of carrying on the coal business without capital, upon the old plan, and the loss is alarming. To wit:

For the hire of 140 hands, at $100	$14,000
For rent on 160,000 bushels coal, at 2 cts. per bus.	3,200
For feeding 60 mules, at $ 75 each,	4,500
Carried forward,	$21,700

(Page 8)

Brought forward,	$21,700
For loss on purchases of supplies by retail, and upon credit, say 5 per cent on $15,000,	750
For loss on discount of drafts, commissions, &c. on $20,400, at 5 percent.	1,020
	$23,470

Thus it is seen, that in a well regulated company, carried on by capital, 160,000 bushels of coal raised and sold, will defray the annual expense of working a force of 140 hands, when a concern carrying on a similar business, with the same force, on the old plan, without capital, and as has often been done, would be hoisting 160,000 bushels of coal, make an annual loss of $23,470; or in other form, it would be necessary for the last concern to hoist about 350,000 bushels of coal to clear expenses.

It is proper here to observe, that no notice is taken in either of the foregoing statements, of the comparative cost of steam and horse power, other than will be found in the charge of feeding mules. The cost of the engine and the expenses of an engineer and attendants, are conceded to be about equal to the cost of 60 mules and their attendants, leaving only the gain of $4,500, the amount for feeding the mules, in favor of steam power per annum.

This amount is known to be below the actual gain.

There are other and strong considerations, shewing that the coal business conducted upon the plan herein proposed, and going into active operation about the time herein before suggested, will yet be more productive than the foregoing statement has shewn, for it is now anticipated with a degree of probability, nearly approaching to certainty, that in three or four years the rail-road company's capital will be redeemed, at which time the transportation of coal on the rail-road will fall from 6 cents per bushel, the present price, to two cents per bushel; and if the location of the rail-road shall be changed, and a branch of the road extended to Warwick, five miles below Richmond, where locomotive engines can be substituted for horse power, as now used, the transportation of coal may be reduced to one cent per bushel; and when Warwick shall become the place of deposite for coal to be shipped from James river, a reduction of at least one cent per bushel in the price of freight will take place, and probably more, for all the coal that shall be shipped to ports where large vessels can go.

(Page 9)

This state of things will then make coal worth as much at the pits in Chesterfield, as it is now worth at the coal yards on James river, opposite to Richmond; giving to the collier an increase of profit of from 40 to $50,000 upon a million of bushels; or enable him to reduce the price at Warwick as low as the present price at the pits (say about 9 cents), leaving the originally estimated profits of $90,000, on a million of bushels; and placing it in the power of the colliers of Virginia, if their product shall equal the consumption, to force from our markets all foreign coal, while they will be enabled profitably to sustain themselves against all competition from new discoveries of coal, be such discoveries where they may.

In addition, no better period could be selected to organize a company and commence preparatory measures, with a view to an active business, commencing with the year 1838, as all the shafts now in operation in this neighborhood will probably be nearly or quite worked out by that time; and no concern except the Black Heath company of colliers, appear to be sinking new shafts to meet that crisis. Then a company at the period at which the rail-road stock will be redeemed, and most of the pits in Chesterfield nearly or quite exhausted, bringing into operation two or more new shafts at that period, may calculate with great certainty upon an extremely active, large and profitable business.

It will be perceived that a force equal to 140 hands is carried out in the preceding estimates. That force is greatly more than sufficient to hoist a million of bushels of coal. Indeed it might, in well arranged new shafts, be equal to one million and a half bushels. Ninety hands in new mines are deemed entirely competent to raise a million of bushels. The capital of $100,000 is not large enough for the other necessary purposes and to purchase more than about 100 hands, nor will this number be actually wanted at the pits for may years. About 25 hands are as many as will be required to sink one shaft during the search for coal; and one shaft, considerably on the dip of the present works at the Midlothian, is now sinking under a contract to carry it 400 feet for $9,000. Indeed the whole number of 100 hands will not be required for several years after the commencement of hoisting coal. The extra hands during these years should be hired out, and the proceeds, with the excess of the profits of the 1-5th peck, (to

Appendix Two ====129

wit, $17,500) after paying the annual expenses, should, as before intimated, form an accumulating fund for the purchase of additional hands over the 100, as they may be required in the future prosecution of (Page 10) the works, and supply any additional engines and shafts that may be necessary.

In conclusion, the proprietors think proper to say, that they are fully aware of the errors into which men are often led by placing too high an estimate upon every thing in which they have a personal interest, and of the uncertainty of mining operations in general. To provide against all undue influences of this character, they sought the advice of such experienced colliers, as they thought best qualified to aid in fixing the value of their lands and mines when they applied for a charter, and having selected the lowest estimate, they have reduced that sum by the amount of one hundred thousand dollars, out of the proceeds of the sale of one half of their lands and mines (which by the terms of their charter they are required to sell,) as a permanent capital, for the benefit of the company they design to form: and in submitting the foregoing estimates and plan to the public, they have been aided by the advice and approval of such experienced and competent judges, as were, in their opinion, best calculated to do equal justice to the proprietors, and such persons as might become interested by the purchase of stock. They now appeal to persons of enterprise and capital to come forward, and to investigate their scheme, examine their lands and mines, and if the result of that investigation and examination should prove satisfactory, to unite and share with the proprietors in the advantages and profits which, in their opinion, are so easily and certainly attainable.

$\Rightarrow$ The shaft now sinking on the dip of the works at the Midlothian, under a contract, is for and on account of the Midlothian Coal Mining Company.

(Page 11)

EVIDENCE *sustaining the* SCHEME *and supporting the value of the forgoing chartered property.*

Dear Sir,

I have duly examined the statement and calculations handed to me, and designed as an exhibit to aid in inducing capitalists to take stock in the Midlothian Coal Mining Company, and upon which you request my opinion, and any corrections that may to me seem proper.

I have given the subject its proper consideration, (so far as I am capable.) I have been engaged in coal business for about fifteen years, and working property in the immediate vicinity and adjoining yours. I find no difficulty in coming to a satisfactory opinion upon the subjects embraced in your project, and submitted to my examination. I think the price put on your lands and coal mines in your charter, reasonable and fair, (the assignment of $100,000 as permanent capital to the company, liberal.) Your statement and calculation I regard as well founded, and subject to no material alteration worthy of note.

In conclusion, as an evidence of what I think of the property, and the confidence I have in my opinion of it, you may consider me a subscriber for ten thousand dollars of the stock, and had I means, would take much more of the stock.

JOHN HETH,
Pits, August 8th, 1835

Dr. Wooldridge.

(A Copy.)

_____

Eliock, Powhatan county,
August 15th, 1835.

I have had submitted to me by the Messrs. Wooldridge, their statement relative to the formation of a joint stock company.

The location of the Midlothian and Grove tracts of coal land, is familiar to me. I have not the smallest doubt about their containing the most extensive and valuable bodies of coal, not surpassed, perhaps, by any other coal field in this region.

(Page 12)

I am equally certain that with good management, with the aid of ample capital, (which is furnished by the liberal terms of their charter,) that an extensive and profitable trade may be carried on.

W.M. FINNEY.*

Messrs. A. & A. Wooldridge.

(A Copy.)

Note – Captain Finney was engaged in the coal business on James river, about four miles from the Midlothian pits, for many years.

_____

Railey's Pits, 23rd July, 1835.

Messrs. Woodridge,

I have examined your statement and calculations submitted to me for my opinion relating to your charter of the Midlothian tract and coal mines, and the Grove tract. Having given to me the subject that reflection so important a concern demands, I now give you my opinion, and as you request, also a statement of the opportunities I have had of forming a correct opinion of the value of your chartered property.

I came to this country from Scotland in the year 1817, and soon after engaged with Mr. Nicholas Mills, as his superintendent of his coal mines. I was from that time principally employed in working Cunliffe's old pits, and the Union pits, until the year 1823, when I took charge of the works at Railey's pits, (then purchased by Mr. Nicholas Mills,) which directly adjoins the Midlothian lands and mines; from that period to the present time, (with the exception of 4 ½ months, when I was absent on a visit to Europe,) I have continued in the management of these mines. I am, therefore, personally acquainted with the mines on the adjoining lands, have been in the mine of the Midlothian, have examined the surface signs and other indications on the Grove tract and the Midlothian tract, all of which tend to convince me of the great value of your property, and satisfies me that the value, as set forth in your charter, is fair and reasonable; and that the appropriation of one hundred thousand dollars as permanent capital to the company, is so liberal as to leave no doubt on my mind that your stock will and ought to be speedily taken up.

As to your statements and calculations upon the subject of the coal business to be conducted upon the principles as laid down by you, I consider them as well founded. Indeed, I see (Page 13) no reason to doubt that the profitable view you present of the future working of your property, (if the charter goes into operation,) will be fully realised.

Although all mining operations are, to a certain extent, doubtful, I consider your scheme, with the field upon which it is to act, as subject to less uncertainty, and fairly promises to be greatly more productive, than any mining scheme I have any knowledge of in this country, and that it is probable a like opportunity of so profitable an investment of capital may not again occur in my time.

Yours, very respectfully,
ALEXANDER REID.
(A Copy.)

————

BELLVIEU, Albemarle county, Va.
July 20th, 1835.

I have received and examined your statement and calculations in relation to the charter of your property, under the title of the Midlothian Coal Mining Company.

I was employed about sixteen years in the superintendence of coal mines in your immediate neighborhood: during that time, I had successively the management of three mines directly adjoining yours, to wit: the Maidenhead mines, Stone Henge mines, and the mines of Mr. Mills, then in the occupancy of Major Heth.

I have therefore been afforded a good opportunity of forming a satisfactory opinion of the value of your mines and lands, and take pleasure in saying, that the price put upon your property in your charter, in my opinion, is fair and reasonable, and that the appropriation of one hundred thousand dollars, out of the sale of one half of your property, as a permanent capital, very liberal.

I concur with you in the view you have taken of the coal business, as set forth in your statement, and have entire confidence in the success of your scheme, if it shall be carried as you design into operation–And that it will be carried into operation, I do not doubt, as I am sure the advantages held out in your scheme are so promising, that capitalistics of enterprise will certainly avail themselves of the present opportunity of investment.

(Page 14)

I regret very much that the extensive purchase I have made of real estate, and upon which I am now settled, (before your charter was obtained) will place it out of my power to purchase as much of your stock as I wish– as it is, I shall go in for as much as my means will enable me.

DAVID HANCOCK.

Messrs. Wooldridge, Chesterfield County, Va.

(A Copy.)

————

Old Pits, 8th August, 1835.

GENTLEMEN,

I have examined carefully the statement and calculations handed me relating to the Midlothian Coal Mining Company. As I have been raised in the immediate neighborhood of the Midlothian tract and coal mines, and the Grove tract, and have been for twenty-five years, immediately engaged in the operations of coal mining, and perfectly familiar with the operations of all the mines in the south side of James river, and particularly having had the direction of two of the adjoining mines to the Midlothian, therefore it affords me great pleasure in having it in my power to say, that I fully concur with Capt. John Heth and others in the favorable opinion they have given of the value of the property chartered as the Midlothian Coal Mining Company, and fully concur in the view as presented in the statement and calculations aforesaid; and were it in my power to do so, would gladly take some of the stock.

Wishing you success in your undertaking,

I remain yours, most respectfully,

C. CUNLIFFE.

Messrs. Wooldridge, Midlothian.

(A Copy.)

Dr. Wooldridge,

In compliance with your request, that I should give you my opinion of the Midlothian land and coal mines, and the Grove tract, regarded as coal property, and that I should state the circumstances that enabled me to form such opinion as I (Page 15) may entertain, I think best to premise that I am a Scotchman by birth; that from early life to the present time, I have been engaged in the calling of a miner. While in Scotland, I was principally employed in the Barther coal mines and iron works; that after I came to America, I was for some time employed in the coal mines of Pennsylvania; from thence I came to Virginia, and was employed a while in Mr. Mill's pits. When my engagements closed with him, I then entered into the business of Messrs. Charles Brown & Co. of Philadelphia, as their principal miner, who were them engaged in working Graham's old pits on the north side of James river. When Mr. Brown closed his business at Graham's pits, I then engaged at the Midlothian coal mines as principal miner. Since my residence at this pit, I have availed myself of the opportunity of examining the evidence of the coal extending through the Midlothian tract and the adjoining tract, called the Grove, and I have obtained all the information I could from conversations with the practical colliers of the neighborhood, all of which have tended to confirm my opinion, that the Midlothian seam of coal, taking into consideration its thickness, quality and position, as far as it has been explored, is decidedly the best and most valuable body of coal I have ever seen; and I entertain no doubt that it extends across the Midlothian and Grove tracts to the south; indeed, I am of opinion that the coal extends through the whole of both tracts, except so far as the usual troubles and difficulties incident to all coal mines may extend. One of these interruptions, in the form of a drop, to west, now presents itself in the Midlothian mines, beyond which, I entertain not the slightest doubt, that the coal will be found of its usual thickness and quality, and as I before said, extending through both tracts. I may have gone too far in my exception of the usual troubles and difficulties, as this coal field is more regular, and presents fewer difficulties and troubles than any mines I have ever been in. This seam of coal averages twenty-five feet thick, and taking the prospects for coal in the two tracts as they appear to me to exist, I may safely say, that I have never before seen any thing of the kind so promising and valuable, and I doubt whether I shall ever again see so large a space as these two tracts present with such good prospect. Indeed, I cannot well conceive how your prospects can be more flattering.

Yours respectfully,
JOHN RENARD.

August 9th, 1835.

(A Copy.)

(Page 16)

To Messrs. A. & A. Wooldridge,

In compliance with your request, I have examined your scheme of the Midlothian Coal Mining Company, and the certificates of Capt. Heth and others, sustaining your statement and calculations, and the value of your chartered property.

I have been generally, for the last seventeen years, engaged in the coal business in your immediate neighborhood–in fact, was born and raised in about a mile of the Midlothian mines, and consequently, must have had a good opportunity of judging correctly as to the value of the Midlothian and Grove lands, and now take pleasure in saying, that I fully concur with Capt. Heth and others in the opinions they have expressed in their certificates.

G. B. WOOLDRIDGE.

(A Copy.)

————

HICKORY GROVE, AUGUST 29th, 1835.

Messrs. Wooldridge,

I have received and examined your statement and calculations in relation to the charter of your property, under the title of the Midlothian Coal Mining Company.

It is proper to say, that I have been employed in coal mining business for ten years: two years for the Messrs. Heth, and eight years at the Stone Henge coal mines, as principal miner, where I left in the fall of 1833, a part of which time I had the direction of the Midlothian mines.

I am well acquainted with the situation of the two tracts or parcels of land embraced in your charter, and have no hesitation in saying, that the Stone Henge bed or strata of coal passes through the Grove tract, entering at the extreme N.E. corner, and have no doubt that the Midlothian bed or stratum passes through it also.

I think your calculations fair, and the estimated value set upon your property, far short of its real value. I have no doubt the stock will be speedly taken, and the profits will fulfil the most sanguine expectations of the stockholders.

Yours, &c.

Z. H. BROOKS.

(Page 17)

Dr. A. L. Wooldridge, Eastlothian,

I have been in employment at the coal mines, as superintendent, for about six years, the last four years at Midlothian–have consequently become well acquainted with the Grove and Midlothian tracts of land, and the Midlothian coal mines. I concur most decidedly in the favorable opinion given by the colliers of the neighborhood, as to the value of the lands and mines, and the future productiveness of the chartered property–and I design particularly to be understood as sustaining the opinion of Mr. Renard.

Z. McGRUDER, JR.

August 31st, 1835.

———

PITS, 10th Sept. 1835.

GENTLEMEN,

I have examined your scheme for the Midlothian Coal Mining Company with care.

You are aware my residence at the Chesterfield mines has only been for two and a half years, but during that time I have given much attention to the course, dip, &c. of the coal in this county. The result of my examinations confirm my opinion of the existence of the Stone Henge seams, and the valuable body of Midlothian coal running through the Grove tract.

It is, I think, almost unnecessary to say any thing of the Midlothian land; the present mine is so well known, and there is not a doubt in my mind, that the same body of coal continued throughout the property, (except where swells, &c. exist).

Your liberal appropriation of so large a capital as one hundred thousand dollars, must ensure the company such advantages as have never yet been enjoyed in the coal business.

I can have no doubt of your success in the sale of stock, (had it been in my power I willingly would have taken some,) after the clear statement you have given.

Very respectfully, yours,

THO. R. POTTS*

---

* Mr. Potts is an Englishman by birth, and has been engaged in the coal business from early life, in the north of England. January 1826, he went to live at Mr. Buddle's Wallsend colliery, and with whom he remained until 1831, when he was appointed by him agent for the extensive collieries of the Marquis of Londonderry–from whence he came to America, and is now the superintendent of the Black Heath company of colliers.

(Page 18)

EVIDENCE OF TITLE.

Chesterfield County, to wit:

I hereby certify that I have surveyed the two tracts of land mentioned in the act of the general assembly of Virginia, passed on the 23rd January 1835, incorporating the Midlothian Coal Mining Company; that the two tracts contain 404½ acres, and that the boundaries of these lands are clear and distinct, and free from all doubt or controversy.

Given under my hand this 25th day of August, 1835.

JORDAN MARTIN,
Surveyor of Ch. Cty.

Virginia, to wit:

At court held for Chesterfield county at the courthouse thereof, on the tenth day of August, anno domini 1835: On the motion of Abraham S. Wooldridge, Archibald L. Wooldridge, Jane Elam, wife of William Green Elam, and Charlotte Wooldridge, wife of Merit Wooldridge, the court doth certify that it appears to them, by satisfactory proof examined in court, that Abraham S. Wooldridge, Archibald L. Wooldridge, Jane Elam, wife of William Green Elam, and Charlotte Wooldridge, wife of Merit Wooldridge, are the only surviving children and heirs of the late William Wooldridge, deceased, who died intestate; and that the said Abraham S. Wooldridge, Archibald L. Wooldridge, Jane Elam, Charlotte Wooldridge, are owners in fee simple in common of the land and coal mines lying in the county of Chesterfield, called "The Midlothian," and that the said Abraham S. Wooldridge is the fee simple owner of the land lying in the same county, called "The Grove," which Midlothian and Grove tracts of land, are the same tracts as described in an act of the general assembly of Virginia, passed on the 23rd day of January, 1835, chartering the Midlothian Coal Mining Company; and furthermore, that it appears by the testimony of the clerk of this court, examined on oath in open court, that the said tracts are free from liens and (Page 19) incumbrances whatsoever, except a lease on the Midlothian tract of land, which will expire on the first day of January, in the year one thousand eight hundred and thirty-eight; which facts are ordered to be entered of record, and certified to all whom it may concern.

Virginia, to wit:

I, Parke Poindexter, clerk of Chesterfield county court, do hereby certify that the foregoing copies are truly and correctly transcribed from the records of the aforesaid county court of Chesterfield, now remaining in my office.

In testimony whereof, I have hereto subscribed my name, and affixed the official seal of said court, this 13th day of August, anno dom. one
(L.S.) thousand eight hundred and thirty-five, and the 60th year of the commonwealth.

PARKE POINDEXTER, *Clerk.*

STATE OF VIRGINIA, *Chesterfield county, to wit*:

I, Eleazar Clay, presiding justice of the peace, in and for the said county of Chesterfield, do hereby certify that the foregoing certificates of attestation is made in due form; that Parke Poindexter, whose name is thereto subscribed, was, at the date of the same, clerk of our said county court of Chesterfield, and that all his legal acts as such, are entitled to full faith and credit. Given under my hand and seal this nineteenth day of August, anno dom. one thousand eight hundred and thirty-five, and in the 60th year of our independence.

ELEAZAR CLAY, *(Seal.)*

⇒ Reference is made to Robert Stanard and Samuel Taylor, esquires, as to the unquestionable fee simple titles to the chartered lands, and the right of proprietors to sink for coal during the residue of the lease on the Midlothian.

(Page 20)

CONDITIONS OF SUBSCRIPTION

TO THE

MIDLOTHIAN COAL MINING COMPANY.

The whole number of shares in the capital stock of the company is three thousand, of one hundred dollars each; of these three thousand shares, Abraham S. Wooldridge will be entitled to five hundred and sixty-two; Archibald L. Wooldridge, to three hundred and thirteen; Jane Elam, wife of William G. Elam, to three hundred and twelve, and Charlotte Wooldridge, wife of Merit Wooldridge, to three hundred and thirteen; making together fifteen hundred shares, or one half of the whole capital stock. The subscribers to the stock of the said company, when fifteen hundred shares shall be subscribed for, will be entitled to that number of shares in the company, which at one hundred dollars per share, will amount to one hundred and fifty thousand dollars. Of this sum, the subscribers will be bound to pay fifty thousand dollars to the proprietors of the Grove and Midlothian tracts of land in equal proportions, that is, to the said A. S. Wooldridge, twelve thousand five hundred dollars; to A. L. Wooldridge, the like sum; to Wm. G. Elam and Jane his wife, the like sum, and to Merit Wooldridge and Charlotte, his wife, the like sum, being thirty-three dollars and thirty-three cents on each of the fifteen hundred shares, on the day of the first general meeting of the stockholders of the said company; on which day deeds will be executed by the proprietors of the said two tracts of land to the subscribers for stock in the said company. The remaining hundred thousand dollars, or sixty-six dollars and sixty-seven cents on each of the fifteen hundred shares subscribed for, being the capital provided by the proprietors of the said two tracts of land, under their charter for carrying on the coal business on the said lands, will be payable within three years from the day of the first general meeting of the stockholders of the said company, or sooner, with legal interest thereon from that day, in such quotas as the president and directors of the said company shall order and direct. The deeds to the subscribers for their shares of the said (Page 21) two tracts of land will provide, that the said president and directors of the said company shall have a lien on each share conveyed, for the payment of sixty-six dollars and sixty-seven cents, with interest thereon, as foresaid, to the president and directors of the said company, as the same shall be ordered by them to be paid in. The subscribers for stock in this company will be entitled to an undivided moiety of the said two tracts of land in fee simple, from the day deeds shall be made to them for their shares, liable only for the payment of sixty-six dollars and sixty-seven cents on each share, to raise the capital of one hundred thousand dollars, which will belong to the shareholders in the company, and will be used in carrying on the coal business on the said two tracts of land for their joint benefit.

(Page 22)

AN ACT

TO INCORPORATE THE

MIDLOTHIAN COAL MINING COMPANY.

[Passed January 23, 1835.]

Whereas it is represented to the general assembly by Abraham S. Wooldridge, that he is the sole fee simple owner of a tract of land lying the county of Chesterfield, containing one hundred and twenty-one and a half acres, called the Grove, and supposed to contain extensive bodies of coal of the best quality; and that his is also the owner of one equal but undivided fourth part of the reversion in fee of another tract of land lying in the same county, containing two hundred and eighty-three acres, called the Midlothian coal pits, now under lease, which has about [blank] years to run; that the other three fourths of the reversion in the tract of land, called the Midlothian coal pits, are owned by Archibald L. Wooldridge, Jane Elam, the wife of William G. Elam, Charlotte Wooldridge, the wife of Merit Wooldridge; that although the extensive and valuable strata of coal, which have been found in the Stone Henge and Midlothian tracts of land, indicate to a moral certainty, that there are like strata of coal in the adjoining tract called the Grove, yet owing to the great depth of this coal from the surface of the earth, mines cannot be opened in either of the said tracts of land, and worked to any thing like the same advantage to the owners or to the public by private and unincorporated as by an incorporated company:

1. *Be it therefore enacted by the general assembly*, That the capital stock, consisting of the Grove tract of land, shall be divided into seven hundred and fifty shares, of one hundred dollars value each; and that so soon as three hundred and seventy-five of the said shares shall have been *bona fide* sold on account of the proprietor, and by him conveyed to purchasers by deeds duly executed and recorded in the county court of Chesterfield, thenceforth all the right, title and interest which the said Abraham S. Wooldridge now has in and to the aforesaid capital stock, shall be vested in the said Abraham S. Wooldridge and the said purchasers, in the proportions of the shares held (Page 23) respectively by them and their heirs and assigns forever; and the said stockholders, their heirs and assigns, shall be a body politic and corporate, by the name and style of *"The Midlothian Coal Mining Company,"* by which style they shall have perpetual succession and a common seal, may sue and be sued, may purchase and hold, sell and convey real and personal property: *Provided*, That whensoever four fifths of the capital stock of said company shall be concentrated by purchase or otherwise, in the hands of less than five members of said company, all the corporate privileges hereby granted shall cease and determine.

2. Twenty-five thousand dollars of the proceeds of sale of the three hundred and seventy-five shares of stock, shall constitute a money capital to be employed by the said company in carrying on the coal business; and the residue of the proceeds of sale, of the said three hundred and seventy-five shares of stock shall belong exclusively to the said Abraham S. Wooldridge.

3. The said company, in addition to the capital stock aforesaid, shall neither purchase nor hold any real estate whatever, except such parcel or parcels of land lying in the said county of Chesterfield, not exceeding one thousand acres, as may be found convenient to supply timber for the said coal lands and coal mines herein before and herein after mentioned, and sites for coal yards and landings, and except also the Midlothian tract of land as is herein after provided.

4. The stock of the Midlothian Coal Mining Company shall be deemed real estate, and as such shall pass by descent, devise and sale, and be subject to dower and curtesy: *Provided however*, That under executions against the said company,

all property owned by them, may be taken and disposed of in the same manner, as if the shares aforesaid had not been declared real estate.

5. As soon as three hundred and seventy-five shares of the capital stock shall have been sold and conveyed by deeds recorded as is herein before mentioned, it shall be the duty of the said Abraham S. Wooldridge to give public notice thereof, for thirty days at least, in some one of the newspapers published in the city of Richmond, and to call a meeting of the stockholders for the purpose of appointing directors and organizing the company, to be held at the Columbian hotel in the said city, at such time as shall be designated in the said notice for that purpose, not less than thirty nor more than sixty days from its date. If a sufficient number of the stockholders shall not attend on the day and at the place aforesaid, to constitute a (Page 24) general meeting, the meeting shall stand adjourned from day to day, not exceeding thirty days, till a sufficient number shall attend.

6. And if three hundred and seventy-five shares of the capital stock shall not be sold and conveyed by deeds recorded as aforesaid, within five years from the passage of this act, or if within six months after three hundred and seventy-five shares shall have been so sold and conveyed, the stockholders shall not assemble in general meeting and appoint directors pursuant to the provisions of this act, then in either of these cases this act shall be utterly null and void.

7. After the first general meeting of the stockholders, the general meeting of the company shall be held annually at the Columbian hotel, on the fifteenth day of January in each year; and the stockholders may hold other general meetings, at such place and at such time as their by-laws and regulations may prescribe. Every general meeting may be adjourned from day to day, and from time to time, at the pleasure of the meeting; and if at any time a sufficient number shall not attend to constitute a general meeting at the time appointed for that purpose, the meeting shall stand adjourned from day to day, not exceeding thirty days, until a sufficient number shall attend.

8. Any number of persons owning or representing a majority of the shares of the company, shall be sufficient to constitute a general meeting. The stockholders may attend and vote at any general meeting in person or by proxy, authenticated as the by-laws may prescribe: the shares of infants shall be represented by their guardians; those of married women by their husbands. The person having the freehold estate in possession shall be entitled to vote upon the stock so held by him or her, in all general meetings, but he or she who has only a remainder or reversion, dependent on a life estate, shall have no vote. In general meeting, each stockholder shall have one vote for each share held by him or her, as far as ten shares, and one other vote for every five shares above ten.

9. The stockholders in general meeting, may pass by-laws and regulations for the government of the affairs of the company, not inconsistent with the constitution or laws of Virginia, or of the United States, as they may think proper.

10. At their first meeting, and at each annual meeting thereafter, the stockholders shall appoint so many directors of the company, not exceeding five, and such other officers and agents as they may think proper, and may prescribe their duties and regulate their compensation. The directors so appointed, shall

(Page 25) continue in office for one year, and until their successors shall be appointed, unless sooner removed from office by the stockholders in general meeting; and the other officers or agents shall hold their places as may be prescribed by the by-laws. Vacancies in the office of director may be supplied at any general meeting of the stockholders, or in such other manner as the by-laws may prescribe.

11. Regular minutes of the proceedings of the stockholders in general meeting shall be kept in well bound books, and carefully preserved, and being read before the adjournment of each meeting, shall be authenticated by the chairman or other presiding officer.

12. The directors shall keep a regular journal of all their proceedings, to be authenticated as the by-laws may prescribe, and shall cause regular books of accounts of all the transactions of the company to be kept, and to be settled and balanced once at least in every year; and there shall be an annual dividend of so much of the profits of the company among the stockholders as the directors may think it advisable to divide, declared on the first Monday in January in each year, or as soon thereafter as may be, and paid in such manner as the by-laws may prescribe.

13. At any time thereafter, the owners of the Midlothian tract of land, (the stockholders of the said company having previously, by an order entered on their records, agreed to admit them into the said company) shall have full power and authority to divide the said tract of land into two thousand two hundred and twenty-five shares of one hundred dollars value each; whereof the said Abraham S. Wooldridge, Archibald L. Wooldridge, Jane Elam, the wife of William G. Elam, Charlotte Wooldridge, the wife of Merit Wooldridge, shall be entitled to one fourth each; and so soon as a number of the said shares, not less than one thousand one hundred and twelve, shall have been *bona fide* sold on the joint account of the said proprietors, and by them conveyed by deeds duly executed to the purchasers, and recorded in the county court of Chesterfield, then all the right, title and interest which the said Abraham S. Wooldridge, Archibald L. Wooldridge, William G. Elam and Jane his wife, and Merit Wooldridge and Charlotte his wife, shall then have in and to the capital stock last aforesaid, shall be vested in the said Abraham S. Wooldridge, Archibald L. Wooldridge, Jane Elam and Charlotte Wooldridge, and the purchasers, in the proportions of the shares respectively held by them, and in their heirs and assigns forever, and the said (Page 26) last mentioned stockholders, their heirs and assigns, shall thenceforth be admitted into the Midlothian Coal Mining Company, with the like rights and privileges, and subject thenceforth to like liabilities in all respects, as the original members of the said company shall thenceforth be entitled or liable to: of the proceeds of sale of the one thousand and one hundred and twelve shares, the sum of twenty-five thousand dollars shall be a money capital, in addition to the capital of twenty-five thousand dollars herein before mentioned, to be employed by the said company in the coal business on the two tracts of land herein before mentioned, and the residue of the proceeds of sale of the said one thousand one hundred and twelve shares shall belong absolutely to the said

Abraham S. Wooldridge, Archibald L. Wooldridge, Jane Elam and Charlotte Wooldridge, each one fourth part.

14. The money capital of the said company, whatever it shall be, whether twenty-five thousand dollars, or fifty thousand dollars,* which shall not have been lost in the business of the company, shall, at the expiration of this charter, be divided among the stockholders of the company at that period, in the proportion that the stock of the company shall be held by them respectively.

15. This act shall commence and be in force for twenty years, and no longer, from and after the passage thereof.

---

*The capital has since been increased to $100,000. See the conditions of subscription and the scheme.

---

[1] Mid-Lothian Coal Mining Company. *Charter, scheme and conditions of subscriptions of the Mid Lothian Coal Mining Company*. Richmond: Printed by S. Sheperd, 1835. Center for American History, The University of Texas at Austin.

APPENDIX THREE

DEATH OF SLAVE LAWSUIT – APPEAL

The Court of Appeals of Virginia documentation has been copied in its entirety. The first case, presumably Hill v. Randolph, was originally heard in Chesterfield County Circuit Court. Apparently the documentation for the first case did not survive to the present.

COURT OF APPEALS OF VIRGINIA

RICHMOND.

RANDOLPH v. HILL[1]

March, 1836.

(Absent *Brooke*, J.)

Plaintiff hires a slave to defendant to work in his coal pits, and the slave being one evening at work in one of the pits with other labourers, they are all sickened by foul air, and are drawn out; next morning the overseer of the pits sends down the foreman, a trustworthy and experienced slave, to examine with a lamp and ascertain whether the foul air has left the pit (which is usual course of examination in such case) and the foreman reports that foul air is gone; the labourers, ten in number, again descend, are again sickened by foul air, and plaintiff's slave is killed by it before he can be drawn out of the pit, which has a single shaft, 70 feet deep, and admitting only one bucket, capable of raising but one or at most two persons at a time: In action on the case to recover damages for the loss of the slave, the jury, on these facts proved by defendant's overseer of the pits, who is plaintiff's sole witness, find a verdict for plaintiff, and the court, overruling defendant's motion to set aside a verdict as contrary to evidence, give judgment thereon for the plaintiff – And *judgment affirmed*, by the equal division of this court.

This was an action on the case brought by Hill against Randolph, in the circuit court of Chesterfield. The declaration alleged, that Hill hired a negro man slave to Randolph for one year, to work in Randolph's coal pits in Chesterfield; and that Randolph was bound to keep all his machinery, utensils and pits, in proper order and repair, to work his pits in a collier-like manner, and to use due and ordinary diligence to prevent accident and hurt to the labourers employed therein; and to Hill's slave among the rest; yet Randolph, regardless of his duty in that behalf, and careless of the safety of Hill's slave, negligently suffered and directed

him to descend into the pits when there was impure and noxious air
herein, whereby the life of the slave was put in great jeopardy; and, well
knowing the pits to be filled with impure and noxious air, caused and
ordered the slave to be kept at work in the pits, until by the impure, and
noxious air, therein he was killed. Plea, not guilty. Trial, and verdict for
Hill for 400 dollars.

Randolph moved the court for a new trial, on the ground that the
verdict was contrary to evidence. The court overruled the motion.
Randolph excepted; and the court certified the facts proved at the trial, as
follows–

It was proved by the testimony of two of Randolph's overseers at his
coal pits, witnesses on the part of Hill–That the slave was hired by Hill to
Randolph, to work in the pits for one year. That it was discovered one
evening, that there was foul air in the pit where this slave of Hill worked,
and he and all the other labourers, were therefore drawn out; and they
were all, and particularly Hill's slave, told by one of the overseers
present (who was one of the witnesses), not to stay in the pits, when they
discovered foul air, long enough to be made sick by it. That, the next
morning, the overseer superintending that pit (who was one of the
witnesses), supposing that the foul air in the pit on the preceding evening,
had been caused by a rain which then fell, and that, the weather being
now clear, the foul air had probably left the pit, sent down one of the
negro labourers at the pit (who, it seems, was a slave belonging to
Randolph) with a lamp, to examine the condition thereof, and to ascertain
whether the foul air was gone so that the labourers could be safely sent
down; which was the usual course in such cases, though the overseers
themselves sometimes went down. That the person sent down was the
foreman, and one of the most experienced labourers at the pits, perfectly
competent to make such an examination, and worthy of full confidence.
That the foreman reported to the overseer, that the foul air was gone, and
that the labourers might go down with safety. That the overseer, placing
as much confidence in that report as he would have had in a personal
inspection, and apprehending no danger, sent the labourers down, ten in
number, including Hill's slave and two of Randolph's own, none of
whom were unwilling to go down; but after working there about half an
hour, they found that there was foul air in the pit, and became sick, some
more and some less, and were drawn out as fast as it could be done, one
or at most two at a time: no preference was given to Randolph's own
slaves, one of whom was the last to be drawn up, sending before him the
body of Hill's slave, who had fallen into some water in the pit, about
eighteen inches deep: he appeared to have been drowned, and could not

be revived: all the other labourers were made sick by the foul air, but none dangerously. That there was foul air frequently in the coal pits; which was sometimes caused or driven down by the rain, soon disappeared. That the shaft at this particular pit, was about seventy feet deep, and a single shaft, which would admit of but one bucket to ascend at a time. That there were several apartments in the pit; the labourers did not all work in any one of them at the same time; and, occasionally, foul air was found in one and not in the others. That such foul air would and occasionally did cause death. And that much greater hire was paid for slaves to work in coal pits, than for ordinary service, the difference being about twenty-five or thirty per cent. And these being all the facts proved in the cause, the court was of opinion, that the jury might lawfully infer from the evidence as delivered by the witnesses,–who might be expected to feel a desire to place their own conduct in the most favourable light,– that the examination made of the condition of the pits by Randolph's slave, was not so careful a one as ought to have been made by a prudent and discreet man, before he exposed so many slaves, most of them belonging to others, to such danger as was proved to have existed; and as a jury had deduced that inference from the facts proved, the court, thinking they had properly done so, overruled the motion for a new trial.

Judgment was then given for Hill upon the verdict; to which this court, upon Randolph's petition, allowed him a *supersedeas*.

Taylor and Johnson, for the plaintiff in error, admitted, that on an appeal from the judgment overruling a motion to set aside a verdict and direct a new trial, on the ground of the verdict being against evidence, it must appear to the appellate court, that the verdict was plainly against evidence. But, they said, this verdict was plainly so. There was no conflict in the testimony; it all came from the plaintiff's own witnesses; he could not have impeached their credit, and if he could, nothing was offered to discredit them. Neither the jury, nor the court, had a right to suppose that the facts were different, in any respect, from what the testimony represented them to be–that the witnesses concealed any fact, or gave a false colour to those they stated, in order to place their own conduct in a favourable light–in effect, that they did not tell the whole truth. Yet it was only upon that supposition, that this verdict could be approved; and this in truth, was distinctly admitted by the circuit court itself. The verdict was not warranted by the evidence, but by facts inferred to exist, which were not proved, and not reconcilable with the facts that were proved. Hill had hired his slave to Randolph to work in his coal pits: there were dangers incident to such labour, from which ordinary labour was exempt; dangers arising from accidents which no human care could always avoid, and among others from foul and noxious air, with which the pits were occasionally infested; dangers not peculiar to Randolph's coal pits, but common to all coal pits, not peculiar to slave labourers, but common to all labourers in coal pits, black or white, bond or free; dangers frequently incident to European coal pits, managed with the utmost skill and care, and having the most perfect fixtures and machinery to draw the labourers to the open air; dangers so well known, that labourers, or the owners of labourers, employed there, received higher wages, as a premium, in truth, for the risque incurred, upon the principle on which higher wages were always given for labour in a gunpowder mill. Hill had been paid for the risque to which his loss was owing. To impute the loss to the want of due care in Randolph or (which was the same thing) in his overseer, was to discredit the testimony, without the least ground for doing so. The circuit court thought that the jury was warranted in inferring from the evidence, that the examination made by Randolph's slave, to ascertain whether there was foul air remaining in the pits, was not so careful a one as ought to have been made by a prudent and discreet man, before he exposed the lives of the labourers, most of whom were the slaves of others, to such a danger. But the person who made the examination was the foreman, and the most experienced labourer at the pits; and he himself was to incur the danger of the foul air, and would, therefore, be very careful to ascertain its existence or absence. There was not the least reason to believe, that a negro man, experienced in the business, who must have often seen foul air in the pits, since it was frequently found in them, was not as capable of ascertaining its existence, as the overseer himself would or could have been. Besides, this was the usual course, in such cases, though the overseer sometimes descended into the pit himself. The usual diligence and care, therefore, was employed to avoid the danger; and Randolph was only bound to bestow ordinary care and diligence. Usual care and diligence was proved by the plaintiff's own witnesses at the trial, but the court thought that the jury was well warranted to discredit the testimony in that particular. If this was proper, they said, no verdict ever could be set aside for being contrary to evidence.

Scott, *contra*, said, that this verdict could not be disturbed, without wholly disregarding the principle stated by judge Roane in Ross v. Overton, 3 Call 319. and so often since approved and acted on by this court. The whole amount of the opinion of the circuit court, which had been so much complained of, was, that the jury, considering the situation of the witnesses, were warranted to take their testimony most strongly for the plaintiff, and against the natural bias of their feelings: and this was true and just. An owner of coal mines ought not to have trusted an ignorant negro, however long he might have been accustomed to work in them, to ascertain whether foul and noxious air had got into them: it was his duty to have experienced colliers to superintend his pits, to impose the duty upon them to make the examination proper in such cases, and to furnish them the proper means to make such examination. Justice as well as humanity required this at his hands. But they required more: as, in spite of all human care and skill, foul air might occasionally collect in all coal pits, it was utterly unsafe to rely on a single bucket in which only one or at most two persons could be brought up at a time, to draw up labourers from a pit seventy feet deep. If there had been two buckets at this pit, Hill's slave would probably have been rescued from death. This alone was sufficient to justify this verdict.

Johnson replied, that it was remarkable, that the circuit court did not give the least weight to the circumstance of there being but a single shaft at this coal pit, and a single bucket worked in it. And the reason was plain enough; it was not shewn, that the circumstance was at all unusual in the working of coal pits, at least, our coal pits, so as to afford an inference of any want of the usual care and diligence to provide against the danger.

BROCKENBROUGH, J. In this case, the court not only certified the facts that were proved at the trial, but also the persons by whom they were proved. They were the overseers employed by the defendant in superintending the labourers at his coal pits. If there was any negligence in the case, they were the persons who were guilty of it. The plaintiff was, however, compelled to make them witnesses, or to lose his testimony altogether, since the labourers were slaves and not competent to give evidence. I agree with the judge of the circuit court, that it was perfectly natural that those witnesses should wish to place their own conduct in the most favourable point of view. They might not have been at all conscious that they were guilty of any neglect, and yet the facts proved by themselves might have been sufficient to convince a jury, composed of disinterested and intelligent men, that they were guilty of gross neglect. The jury might have been satisfied, that a single examination, even by a careful and trustworthy person, with a single lamp, to ascertain whether it would be extinguished by mephitic gas in a pit seventy feet deep, was not sufficient; that where human life was to be risked, repeated and successive experiments should have been made, with torches or lamps, at regular intervals, before the lungs of men should be required to inhale that air; or that other more complete experiments should have been made to ascertain the condition of that subterranean abode; that an hour or two would not be unprofitably thrown away, in determining the condition of the pit. The jury might reasonably have concluded, that to guard against the danger of mephitic gas, it was the duty of the defendant to provide a larger bucket and a stronger rope, to enable more than one or two persons, at a time, to ascend the shaft, and thus escape from death. The jury might fairly have inferred, from the evidence given, and allowing it full credence, that the defendant and his agents were guilty of the negligence charged. They were the proper judges of this matter; the judge who tried the cause thought they had decided rightly; and I am sure I can see no ground on which to say that they were wrong. I am for affirming the judgment.

CARR, J. The principles that govern cases of this kind (of which we have had several lately) are well settled. It is agreed, on all hands, that when a court is applied to for a new trial because the verdict is contrary to evidence, "the court ought to grant it, only in case of a plain deviation, and not in a doubtful one, merely because the judge, if on the jury would have a different verdict; since that would be to assume the province of the jury, whom the law has appointed the triers." The difficulty lies in applying this law to the facts of the different cases brought before us. We ought, I think, to exercise the power given us with a jealous caution of ourselves; for if we do not agree exactly with the jury, we are naturally too apt to overlook the distinction between a plain and a doubtful deviation; and thus to invade the province of the jury. The facts before us present to my mind one of those doubtful cases. The defendant having hired the slave to work at his coal pits, which are known to be subject occasionally to the visitation of this foul air, and having given the additional hire which is laid on to meet this risk, ought not to be charged with the loss of the slave, unless he was in some default. If he has been negligent in any thing, it was either in sending the hands into the pits without a sufficient examination, or in failing to provide sufficient means of escape in the moment of danger. The hands had all been more or less sickened the evening before by foul air in the pit, and had been taken out. The next morning they were sent down again, after an examination by a single person, and that the person a negro slave, but experienced and confidential: was this taking sufficient precaution, where so many human lives depended on the issue? Again: the pit was seventy feet deep, and there was but one shaft, allowing but one bucket to pass up and down: was this providing sufficient means of escape? These, I confess, are doubtful points with me. Perhaps they might not be so, if I were better acquainted with the working of coal pits, the nature of this mephitic air, the customs and habits of the business, and the precautions commonly used; but of these I am wholly ignorant. Here are twelve men, most of them probably citizens of the county, some perhaps from the neighbourhood of these pits, and well acquainted with all these facts; every one of them, I apprehend, a better judge of these matters than myself. They are too, the appropriate triers of facts. With the witnesses before them, and no bias to mislead their judgments, they have found for the plaintiff. And the judge who heard the whole case has refused a new trial. Shall I understand to say, that this is a finding against the evidence, so gross and palpable as to justify me in setting all aside, and sending the parties back? I certainly cannot. Let me not be misunderstood: I do not mean to say, that the defendant has actually been negligent; that he has deserved the verdict; but that it is one of those cases where the jury's verdict is decisive with me; for I am free to declare that if, on the same facts, the case had come up with a verdict for the defendant, I should, as at present advised, have refused a new trial. I am affirming the judgment.

TUCKER, P. I am of opinion, that the verdict of the jury, upon the facts appearing before them, was clearly wrong; and unless it be conceded, that a court is never to grant a new trial in a case which is peculiarly appropriate for the decision of the jury, a new trial ought to be granted in this. But, whatever the nature of the case, if the jury have plainly deviated from the conclusion to which the facts proved ought to have led them, the court ought to exercise it superintending power, by granting a new trial. Such I conceive to have been the case here. The verdict is altogether unsustained by the facts, and the court would not take upon itself to decide upon the weight of evidence; the facts proved, and not the evidence, having been certified by the circuit court. I have therefore no difficulty in saying, that the judgment should be reversed, and a new trial awarded.

CABELL. J. I concur in the opinion of the president.

The judges of this court being equally divided in opinion,–judgment of the circuit court affirmed.

---

[1] State of Virginia and Benjamin Watkins Leigh. *Reports of cases argued and determined in the Court of Appeals, and in the General Court of Virginia.* Richmond: Gary & Clemmitt, 1867, second ed.

APPENDIX FOUR

March 19, 1855, Explosion Article

The article below encompasses all the components involved in the coal mining business in Chesterfield County. Although this is the second article in a series written about the March 19, 1855, explosion at the "Midlothian Coal Pits," it says a great deal.

1) *Death as a result of the explosion*
2) *White individuals discussed first*
3) *Boys worked in the pits*
4) *Burned as a result of the explosion*
5) *Blacks, including slaves, discussed after whites*
6) *Not all were killed instantly, implying painful short and long term suffering*
7) *Slave insurance and the resulting insurance payout after the slave's death*

In a truly capitalistic style, the slave owners "can get their money at once, by making proper application."

DAILY DISPATCH
RICHMOND, THURSDAY, MARCH 22, 1855

"LATEST FROM THE MIDLOTHIAN PITS"

We are indebted to Dr. F. W. Hancock, of this city, for the following list, which is strictly correct. Dr. H. left the pits at a late hour yesterday evening. We regret to learn that two more white persons have died since we left the pits last Tuesday evening, making 9 [whites] in all. Their names are: John Lester, Joseph Howe, John Evans, Jonathan Jewitt, a boy, William Wright, a boy, Samuel Gouldin, gas attendant, Thomas Dunn. The above persons were dead when taken out of the pit. Nicholas Ham and Thomas Kennedy, who were taken out alive, have since died.

John Howe's injuries are not considered dangerous. Samuel Hart, a boy, is badly burned.

NEGROES TAKEN OUT DEAD

Lewis Jackson, Issac Johnson, Robert Adams, Armistead Ritchie, Charles Wilson, Edwin Carter, Philip Forsee, Fendal Riley, Henry Spears, William Percell, Isacc Galt, and Charles Williams, were all owned by the "Midlothian Company."

Henry Pickett, Patrick Mills, William Mills, Francis Mills, (in a dying condition) and Billy Herrod, were owned by Mr. Nicholas Mills.

Jordan and John, were owned by William Goode, Jr. and insured in the U. S. Life Insurance office.

Alfred, Archer, and Israel, (in a dying condition) were owned by A. S. Wooldridge.

Herod, owned by Charles Pope, and insured in the U. S. Life Insurance office.

Dick, (in a dying condition) owned by Gustavus Depp, and insured in the U. S. L. I. office.

Stephen, Orange, and Bob, owned by Dr. Hancock, and insured in the U. S. L. I. office.

Frederick Harris, owned by George Harris.

David Depp, owned by William Robertson.

Dick Hancock, owned by Dr. Hancock, and insured in the U. S. L. I. office.

Patrick Wincheloe, owned by Wincheloe's estate.

Jasper Forsee, owned by Thomas Forsee's estate.

William Kenney, owned by Dr. Wooldridge's estate.

NEGROES INJURED

Joe White, (recovery doubtful) Frederick Jones, Dick Smith, Lewis Monroe, Isaac Minor and Henry Taliaferro, all slightly injured, and owned by the Midlothian Company.

Anthony Jones, owned by Nicholas Mills.

John Gray, owned by A. S. Wooldridge.

Making in all *nine* whites dead, and *two* injured. – *Thirty* negroes dead, *three* dying, and *eight* injured but will recover.

Those persons having insurance in the U. S. L. I. office, can get their money at once, by making proper application.

APPENDIX FIVE

SERIES OF MINE DISASTER ARTICLES

Each article was copied in its entirety, unless noted, including misspellings.

Please note the comments alluding to controlling science.

Richmond Enquirer
Saturday, March 23, 1839

"THE BLACK HEATH COAL MINE"

The Black Heath Mine, worked by the "Black Heath Coal Company," is one of the richest and most extensive in this country. It is 12 miles from Richmond, in nearly a Western direction, and is situated in the midst of bituminous coal fields of unknown extent. The shaft from which the explosion of Monday took place, has not been long sunk, and we believe is the deepest in the Union – being more than 700 feet to its bottom. Upwards of 10,000,000 bushels of coal had been explored in the pit reached by it; and none can conjecture how much more a further exploration would discover.

The Steam Engines and apparatus for hoisting coal from this shaft were excellent; and the system and facility with which the hoisting process was conducted, produced an average of about 2,500 bushels of coal per day. It is to be regretted that these operations have been interrupted – throwing so much weight in the scale of our productions, and aiding essentially to increase our capital and commercial strength as they did – and this regret is added to by the afflicting event which has caused the interruption. However, the intelligent and active men who are superintending the Mine, say this it will be reclaimed in a short time.

The explosion was one of a most violent nature. – How it happened there is no telling. But that it occurred from neglect or disregard of positive orders and regulation of the pit, is beyond all doubt. The drifts and *"air coasts"* (passages for the air from chamber to chamber) were so arranged as to keep up constant ventilation. It is the general opinion, that one of the doors of the *air coasts* must have been closed, and that thus the "inflammable gas" accumulated on Sunday to such an extent as to produce the explosion soon after the laborers entered the Pit, on Monday morning. Sir Humphrey Davy's lamp was regularly used in the Mine, and no doubt is entertained, but that it was used on Monday morning. It was commonly carried forward to test the presence of the gas. It may have been out of order; if a slight rent should have been in its wire gauze covering it would readily ignite the gas – Other lamps were used; and one of these may have been taken into a chamber or drift where the safety lamp had not been presented. Either of these causes would have involved carelessness. The density and inflammability of the gas might have caused the wire to have become oxidated, and fall to pieces; but that could not have occurred till after indication by flame inside the gauze, of a danger, in the face of which it would have been madness in the laborers to remain. Whatever may have been the immediate cause, the arrangements and rules of the pit, drawn from the lights of science and experience in mining, were such as to have ensured safety, if properly attended to. But would it not be well, in order to diminish the chances of danger from even *carelessness* itself, to use Davy's lamp *exclusively*, in all pits where there has been any exhibition of carburetted bydrogen [hydrogen] or "inflammable gas?"

One of the superintendents of the operations in the pit, who was below when the explosion took place, was a man of great skill in his profession, having been many years engaged in it in some of the most famous of the English Mines. He was a Scotchman, named John Rynard. It is hard to account for how he should have permitted the cause of the occurrence; but even in the midst of an effort to correct the omission or neglect of Saturday night, the explosion may have taken place.

Mr. John Hancock, a native of Chesterfield, of respectable family, was the other unfortunate superintendent.

The laborers were all colored men. The superintendents above the shaft say that about forty were below.–They cannot speak with certainty. Many had gone to see their wives at distant plantations, and it was not known how many had returned. Those who had not, do not yet appear from terror at the news of the explosions; but *forty* is the *maximum*.

The explosion was so powerful as to blow pieces of timber out of the shaft to a distance of a hundred yards from it. Three men were blown up it in a coal hamper to a height of some thirty or forty feet above its top:– two of them fell out of the hamper in different directions, and were immediately killed – the third remained in it, and fell with it, escaping most miraculously with his life, having both legs broken. He is now doing very well. Much loose coal was blown from the drifts to the bottom of the shaft, and four of the bodies, as we have already stated, were taken from beneath a large bulk there, in a mutilated state. Four were taken out shortly after the explosion on Monday – one of whom died. – The others are in a fair way to recover.

Every exertion has been made, which could be made consistently with safety, to rescue the unfortunate beings. It appeared upon going down the shaft, that much carbonic acid gas (the product of combustion) was present. This is called at the mines "black damp," and though not inflammable, is destructive to human life. – This, then had first to be dispersed. The partitions too, in the shaft, necessary for the ingress and egress of air in the pit, were much torn to pieces by the explosion and had to be repaired as the shaft was descended, or death would have resulted to those who went down.

These explosions were formerly very common in the North of England. One occurred at the Felling colliery in Northumberland, England, on the 25th of May, 1812, in which 92 lives were lost. This is the greatest destruction ever known from the same cause. In 1815, an explosion occurred in a mine at Durham, in which 57 persons were destroyed, and in another, 22 were killed in the same manner. The discoveries of Sir Humphrey Davy and other contributors to science and benefactors of mankind have since rendered the avoidance of these destructive explosions certain.

In our mines, no explosion of any extent have ever occurred, from the ignition of inflammable gas. Such are as certainly to be guarded against as the bursting of steam boilers. The safeguards are as simple as effective.

Let the unfortunate event which has just occurred be a lesson and warning, as we are sure it will be; and if possible, cause a more constant and rigid observance of the rules which science and experience have pointed out as the sure and unerring guarantees of safety.

[*Richmond Compiler, March 21*]

The South-Side Democrat *printed this article about the December 12, 1856, disaster quoting the* Richmond Dispatch *as its source. Although a better description was provided on December 15, this article presented a different perspective. The laborers dug into old mining works, causing a terrible flood in the shaft. While giving an example of another type of hazard causing loss of life, this article also offers an interesting social commentary the Records of Death cannot fully convey. Notice the comment, "All the white men…"*

South-Side Democrat
Tuesday Morning, December 16, 1856

"THE MIDLOTHIAN COAL PITS ACCIDENT"

In addition to the particulars given yesterday we to-day subjoin the names of the unfortunate men killed by the rush of water. The relief party…descended the pits and rescued two white men, William Barnes and Beuben Burton, who had made their escape from the submerged drift along the highest or "rise." The relief party proceeded into the workings as far as they were accessible, but failed to find another human being, leaving but little doubt on the mind of any one connected with the work, they had all perished in the deluge. Those now missing are: William Dunn, James Farley, Thos. Lester, J.W. Pringle and Edward Dawson, white men; and Bristol White, Thos. Jackson, Daniel Washington, slaves of the Midlothian Company; Edward Mills and Henry Dickenson, slaves to Nicholas

Mills, Esq., of this city; John Goode, the property of Mr. Goode; and Mark Martin, owned by William E. Martin, of Chesterfield.

All of the white men have left helpless and dependent families, whose situations will be truly deplorable, if prompt aid is not rendered them from those who have means to subscribe to the relief of the disconsolate widow and sorrowing orphan. Bereft of protection and support by a sudden affliction, theirs is truly a hard lot.

The mining company will be at immense expense to get the pits clear of the water, &c.

Notice the statement regarding the five slaves being insured.

The Daily Express
Friday Morning, April 15, 1859

"THE EXPLOSION AT THE BRIGHT HOPE PITS"

The dreadful explosion of gas at the Bright Hope Pits, in Chesterfield, on Wednesday morning, by which nine human beings were killed, continued yesterday to be the source of much excitement to the vicinity of the *locale*. At five o'clock yesterday morning, the shaft was sufficiently free from the [illegible] effects of the gas to be entered, when the bodies of the unfortunate miners were found…[description omitted in respect of the deceased]. The four whites were GEO. SMITH, ISAAC PALMER, RICHARD BLANKENSHIP, AND ALBERT CRUMP. The five negroes were slaves, two belonging to S. D. WOOLDRIDGE, Esq., two to MR. CHAS. BREWER, and the fifth to MR. ABSOLUM MARTIN. They were taken out and properly attended to by the company's managers, in the preparation for burial.

Through the kindness of a friend, which we shall gratefully remember, the following particulars concerning the killed, reached us last night, by telegraph:

GEORGE SMITH was thirty-five years of age, and leaves a wife and four children; ISAAC PALMER was forty-five years of age, and leaves a wife and no children. RICHARD BLANKENSHIP, twenty years of age, single. ALBERT CRUMP, widower, about thirty-five years of age, and leaves two children. All the negroes were insured.

To form some idea of the nature of this explosion, the reader may compare it to the discharge of a cannon loaded with powder only, and before which the victims may have stood. The concussion strikes them lifeless, and in the confinement of the mine, the fatal gas suffocates and kills them, before relief of any kind can be made available. – This is truly a sad case.

Daily Dispatch
Tuesday Morning, December 15, 1863

"COALPIT EXPLOSION"

An explosion occurred at the "Raccoon Pit," in Chesterfield county, on Thursday last, which resulted in the death of sixteen men and the fatal injury of three others. The accident was caused by the ignition of gas in the pit and was followed by a tremendous explosion, which shook the earth for miles around.– At the time of its occurrence there were seventy or eighty hands at work in the pits, all of whom, save nineteen, escaped serious injury. Much excitement prevailed in the neighborhood after the explosion and great anxiety was manifested to know who were injured. As soon as the shaft could be descended working parties were sent down, and discovered that Mr. Barham, the overseer, and fifteen negroes were dead, and three other negros fatally injured. The balance were safe. Most of the slaves were owned by the Chesterfield Coal Mine Company. The injury to the works was comparatively small, and can be repaired in a short time.

Raccoon Pit is but a short distance from Clover Hill Pits and about nine miles from Petersburg. How the accident occurred no one can tell, as most of the parties in its immediate neighborhood were killed.

The Daily Dispatch printed several articles after the Friday, February 3, 1882 explosion at the Grove Shaft mines in Chesterfield County. Each article conveys pain and compassion for the victims and their loved ones left behind. Note the "CONSIDERED 'GASSY'" reference in the first article. The omen once again appears, 72 years after the first documented explosion.

Daily Dispatch
Saturday Morning, February 4, 1882

"FEARFUL FATE"

Thirty-two Men Entombed in the Midlothian Mines, in Chesterfield County.

Explosion in the Grove Shaft; Cinders and Smoke Bursting Out the First Inclination of the Terrible Catastrophe – Names of Those who were in the Mine at the Time – Conjectures as to the Cause of the Accident – Efforts to Penetrate the Shaft to Ascertain the Fate of those Unfortunate Beings who Have Been Either Killed Outright or are Entombed Eight Hundred Feet Below Ground – Facts About the Midlothian Mines.

Soon after 1 o'clock yesterday afternoon an explosion occurred at the Grove shaft, Midlothian mines, near Coalfield, in Chesterfield county, resulting in the loss of about thirty lives.

The mine where the unfortunate accident occurred is known as the Midlothian Coal-Mining Company's, and is situated in Midlothian district, Chesterfield county, on the Richmond and Danville railroad, about thirteen miles from Richmond, and is owned by the estate of the late William R. Burrows, of Albion, N.Y. It is, and has been for the past five years, under the superintendency of Mr. Dodd, an experienced miner.

The Grove shaft is some four hundred feet deep. From the bottom of the shaft there is a tunnel of 450 feet, at the end of which

THERE IS AN INCLINE

descending at an angle of about twenty-eight or thirty degrees to the extent of about 2,000 feet in length. The work of driving the incline has been suspended for some time, it having proved unprofitable. Where the men have been working there are two engines of about forty-horse-power each in the bottom and at the further end of the tunnel for the purpose of raising coal from the incline, and four mules to haul the boxes of coal to the bottom of the shaft, when it is raised to the surface by an engine on top.

The pit has been

CONSIDERED "GASSY"

for some time, but has been ventilated by a fan, with the aid of the exhaust and smoke from the steam-boiler in the bottom.

One of the miners, named Benjamin Johnson, was badly burned by gas last week.

The total number of hands employed on the top and bottom has been about 120, of which about 40 are white and the remainder colored. Most of the men are married and have families residing in and about the village of Midlothian, or Coalfield, as it is sometimes called. The pit has been

WORKED NIGHT AND DAY,

changing at 6 o'clock A.M. and 6 o'clock P.M. and about fifty men have been employed on a shift. The working forces in the bottom have been under charge of two brothers, William Marshall and Johnson Marshall, alternating night and day-both old miners and considered excellent gas-men. They have been in the employment of the company for a long number of years, and both of them have families. William Marshall lost a son in the same pit by the explosion of 1876.

The thickness of the seam in which the miners have been at work would average about four feet, and by a perpendicular descent it is likely that the men were 800 feet below the surface.

THE PAY OF THE MEN

at work in these mines averaged about $1.50 per day. They had a task of about 100 bushels per day, and were generally able to get through with it in eight or nine hours.

It is estimated that these Midlothian Mines have cost about $500,000 since Mr. Burrows acquired them about twelve years ago.

BLACK DAMP.

It is quite likely that after the explosion the shaft was filled with black damp, through which the fresh air could not easily be forced with the fan. In 1856 this black damp had to be broken with water.

The air from the surface had to be driven a distance of about 2,800 feet, as follows:

	Feet.
Shaft, perpendicular..................................	400
Tunnel from bottom of shaft remaining horizontally about	400
Incline commencing at end of tunnel had been driven for about 2,000 feet, dipping at an angle of about 30 degrees............	2,000
Total..	2,800

The men were probably about 200 feet from the extremity of the incline, say about 2,600 feet from the fan on the surface. The shaft was in two chambers; the theory of it was that fresh air would go down one and foul air rise out of the other. The "upcast" was simply a third chamber penetrating from the surface to the tunnel. The heat from the boiler and the work of the fan created a draft which carried off bad air.

A VOLCANIC OUTBURST.

The first evidence of what had occurred in the pit was a volume of smoke, cinders, wood, and bark thrown up from the shaft, which thereupon became choked up and closed.

Intense excitement ensued, as it was known that a large number of men were at work in the pit.

Several efforts were made yesterday afternoon to test the pit and to reach the imprisoned workmen without success.

A telegram from Coalfield to this paper, filed at 8:45[?], said: People from all quarters are flocking to the explosion. There are various reports as to the

NUMBER OF WORKMEN IN THE PIT.

Some say 35, some 40, and others say, with more correctness, 32. The coal-pits are about one mile and a half from this point [Coalfield], and it is difficult to get information.

No one seems to know how the explosion happened, whether it was the result of foul air or carelessness on the part of some of the unfortunate men. The superintendent says he cannot account for it. He adds that it is supposed that the falling slate came on the brattishs which carried the air, stopping the ventilation. This may have occurred while the men were eating their dinners. No doubt they went back to their work, and may have lighted up the mine.

The following is a list of the men in the pit at the time of the explosion:

William Marshall, foreman,
James E. Hall,
Thomas E. Hall
George Jewett, Jr.
A. W. Jewett, Jr.
James Brown
Joe Cournow
John Morris
Joseph Shields
Richard Cogbill
(all white);
Richard Morgan,
Bob Bereford,
Sam Cox,
Pleasant Stewart,
Joe Cunliff,
Beverly Brooks,
Alexander Logan,
Peter Hoffer,
Major Pollard,

Solomon Taylor,
Squire Bright,
John Green,
Lewis Hobbs,
Daniel Hammond,
Isham Graves,
Ed Ross,
Robert Booker,
Thomas Summels,
Albert Hughes,
James Mills,
Jeff Coleman,
Fred Anderson
(all colored),

SOME OF THE SUPPOSED DEAD,

W.H. Marshall, "the bottom boss," was the son of an old English miner brought over here by the English company almost fifty years ago. He was about forty-five years of age, had a wife and four children, and was considered one of the best miners in the field.

James E. Hall was the deputy bottom boss, was a native of Chesterfield, and a cousin of Marshall, and was about forty years old.

The Jewetts were the sons of English miners.

Brown was an Irishman.

Cournow was the son of a man who was killed by the explosion in 1876 in the same pit.

John Morris was a lad, son of an Englishman who lost his eyes in the pits.

AN EXPLOSION IN 1876

occurred at these pits, when nine men were killed, details of which were published in the *Dispatch* at the time.

THIRTY-TWO UNDER GROUND.

Mr. Albert Blair received the following last night:

COALFIELD, VA., February 3, 1882.
Explosion at Grove shaft. Thirty-two caught under ground.
E.W. Crew, Operator.

The Situation at Midnight.

COALFIELD, 12 o'clock.

It is now believed beyond doubt that the thirty-two men who were in the pit are all dead. It is supposed they were instantly killed by the explosion. If any survived it, they were suffocated by carbonic-acid gas soon afterwards.

THE NIGHT TURN

came off this morning at 6 o'clock, and were relieved by the men now entombed in the mine. A machinist and assistant brought the latest news from the mine at 12 o'clock. They say the pit was clear, and that William Marshall, the pit boss, told the assistant he could come down in the evening and feel perfectly safe.

The night-pit boss also reported to the superintendent that the pit was free from gas, but that during the night they had had

A TUMBLE OF SLATE,

which knocked down a portion of the brattishs, a wooden partition for conveying[?] the air to the miners. This was repaired, and all was free when the day turn went in.

Soon after the explosion, at 1 o'clock, the people knew that something appalling had occurred, and an alarm was given, and in a short time the wives and families of the miners, most of whom reside in the vicinity, were on the ground. All realized the great danger, but hope was strong that the men would be rescued.

THREE ATTEMPTS WERE MADE

by the superintendent and two brave miners to establish communication with the doomed men, but without success. They tried to unite the signal cord, which was broken about four hundred feet from the surface, but were driven back by carbonic-acid gas.

In despair, about 2 o'clock all hope was abandoned. When the men descended beyond four hundred feet they listened for any sound, but all was

SILENT AS THE GRAVE.

Twenty-four of the thirty-two unfortunate men were married. Soon their wives and children were assembled around the mouth of the awful tomb, and the most

HEARTRENDING SCENES

took place.

Further efforts to reach the bottom of the mine had to be abandoned, as there was danger of a general conflagration from the fires of the engine-boilers below, if ventilation was restored until these have time to expire. Nothing further can now be done. To-morrow an effort will be made to reach the mine.

Daily Dispatch
Sunday Morning, February 5, 1882

"GROVE SHAFT HORROR."

Determined Efforts to Descend Into the Mine and
Learn the Very Worst

Full particulars of the Great Disaster of Friday; Twenty-seven Widows, One Hundred and Eight Children Fatherless–Volunteers from Other Mines Present to Give What Assistance They Can–Repairing of the Shaft Begun; Descent of Working-Parties–Probable Cause of the Explosion–List of the Men Caught Underground, with Places of Nativity, Ages, and Family-History–The Latest from the Relief Parties– Mr. Cuthbert's Account–Down in a Coal Mine; A Description Written in 1843–One Body Discovered.

Though there was little outward evidence of it, yesterday was a day of great sorrow at the Midlothian mines.

Around the mouth of Grove Shaft there was no crowd; only men at work. The widowed women and the children made fatherless by the great calamity of Friday generally remained at their homes, suffering the agony of frightful suspense and hoping against hope, while courageous men, with all the means at their disposal, went hard to work to penetrate the mine and discover the worst. It can hardly be possible that any of those entombed by the explosion of Friday can be alive, but their friends feel it a duty to labor with as much zeal and energy as if by so doing they might rescue them from impending death.

The explosion blew out the brattice of the shaft. The brattice is a partition dividing the shaft into two chambers, and is necessary in order that an atmospheric current may be created and the fresh air let in by the aid of the fan, and the foul air let out. Wherever the mines proceed in the bowels of the earth, in mining of the character done in Chesterfield, this brattice-work in some form or other must be put up. The explosion broke it up in the shaft, and the relief parties yesterday had first to repair it. To do it quicker canvas was used. As the men went lower and lower into the shaft they cleared the *debris* away, and our latest accounts give, considering all the circumstances, a satisfactory account of their progress.

The disaster makes 27 widows and 108 children fatherless. Ten of the thirty-two men lost were white.

The following information about the shaft is accurate:

	Feet.
Depth of shaft..	640
Length of tunnel (through bed of granite)........	600
Length of incline.....................................	2,000
Total distance from mouth of shaft to the extremity of the incline.......................	3,240

VISIT TO COALFIELD.

Mr. J. B. Lightfoot, the agent here of the Midlothian coal-mines, knew nothing of the disaster until he learned it from the *Dispatch* of yesterday morning. Then, impatient to get to the spot, and being unwilling to wait for the train, he drove to Coalfield, and was at the shaft all day.

Mr. William R. Burrows, one of the owners, went to Coalfield yesterday by train, and returned in the afternoon.

The vein of coal which the men were working was about four feet in thickness, and was of very good quality. It sold for $3 per ton at the mine.

The outlay in preparing these mines during the past twelve years was about $300,000. A great deal of money was spent in driving the tunnel through solid rock from the bottom of the shaft to the coal-vein.

The Herald's Account.

When news of the disaster reached Rich[mond] Mr. Cuthbert hired a locomotive and hastened to Coalfield and sent the following account:

The Grove shaft of the Midlothian mine is situated about thirteen miles from Richmond, on the Richmond and Danville railroad, having a tract one mile in length running from the railroad to the mine. The shaft is 600 feet perpendicular depth. From that point there is a stone tunnel 600 feet more to the coal-vein. From this point an incline is driven south 54 degrees west, dipping at an average angle of 17 degrees for 2,000 feet, which makes a total depth of 1,400 feet. There are six levels working, the first commencing at 1,250 feet from the top of the incline.

WHERE THE MEN WERE.

In these six levels there were fifteen coal-diggers working. The remaining seventeen were in other portions of the pit. One of the seventeen, the engineer, would be with his engine at the head of the incline. A banksman, a driver, and a fireman would be in the vicinity of the engine. The others, who were timber hands, gasmen, and assistants, would be in the levels, where the diggers were. The night shift or turn had come off work that morning at 6 o'clock, and were relieved by the men who are now inevitably lost.

THE LAST MEN OUT.

About the same time there went into the pit a machinist and assistant. They went to remove an engine, and came out to dinner at 12 o'clock noon, thus bearing the last intelligence from the lost men. The machinist says that he saw the pit boss and gasman near the engine-room at 10 o'clock, having come up to eat their breakfast. The pit boss, whose name was William Marshall, told the assistant of the machinist that he could come down the incline in the evening and feel perfectly safe, but that he should observe due caution in coming down the incline. He said he should keep a sharp lookout for the train and not be caught by it. The trains are hauled up the incline by a wire rope. A nephew of Marshall was also to have come down with the assistant, neither being accustomed to the pit–which is an additional proof that no fears were entertained by the workmen below.

A TUMBLE OF SLATE.

The night pit boss reported to Superintendent Dodds that the pit was free of gas, but that during the night there had been a tumble of slate which knocked down a portion of the brattice, which is a wooden partition for conveying the air to the face of the coal. This caused an accumulation of a small quantity of gas in this level which was removed before he left and the brattice restored. This is all the information that is attainable from the men, or as to the condition of the pit when they went into, or up to the time the machinist and his assistant left the pit. Work was suspended for dinner until 1 o'clock.

THE EXPLOSION.

Precisely at that hour there was a report of an explosion in the shaft, followed by a cloud of dust from its mouth. A large number of top-hands, who were near at the time, realized that something appalling had happened. They said at once that it was either an explosion of gas or that the boiler had burst.

A HORROR-STRIKEN CROWD.

An alarm was soon given, which brought a crowd to the scene. The wives and families of the miners and hands, most of whom reside in the vicinity, were soon on the ground, and all of them realized that there was great if not the most imminent danger to the men in the mine. The most distressing scenes followed, but still some of the relatives and friends of the doomed men were not without hope of their rescue or escape from a terrible death. Among others Superintendent Dodds was promptly on the ground.

A PERILOUS DESCENT.

Safety lamps were at once procured, and the Superintendent and Pit-Boss Marshall, brother of William Marshall, and Edward Coxon went aboard the cage, and descended to the point about three hundred feet down the shaft. At that point they discovered that the signal wire was broken, and their lights were extinguished by a strong current of air from above. After attempting to relight the lamps they returned to the top of the pit. Superintendent Dodds and his companions then concluded that the brattice in the shaft was damaged, in consequence of which the current of air did not descend further than that point.

A SECOND ATTEMPT.

Marshall and Coxon, then descended a second time to the bottom of the shaft. The superintendent remained at the top giving directions and procuring lamps. It was arranged that they should signal from the bottom, if practicable, and send the cage back for Dodds. If not practicable, the cage was to be brought back. At the expiration of one minute it was found the signal-wire was broken, and the men were of course drawn up again. This was the second attempt to penetrate the mine.

AN AWFUL SILENCE.

They reported a large portion of brattice in the shaft broken out and a considerable quantity of *debris*, consisting of timber, coal-boxes, water-barrels, and other articles, at the bottom of the shaft. All was silent as the grave. They listened eagerly for some sound from the entombed men, but could hear none. Ventilation was entirely cut off, and "after-damp," or poisonous carbonic-acid gas, had rolled back in volumes to the shaft-bottom. In absolute despair of being able to render any assistance, Marshall and Coxon came up. It was then about twenty minutes past 1 o'clock.

ATTEMPTING TO SIGNAL THE MEN.

Another and third attempt was then made to obtain some communication with the men in the pit. This was an effort to repair the signal wire. In order to do this it was decided to endeavor to attach a cord to the broken wire and carry it down with them. The wire was intact to a point four hundred feet below the surface. The first impulse was to cover the break in the shaft brattice with canvas or sail-cloth for the purpose of restoring ventilation. Superintendent Dodds objected to that proposition on the ground that whatever gas might be between the shaft and the boiler, a distance of 500 feet, would be carried on to the boiler fires and would probably result in another explosion. After making known his fears to the men on the ground they quite coincided with his opinion and the plan was abandoned.

DRIVEN BACK BY AFTER-DAMP.

Nothing then remained but to try and restore the signal. Marshall, Coxon, and a man named Crump then went down again for a third time. They carried a rope with them which they attached to the signal wire, and after descending a short distance beyond that point were forced to return by encountering carbonic-acid gas. This was the final effort to reach the mine or open communication with it. It then became awfully apparent to those engaged in these efforts that all the inmates of the pit were dead.

HOPE ABANDONED.

Upon their return, which was about 2 o'clock, all hope was abandoned, and the most harrowing scenes of wailing women and children and grief-stricken men followed.

Ventilation Restored.

COALFIELD, 9 P. M. – Miners are steadily at work in the shaft repairing the brattice-work, and ventilation is now restored to the bottom of the shaft.

None of the bodies have yet been recovered.

The Descent Into the Mine in Search of the Dead.
(Special telegram to the Dispatch)

COALFIELD, February 4. – Snow to the depth of about six inches fell during the night, and the morning broke drear and dismal over the Grove shaft of the Midlothian coal-mines, with its tomb of thirty-two men.

Miners from the Deep-Run, Etna, Jewett, and other mines in the county came early, plodding through the snow, to render any assistance in their power towards the recovery of the bodies of the unfortunate men, whom all generally concede to be dead.

The Burrows Midlothian coal-mine of the company employed at the time of the accident including the thirty-two

BURIED IN THE SHAFT.

Nearly all of those living were on the works in the structure surmounting the shaft this morning, besides some dozen or two experienced miners from the neighboring mines.

It was easy to discover from the solemn aspect of the coal-begrimmed visages of the latter, and also of the grave miners, that a descent into the shaft with its treacherous after-damp was looked upon as an undertaking of great personal risk. Notwithstanding this fact there were numerous volunteers ready at a moment's notice to descend and ascertain the doom of the miners and commence the work of searching for the bodies.

During the morning, Superintendent Dodds and other experienced miners held frequent

CONSULTATIONS

as to what was best to be done. The apprehension seemed to be that there was danger from the fires under the engine boilers, which, if not extinct, would cause a fresh explosion, if not already done, as soon as ventilation was restored. The morning hours wore on, and it was as late as 11:40 A.M. when Superintendent Dodds himself, accompanied by George Conrad and E. Coxon, got into the bucket, and amid breathless excitement, commenced a voyage of exploration into the dangerous regions below. The party carried safety-lamps and a signal hammer. The order was given

"LOWER AWAY STEADY."

The perilous journey was begun, and in an instant almost the bucket with its human freight disappeared out of sight. Every eye was fixed upon the slowly-moving rope. An intense stillness was observed to catch any sound that might come from the descending party, when the loud and piteous lamentations of a woman on the outside of the building pierced the very heart of every man there. There was an immediate movement to take her away, as her cries disturbed those who were eagerly awaiting a signal from below.

Down, down, the rope continued to go, and not until ten minutes had been consumed in the descent did the signal to stop come to the ears of those at the mouth of the shaft. In about three or four minutes more

THE SIGNAL CAME TO HAUL UP,

and in a few more minutes the exploring party appeared at the surface. Superintendent Dodds reported that they had descended to within one hundred feet of the bottom, and that the shaft was perfectly clear of carbonic-acid gas.

THIS WAS CHEERING NEWS.

The spirits of all hands revived, even under such mournful circumstances, and a party, consisting of Pit-Boss Johnson Marshall, George Conrad, Royall Johnson, and John Mallory, was at once organized to go down and begin operations with a view to the discovery of the bodies, and, if possible, ascertain the actual cause of the catastrophe.

It may be here remarked that the general

THEORY OF THE EXPLOSION

is that it resulted from a tumble, which carried away the brattice, cutting off ventilation, and causing an explosion of carbonic gas, and thereby closing up the shaft and cutting off every avenue of escape. This is almost the unanimous belief here.

John Marshall and party remained below some twenty minutes, and reached the first break in the brattice. They made a thorough examination of that portion of the shaft which was free from after-damp, and again ascended to obtain the necessary materials for the purpose of repairing the brattice, which will be done temporarily with sail-cloth. If this experiment is successful, operations will be vigorously pushed until the lower tunnels are reached, when the bodies will be discovered.

It is the settled opinion of the leading miners on the ground that

THERE IS NO FIRE BELOW,

and as soon as this prevails with any degree of confidence among the mine hands the work of removing *debris* and opening the avenues to the coal-face will be commenced in good earnest.

At 2 P.M. another party, consisting of Thomas Jones, William Jewett, and John King (white), and Thomas Pollard (colored), went down. They carried all the necessary materials, and such tools and implements as were required to make the repairs to the brattice.

Report of the working party at 3 P.M. states they had repaired about forty feet of the first break-in. It was found that the damage to the brattice was greater than had been anticipated, and it will require considerable labor and time to reach

THE BOTTOM OF THE SHAFT

and beginning of the tunnel. The shaft is very damp and making a great deal of water, which retards the workmen in their operations. It is the opinion of the superintendent that the prospect for reaching the bodies of the mine to-night is not very good. Still it may be accomplished, as all the men are eager to do what they can. The following is a

LIST OF THE MEN LOST

in the mine, giving their supposed ages, places of nativity, whether married or single, and number of family of the former:

William Marshall, aged forty-five years of Percy Main, England; has wife and four children.

Thomas Hall, thirty-five years, Chesterfield, Va.; his wife and four children.

George Jewett, Jr., twenty-one, Chesterfield, Va., wife and one child.

A.A. Jewett, thirty, Chesterfield, Va., wife and one child.

James Brown, thirty-three, probably from Georgetown, D.C.; wife and three children.

James Hall, thirty-three, Chesterfield, Va.; wife and five children.

James Cournow, twenty-one, Chesterfield, Va.; single, but leaves a widowed mother with seven children.

John Morris, twenty-three years, Chesterfield, Va.; single.

Joseph Shields, fifty years, Durham, England; wife and eight children, now in England.

Richard Cogbill, sixty-six years, Chesterfield, Va.; one child living.

Richard Morgan, forty years, a native of Chesterfield, Va.; wife and four children.

Bobert [Robert] Binford, forty, Chesterfield, Va.; wife and seven children.

Samuel Cox, forty-five, Chesterfield, Va.; wife and one child.

Pleasant Stewart, thirty, Chesterfield; wife and one child.

Joseph Cunluff, sixty, Chesterfield; wife and three step-children.

Beverly Brooks, fifty, Chesterfield; wife and several children.

Alexander Logan, forty, Chesterfield; wife and children.

Peter Harper, forty years, Richmond, Va.; wife and children.

Major Pollard, thirty, Chesterfield; wife and three children.

Solomon Taylor, forty, Chesterfield; wife dead. five children living.

Squire Bright, fifty-five, Chesterfield; wife and six children.

John Green, fifty-five, Chesterfield; wife and one child.

Lewis Hobbs, fifty-five, Dinwiddie, Va.; wife and six children.

Daniel Hammond, thirty-two, Powhatan, Va,; wife.

Isham Graves, twenty-one, Chesterfield; single.

Edward Ross, fifty-five, Chesterfield; single.

Robert Booker, eighteen, Chesterfield; single.

Thomas Summels, forty; wife and five step-children.

Albert Hughes, thirty; wife and seven children.

James Mills, thirty, Chesterfield; wife and two children.

Jeff Coleman, forty-five, Chesterfield, wife and three step-children.

Fred Anderson, twenty-three, Chesterfield; single.

The following were

IN PREVIOUS DISASTERS:

John Green (colored) was in the upper portion of the same shaft in May, 1876, when the explosion then occurred. He was working with Charles Holder, who was killed. Holder was thrown out of the bucket; Green held on to the rope and was hauled out. Ned Ross, also colored, was in the shaft in May, 1876. He was working at the bottom, and was rescued barely alive. He was about the same place yesterday when the explosion occurred by which he lost his life. Joseph Cournow (white) is the son of Thomas Cournow, who was one of the pit bosses and lost his life in the explosion of May, 1876. Solomon Taylor (colored), among the killed Friday, was also in the explosion of 1876, but escaped with others.

THE LATEST

Discovery of One of the Bodies Not Very Far
From the Bottom of the Shaft.
(Special telegram to the Dispatch.)

COALFIELD, Va., February 4. – Have just (at 10:30 P.M.) arrived from Grove shaft, Midlothian pits.

At last the persistent efforts of the miners have been rewarded by reaching the bottom of the shaft, and by consumate daring discovering the body of one of the unfortunate men about one hundred and fifty feet from the base of the shaft. This was Ned Ross, the colored hanger-on at the shaft bottom. His body was considerably bruised, and showed unmistakable evidence of his having died from the effect of after-damp or carbon gas. The hardy miners who made this success proved themselves heroes, and deserve the highest consideration for their

GALLANT CONDUCT.

Two of them came near losing their lives. The party consisted of John Kendler, George Conrad, Thad. Crump, and Johnson Marshall. These were the last party that went down to-night, and they fought their way against the insidious "after-damp" after they reached the bottom. The two latter, Crump and Marshall, while out of the cage, or bucket, exploring a tunnel, encountered "after-damp," and were overcome by it. Their companions succeeded in bringing them back to the cage, and after placing them in the [bucket] the signal to haul up was given, and luckily they arrived at the top, to be brought too [*sic*] by restoratives. Both the men are still in a feeble condition. In all, nine turns went down this afternoon, relief after relief, until the brattice was all repaired, the ventilation restored, and the bottom reached, with the results as given above.

It is not known whether further operations will be continued to-night. The probability is they will be

SUSPENDED UNTIL MORNING,

as the men are nearly all exhausted.

There will be great suffering among the stricken families unless benevolent people come promptly to their aid with substantial relief. This community is very poor, and is already encumbered with widows and orphans, victims of the previous mine disasters.

Let something be done for these destitute people.

Going Down into a Coal-Mine.

The following letter, written in 1843, is published in Howe's Historical Collections. Making allowances for the fact that since that date there have been great improvements in machinery, the description is a pretty fair one of the mining operations of the present day. The Midlothian mines referred to were in the same coal-fields, but not reached by the same shafts now worked. The Mr. Marshall mentioned was doubtless the father of Mr. Marshall, the foreman, who lost his life at Grove shaft Friday:

Learning that the Midlothian mines were the most extensively and as skillfully wrought as any, I paid them a visit. Four shafts have been sunk by this company since 1833; in two coal has been reached, one at a depth of 625 and the other at 775 feet. The sinking of the deepest occupied three years of labor, at a cost of about $30,000. The materials were raised by mules, and it is supposed a like depth was never before attained by horse-power in any country. These shafts, 11 feet square each, are divided by timbers into four equal chambers. At the deep shaft two steam-engines on the surface operate in raising coal; at the other, one. The extra engine at the deep shaft draws coal up an inclined plane down in the mine to the bottom of the shaft. This plane reaches the lowest point of the mine about 1,000 feet, or a fifth of a mile, from the surface. The coal having thus been brought to the pit, the other engine raises it perpendicularly to the surface, when the baskets containing it are placed on little cars on a small hand-railway, and are pushed a few rods to where it is emptied, screened, and shoveled into the large cars on the railroad connecting with tidewater near Richmond. While the engine attached to the plane is drawing up coal it is so arranged that pumps, by the same motion, are throwing out the "surface water," which, by means of grooves around the shaft, is collected in a reservoir made in the rock 360 feet below the surface. This water is conducted about 20 feet above ground to a cistern, from which it is used by the different engines.

Through the kindness of the president of the company I was allowed to

DESCEND INTO THE MINES.

My friend, guide, and self, each with a lighted lamp, sprang into a basket suspended by ropes over pulleys and framework above a yawning abyss 775 feet deep. The signal was given – puff! puff! went the steam-engine, and down, down, went we. I endeavored to joke to conceal my trepidation. It was stale business. Rapidly glided past the wooden sides of the shaft – I became dizzy – shut my eyes – opened them and saw far, far above the small faint light of day at the top. In one minute – it seemed five – we came to the bottom with a *bump!* The underground superintendent made his appearance, covered with coal-dust and perspiration; his jolly English face and hearty welcome augured well for our subterranean researches. Him we followed, each with a lighted lamp, through many a labyrinth, down many a ladder, and occasionally penetrating to the end of a drift, where the men were at work shoveling coal into baskets on the cars running on railroads to the mouth of the pit, or boring for blasts. We witnessed one or two. The match was put, we retreated a short distance, then came the explosion, echoing and reechoing among the caverns – a momentary noise of falling coal, like a sudden shower of hail, succeeded, and then all was silence.

THE DRIFTS, OR PASSAGES,

are generally about 16 feet wide, and 10 feet high, with large pillars of coal intervening about 60 feet square. I can give the idea by comparing the drifts to the streets and the pillars to the squares of a city in miniature. When the company's limits are reached the pillars will be taken away. The general inclination of the passages is about 30°. Frequently obstacles are met with, and one has to descend by ladders or by steps cut in solid rock. Doors used in ventilation were often met with, through which we crawled. Mules are employed underground in transporting the coal on the small railways coursing nearly all the drifts. They are in excellent condition, with fine glossy coats of hair, nearly equal to well-kept race-horses, which is supposed to result from the sulphur in the coal and the even temperature of the mines. Well-arranged stables are there built, and all requisite attention paid them. Some of the animals remain below for years, and when carried to the strong light of day gambol like wild-horses.

PARTITIONS OF THIN PLANK

attached to timbers put up in the centre of the main drifts are one of the principal means by which the mines are ventilated, aided by a strong furnace near the upcast shaft. Near this, is a blacksmith-shop. The atmospheric air is admitted into the mines down the deepest shaft, and, after coursing the entire drifts and ascending to the rise-workings of the mines, is thence conducted to the furnace, where it is rarefied and ascends to the surface, having in its progress become mixed with carbureted hydrogen gas emitted from the coal. When the gas is evolved in unusual quantities greater speed is given to the air by increasing the fire. If the partitions in the drifts (known as brattice-work) should be broken, the circulation would be impeded, and the gas so strongly impregnate the air as in its passage over the furnace to ignite, and result in destructive consequences. Or, should too much gas be thrown out of the coal when the circulation is impeded from any cause, it would explode on the application of a common lamp. In such cases the Davy lamp is used. I heard the gas from the coal make a hissing noise, and I saw it set on fire in crevices of the walls by the lamp of our conductor; and although a novice in these matters enough was seen to convince me of the skill of Mr. Marshall, the company's underground superintendent, in managing the ventilation.

Some years since, when ventilation was less understood than at present,

AN EXPLOSION

took place in a neighboring mine of the most fearful character. Of the fifty-four men in the mine only two, who happened to be in some crevices near the mouth of the shaft, escaped with life. Nearly all the internal works of the mine were blown to atoms. Such was the force of the explosion that a basket then descending, containing three men, was blown nearly one hundred feet into the air.

Two fell out and were crushed to death and the third remained in and with the basket was thrown some 70 or 80 feet from the shaft, breaking both his legs and arms. He recovered, and is now living. It is believed the number of bodies found grouped together in the higher parts of the mine, that many survived the explosion of the inflammable gas and were destroyed by inhaling the carbonic-acid gas which succeeds it. This death is said to be very pleasant; fairy visions float around the sufferer, and he drops into the sleep of eternity like one passing into delightful dreams.

Some years since a gentleman was one autumnal evening hunting in this county in the vicinity of some old coal-pits. Straying from his companions, he accidentally slipped down the side of an

ABANDONED PIT

and caught by one arm a projecting branch on its slope. The pit was supposed to be about 200 feet in perpendicular depth, and its bottom a pile of rocks. He heard in the distance the cries of his companions and the yell of the hounds in the chase. He shouted for help, but no answering shout was returned save the echo of his own voice among the recesses of the surrounding forest. Soon his companions were far away. Death awaited him – an awful death. His mind was intensely excited, and keenly alive to the terrors of his situation. He thought of his friends – of all he loved on earth! And thus to separate; oh, 'twas agony. Hoarsely moaned the wind through the dying leaves of autumn; coldly shone the moon and stars on high, inanimate witnesses of human frailty fast losing its hold upon this life. Nature could sustain herself no longer, he bade "farewell to earth," grew weaker and weaker, released his grasp and fell – fell about *six inches!* This brought him to the bottom of the pit, as you patient reader, are at the bottom of a long letter – all about *coal,* too.

APPENDIX SIX

Baltimore Life Insurance Company Records[1]

Part of the correspondence material referenced in Chapter Three is provided below for your discernment. In the letter dated January 11, 1855, "Dear Sir" refers to Mr. Henry F. Thompson, Secretary of the Baltimore Life Insurance Company. Accompanying the letter were life insurance rate schedules, including for slaves, for The Richmond Fire Association, The National Safety Life Insurance and Trust Company out of Philadelphia and the National Loan Fund Life Assurance Company, of London, which are not included as part of this documentation. The latter two companies' information included names of their General Agent and Medical Examiner. In the case of the National Safety Life Insurance firm, the doctor was the agent.

Accurate interpretation of original script was attempted, yet is not guaranteed.

Richmond Jany. 11 '55 [1855]

Dear Sir,

       Your letter to Mr. Darracott was read last evening. In reference to additional risks in coal pits I have conferred with several gentlemen who have experience on this subject. Major Wooldridge, President of the Midlothian Coal pits informs me that they have never lost any hands in his pits from gas since he has been connected with them (for 20 years). He thinks the risk from accidents from machinery not greater than in ordinary labour. "Ludlam & Watson" formerly agents here for the "Life Assurance Co: of London" say that they do not consider the risk in coal pits so great as on public works generally, particularly R. Roads. They insured here annually, about 600 negroes, some of them in coal pits. Mr. Nicholas Mills of this city has hired some 15 or 20 hands in the Midlothian pits for a number of years & has lost none from accidents. In the Black Heath pitts near Richmond, a number of accidents have occurred from gas. As at present advice I would not recommend insurance on hands in these pits at any premium.

In the pits on the <u>North</u> side of James River, lying in Henrico and Goochland, they have <u>never</u> had any accidents from gas. In Kanawha in digging [illegible] coal there is no gas. There is I am informed no pitting there. This is the place where the hands of Mr. Doswell where application for policies is now before you has hired his hands. The only additional risk there is from the climate being somewhat colder than here.

I have thought for a long time that coal pitts are more healthy places for negroes than factories or R. Roads. They have sufficiently active labour there without exposure to the vicissitudes of weather. To negroes predisposed to <u>consumption</u> – of this disease a great many die in Va:

I think the location is particularly favourable.

From the enclosed rates of three Co's you will perceive your rates are considerably higher than theirs. Comparing yours with the "Richmond Fire Association" for one year, a servant may be insured in their Co. at 30 years of age for $500 for $7.95 – adding 1 per cent Extra for Coal pits – it would be $12.95. In your Company it would be $12.00 without any Extra premium. The nos. of Coal pit hands being small in proportion to other hands you might afford to insure at the same rates or very small Extra premium. I would suggest you should not charge more than 1/4 per cent Extra premium on coal pit hands. Insurance on negroes can only be made profitable by insuring a large number. If the premiums are too high in proportion to the other Co's we shall be precluded from doing much.

We hope to get some insurance now on <u>white</u> persons. If we can once commence on this Species of insurance we should hope to do well with it. Please send some Blanks for negroes. Also send Mr. Doswells policies as soon as practical.

I should be glad to have <u>my a/c</u> settled from money's now in Mr. Darrocotts hands. We send a application for negro Horace of Wm. Jones. We were under the impression it was sent before this with other applications. We send an application for Wm. D. Winston. Mr. Darracott is his Bro: in Law & signs for him. He wishes a policy sent, and if it suits Mr. Winston as well as the Co: in which he is now insured he will accept it.

Yrs: Very Respectfully,
Ths. [Thomas] Pollard

Mr. Henry F. Thompson Sec.
Balt. Life Insur. Co:

Thos. Pollard
Richmond
11 Jany 1855

Two years later the BLIC was still insuring coal pit hands and the recommendation to the Company was that they increase the rates on the slaves in the pits. The applicable series of correspondence documenting the discussions are included for review. Mr. Coulter is addressed as "Secretary" in another letter not included in this appendix, indicating he is an officer with BLIC. Notice the "hands are idle about ground reference" in the February 5, 1857, letter. The slaves were not sent into the pits unless life insurance had been purchased on them, providing reimbursement for the owners in the event of the slave's death.

Richmond Feb. 3 1857

Mr. A. B. Coulter
    Dear Sir,
        Enclosed please find 13 applications for insurance of coal pit hands now in the employ of Tompkins & Co.

Dr. Pollard who had had the misfortune recently to break his right wrist which interferes with his writing requests me to say to you that he is convinced that the risk attending the insurance of Coal Pit Hands hereabouts is such as to render it desirable for the Co. to increase the extra Premium to al least 2 per cent.

He also requests that you will renew your instructions as to the maximum amt for which we are allowed to insure. He would suggest that I should not exceed $900.

Very Truly Yours,
P B Price

If you make changes please send us new rates.

Richmond Feb. 5 1857

Mr. A. B. Coulter
    Dear Sir,
        Yours of Jan. 29 & Feb [illegible] are to hand. Also the package of Policies by Express. I will send you in two or three days my report for January.

Mr. Bolling claims that as I was acting under your printed instructions in giving ¾ of the value of his servant woman as the [illegible] to be insured. The Co. cannot plead another regulation of which no mention had been made to me.

He had made his arrangements to begin his Policy on this, the day of the purchase and was not a little disturbed by your refusal. His girl is perfectly sound & would bring on the block $1000 to $1100 Dollars I suppose. Being his only property of the kind he is particularly anxious to have her secured. [Illegible] to his relatives[?] as an acquaintance & friend of mine & Dr. Pollard's & the length of time granted to insure in your Co. he preferred it & applied to no other. His purchase of the negro girl no doubt was influenced by the fact that he could make such arrangements as your published terms afford.

Under the circumstances Dr. P. and my self both suggest that he be granted $800.

The parties who apply for insurance of the Coal Pit Hands are very anxious to get the Policies as they are keeping the hands above ground and idle till they get them insured.

If they have not been forwarded please send them as soon as you can.

Yours Truly,
P B Price

I enclose the application of J. H. Mayo for insurance on his slaves Nelson & Israel.

Query – Mr. Benjamin Pollard paid me Premiums on 14 Policies in January for himself & Ella Temple Mary Re. Thorton [?], $208.92. I sent the policies in for exchange & on receipt of the new ones at reduced rates found that they amounted to $168.10 so had to refund $40.82 Mr. D. Lee Powell paid me on four old ones. $46 & the new ones substitute amount to $44.98.

Reduction on 14	40.82
" " 4	1.02

Was the difference [illegible] to accidental circumstances or age? Not being familiar with the D. rates I don't know whether there is greater red[uction] on some ages than others.

Richmond Feb. 6 1856 [Error – correct year is 1857]

Mr. A. B. Coulter
    Dear Sir,
        I exceedingly regret the omissions about Tompkins & Co.'s hands <u>all one year</u>. I telegraphed you to that effect this morning so that I might get all the policies tomorrow.

I return the papers for Henry.

I send application for C.[?] E. Snodgrass [?] slave Peter.

Yours of the 29th & 30th to hand [?].

What were contents of yours of 31st.

Thanks for the instructions.

What is the <u>maximum</u> on negro men.

Yours in [illegible],
P B Price

This next letter discusses the rates for coal pit hands, taking into consideration the explosions in the coal pits. Please note the same Mr. Pollard, who wrote the January 11, 1855 letter, is the author of this correspondence also. The recipient of the letter is unclear, however he is either a BLIC representative, or an individual asking for coal miner slave insurance.

A risk comparison between coal mines places Black Heath as the most dangerous, then Mid Lothian Mines, and Clover Hill. The mines north of the James River were considered the least dangerous and at the end of the list. The first three mines are south of the James in Chesterfield County. Note the use of the word "species" to categorize the type of insurance.

Richmond Dec. 30 '57 [1857]

My Dear Sir,

      Mr. Price handed me your favour of the 29th just today. I had previously thought on the subject referred to in your letter, and made the suggestion to him, concerning the change in the rates of coal pit hands, which he communicated to you.

When I first made enquiries concerning these risks I came to the conclusion that they were less, than I now think them. I convened at that time with the Pres. of the "Midlothian Coal Pit Co:" who told me there had been no accident from gas since he presided over the Co:– a period of 20 years. In the second year after this they had an explosion which destroyed 20, or more of their hands. The "Black Heath pits," the Co; in which we have insurance, had an Explosion about 2 years since in which they lost some 12 or 15 hands. They were insured in a Co: here, at about 1 ½ per ¢ Extra. This Co: immediately raised their rates to 4 per ¢ Extra. In a conversation with the agent of this Insurance Co: he states it as his opinion that they could make money at this Extra percentage which however is to high that it has driven off the insuring parties. Another Co: here whose published rates are 1 ½ per ¢ Extra for mining hands, say they will not insure coal pit hands at all, and another Co: with the same published rates, say they do not wish the risks on coal pit hands & have under the "Richmond Fire Assoc:" (part life Co:) have some risks in coal pits, but at what rates I do not know.

It is impossible to make any accurate calculations on this species of Insurance. You may have no accident for 20 years, and then again you may have accidents the first year of the insurance. In the first case of course money would be made, and where no risks would occur for this time, the Co: could stand a considerable loss of hands. If you conclude to insure in mining at all I would advise the rate of 3 per ¢ Extra which perhaps is not so heavy so at to drive off the parties & sufficient with good fortune, probably ordinary fortune, to make money. If you determine to adopt this rate we will Endeavour to get the hands put down in valuation as low as practicable, so as to make the parties more interested & more particular in preserving life.

With the compliments of the season I am, yours most respectively,

Th: [Thomas] Pollard

P.S. Since writing the above I have ascertained that the "Richmond Fire Assoc." have hands insured only in the "Clover Hill" Coal Pits – and at the rate of 1 ½ per cent Extra. I presume from this they think the risk there is small, and large in the other Co's – as I have no idea they would insure at the same rate in those other pits. With these facts before you I hope you will be able to come to a conclusion in the matter. The idea seems as near as I can learn now, that the risk is greatest in the "Black Heath pits", next in the "Midlothian" & least in the "Clover Hill", and the pits on the North Side of James River.

I take this opportunity of enclosing my a/c – it is probably better to do so at the End of the year.

Yrs: Truly
Th: Pollard

---

[1] The Baltimore Life Insurance Company Papers, MS 175, H. Furlong Baldwin Library, Maryland Historical Society.

APPENDIX SEVEN

ADDITIONAL LISTS OF SLAVES

The following documentation provides information from a selection of sources showing slave involvement in the mines. Only a small sample of the material available has been included in this appendix. The first manuscript is a document written between 1810 and 1819 found in the special collection of the "Papers of Henry [Harry] Heth."

A portion of the Chesterfield County Slave Census Records is listed to show the continued use of slaves in the coal mines. The slave houses owned by the companies are also included. The year of the census is 1860, which was chosen specifically to highlight the continued use of slaves fifty years after the first documented explosion. As noted in the Records of Death slaves continued to perish in the mines after 1860.

Accurate interpretation of original script was attempted, yet is not guaranteed.

HANDS PURCHASED AT MY FATHER'S SALE (181_)[1]

B.R. – H.H. J.H. – at B.H.

[Possible interpretation of initials: Beverly Randolph – Henry (Harry) Heth, John Heth – at Black Heath. The numbers listed would indicate the purchase price (or value ?) of each slave(prior to death). Note the wagons, bushels of coal, and mules in the accounting indicating the coal-mining relationship.]

M__ Den_ [Illegible] Dead
Bob   570
Daniel _ [?]   250

Ceasar	90		
Billy B.	100 Dead		
Sam	100 Dead		
Phil _ [?]	150		
Frank A	100		
Davy - B	410		
Peter	175		
Oba	90		
Neal [?] C.	200		
John J.	420		
Chester	50		
Morgan	400		
Ben	250	Rueben	$375
Jim _ [?]	300		
Daniel W.	450		
Abram	100		
Nelson	250		
Shadrack [?]	310		
Jacob	200 Dead		
Abraham	130		
John Trabue	260		
Billy	450		
Jefferson	335		
William	310		
Phil C.	85		
Jack _ [?]	200		
Reuben	215		
Jack Trent [?]	130		
Jim B.	460		
Murdock [?]	585		
Phil [?] Lewis	455		
Richard	310		
Frank	310 Dead		
Waggon & Team	495		

9895

34 – Mules	$1475
3500 bus coal	1050
	———
	12,420

Mr.[?] Heth	2875
J. Heth	535
	———
	75,830
hire pit hands & [?]	1778
	———
	17,608

Charles	500
Harry	250
Nate Bel__[?]	205
Elizabeth & child	480
Nancy & 3 chl	800
Waggon & 40	
	———
	2,875

1860 SLAVE CENSUS
Chesterfield County Southern District

CLOVER HILL COAL MINING &
IRON MANUFACTURING CO.[2]

NUMBER OF SLAVE HOUSES – 12

[Names: All unknown, Color: B – Black, M – Mulatto]

Number of Slaves	Age	Sex	Color
[Owned]			
1	40	M	B
1	30	M	B
1	45	M	B
"are employed"			
1	25	M	B
1	55	M	B
1	25	M	B
1	14	M	B
1	45	M	B
1	45	M	B
1	13	M	B
1	20	M	B
1	11	M	B
1	40	M	B
1	40	M	B
1	31	M	B
1	50	M	B
1	40	M	B
1	14	M	B
1	26	M	B
1	47	M	B
1	18	M	B
1	55	M	B
1	45	M	B
1	45	M	B
1	35	M	B
1	46	M	B
1	26	M	B
1	55	M	B
1	15	M	B
1	35	M	B
1	17	M	B

Number of Slaves	Age	Sex	Color
1	40	M	B
1	37	M	B
1	33	M	B
1	46	M	B
1	20	M	B
1	23	M	M
1	16	M	B
1	36	M	B
1	34	M	B
1	21	M	B
1	20	M	B
1	35	M	B
1	47	M	B
1	50	M	B
1	41	M	B
1	47	M	B
1	46	M	B
1	21	M	B
1	46	M	B
1	57	M	B
1	45	M	B
1	46	M	B
1	23	M	B
1	27	M	B
1	45	M	B
1	60	M	B
1	35	M	B
1	26	M	B
1	60	M	B
1	27	M	B
1	28	M	B
1	55	M	B
1	45	M	B
1	27	M	B

1860 SLAVE CENSUS
Chesterfield County Northern District

MIDLOTHIAN COAL MINING CO'P.[3]

NUMBER OF SLAVE HOUSES – 35

[Names: All unknown, Color: B – Black, M – Mulatto]

Number of Slaves	Age	Sex	Color
[Owned]			
1	35	M	M
1	35	M	M
1	25	M	B
1	45	M	B
1	40	M	B
1	40	M	B
1	65	M	B
1	35	M	B
1	45	M	B
1	20	M	B
1	30	M	B
1	30	M	B
1	35	M	B
1	35	M	B
1	45	M	B
1	45	M	B
1	40	M	B
1	35	M	B
1	40	M	B
1	35	M	B
1	35	M	B
1	40	M	B

Number of Slaves	Age	Sex	Color
1	35	M	B
1	45	M	B
1	25	M	B
1	50	M	B
1	45	M	B
1	28	M	B
1	40	M	B
1	35	M	B
1	55	M	B
1	35	M	B
1	65	M	B
1	40	M	B
1	55	M	M
1	55	M	B
1	42	M	B

Emp. *[Employed]*

1	30	M	B
1	33	M	B
1	50[?]	M	B
1	26	M	B
1	30	M	B
1	45	M	B
1	22	M	M
1	22	M	B
1	25	M	B
1	65	M	B
1	30	M	B
1	30	M	B
1	35	M	B
1	26	M	B
1	55	M	B
1	45	M	B
1	40	M	M
1	30	M	B

Number of Slaves	Age	Sex	Color
1	25	M	B
1	21	M	B
1	16	M	B
1	18	M	B
1	27	M	B
1	34	M	B
1	35	M	B
1	28	M	M
1	40	M	B
1	26	M	B
1	26	M	B
1	45	M	B
1	35	M	B
1	40	M	B
1	35	M	B
1	40	M	B
1	40	M	M
1	55	M	B
1	45	M	B
1	35	M	B
1	55	M	B
1	28	M	B
1	80	M	B
1	22	M	B
1	25	M	B
1	30	M	B
1	45	M	B
1	45	M	B
1	46	M	B

[Employment notation removed at beginning of list on page 9 – unclear if owned or employed by the Midlothian Coal Mining Co., however their owners probably hired out their slaves.]

1	60	M	B
1	50	M	B

Number of Slaves	Age	Sex	Color
1	45	M	B
1	65	M	B
1	62[?]	M	B
1	19	M	B
1	25	M	B
1	30	M	B
1	20	M	B
1	35	M	B
1	13	M	B
1	13	M	B
1	30	M	B
1	45	M	B
1	18	M	B
1	60	M	B
1	40	M	B
1	30	M	B
1	28	M	B
1	65	M	B
1	55	M	B
1	65	M	B
1	65	M	B
1	50	M	B
1	45	M	B
1	35	M	B
1	55	M	B
1	55	M	B
1	60	M	B
1	45	M	B
1	55	M	B
1	40	M	B
1	35	M	B
1	25	M	B
1	45	M	B
1	35	M	B

Number of Slaves	Age	Sex	Color
1	30	M	B
1	35	M	B
1	40	M	B
1	30	M	B
1	65	M	B
1	18	M	M
1	50	M	B
1	45	M	B
1	40	M	B
1	25	M	B
1	15	M	B
1	35	M	B
1	45	M	B
1	40	M	B
1	20	M	B
1	19	M	B
1	45	M	B
1	16	M	B
1	35	M	B
1	35	M	B

[1] Papers of Henry Heth, Acession #33-114, Special Collections, University of Virginia Library, Charlottesville, Va.
[2] United States. *Population schedules of the eighth census of the United States, 1860, Chesterfield County, Virginia, slave schedules.* From originals in the U. S. National Archives, Washington, D.C. Page 20.
[3] United States. *Population schedules of the eighth census of the United States, 1860, Chesterfield County, Virginia, slave schedules.* From originals in the U. S. National Archives, Washington, D.C. Pages 7–9.

BIBLIOGRAPHY

Manuscripts and Special Collections

Bickerton Lyle Winston ledger, 1846-1859, Virginia Historical Society, Richmond.

James H. Moody. Insurance Policy, 16 February 1847. Accession 34643. Personal papers collection, The Library of Virginia, Richmond, Va.

Mid-Lothian Coal Mining Company. *Charter, by-laws, &c. of the Mid Lothian Coal Mining Company*. Richmond: Printed by Gary & Clemmitt. Special Collections, University of Virginia Library, Charlottesville, Va., 1866.

Mid-Lothian Coal Mining Company. *Charter, scheme and conditions of subscriptions of the Mid Lothian Coal Mining Company*. Richmond: Printed by S. Sheperd. Center for American History, The University of Texas at Austin, 1835.

Mid-Lothian Coal Mining Company. *Mid-Lothian Coal Mining Company Circular*. Special Collections, University of Virginia Library, Charlottesville, Va., 1840.

Mid-Lothian Coal Mining Company. *Mid-Lothian Coal Mining Company Circular*. Virginia Historical Society, Richmond, 1851.

Papers of Henry Heth, Accession #38-114, Special Collections, University of Virginia Library, Charlottesville, Va.

Policies, 1864, issued by the Virginia Life Insurance Company on the lives of Alfred, Charles, and Stephen (slaves), Virginia Historical Society, Richmond.

Nautilus Insurance Company Slavery Era Ledgers, Sc MG 715, Manuscripts, Archives and Rare Books Division, Schomburg

Center for Research in Black Culture, The New York Public Library, Astor, Lenox and Tilden Foundations.

The Baltimore Life Insurance Company Papers, MS 175, Maryland Historical Society.

Wooldridge (A. & A.) and Company. *Proposals for incorporating the Ben Lomond Coal Company.* Richmond: T.W. White. Special Collections, University of Virginia Library, Charlottesville, Va., Virginia Historical Society, Richmond, 1837.

Online Sources

California Department of Insurance. http://www.insurance.ca.gov (accessed 11-10-2007).

http://arllib.msha.gov/awweb/main.jsp?smd=2&nid=$1/2644,1738 /3598 (accessed February 7, 2008).

http://www.behindthename.com/godfrey (accessed October 26, 2007).

methane. Dictionary.com. *The American Heritage Dictionary of the English Language, Fourth Edition.* Houghton Mifflin Company, 2004. http://dictionary.reference.com/browse/methane (accessed: May 15, 2008).

Public Records

Chesterfield County Marriage Records and Vital Statistics, Register of Deaths, Lower and Upper Districts, 1853 – 1896.

Chesterfield County Marriage Records and Vital Statistics, Register of Deaths, Lower and Upper Districts, 1855 – 1870, Bar Code 1124561, Library of Virginia, Richmond.

City of Richmond, Virginia. Department of Recreation & Parks. Bureau of Cemeteries. "UNKNOWNS." Maury Cemetery, Richmond, Va., September 1986.

United States. *Population schedules of the seventh census of the United States, 1850, Chesterfield County, Virginia, slave schedules.* From originals in the U. S. National Archives, Washington, D.C., 1850.

United States. *Population schedules of the eighth census of the United States, 1860, Chesterfield County, Virginia, slave schedules.* From originals in the U. S. National Archives, Washington, D.C., 1860.

Virginia Associates, v. Irving H. Cosby, Jr. et al., Chancery No. 4362-86, Circuit Court of the County of Chesterfield, 1986.

Virginia. Auditor Public Accounts (1776-1928), Personal Property Tax Books, Chesterfield County, 1810.

——. Chesterfield County, 1811.

——. Chesterfield County, 1818.

——. Chesterfield County, 1826.

——. Chesterfield County, 1827.

——. Chesterfield County, 1828.

——. Chesterfield County, 1829.

——. Chesterfield County, 1830.

——. Chesterfield County, 1831.

———. Chesterfield County, 1832.

———. Chesterfield County, 1833.

———. Chesterfield County, 1834.

———. Chesterfield County, 1835.

———. Chesterfield County, 1836.

———. Chesterfield County, 1837.

———. Chesterfield County, 1838.

———. Chesterfield County, 1839.

———. Chesterficld County, 1840.

———. Chesterfield County, 1841.

———. Chesterfield County, 1842.

———. Chesterfield County, 1843.

Virginia. Auditor Public Accounts (1776-1928), Personal Property Tax Books, Powhatan County, 1837.

———. Powhatan County, 1838.

———. Powhatan County, 1839.

———. Powhatan County, 1840.

———. Powhatan County, 1841.

———. Powhatan County, 1842.

———. Powhatan County, 1843.

Virginia. General Assembly. Legislative Petitions of the General Assembly, Chesterfield County, 1836.

———. Chesterfield County, 1851.

Published Works

Bird, Samuel O. *Virginia's Coal Ages*, Virginia Division of Mineral Resources publication, 149. Charlottesville: Va: Commonwealth of Virginia, Dept. of Mines, Minerals, and Energy, Division of Mineral Resources, 1997.

Eavenson, Howard Nicholas. *The first century and a quarter of American coal industry*. Pittsburg, Pa: Koppers Building, 1942.

Heinrich, Oswald J. "The Midlothian, Virginia, Colliery in 1876", Transactions of the American Institute of Mining Engineers, Vol IV, Easton, Pa., American Institute of Mining Engineers, 1876.

Howe, Henry. *Historical Collections of Virginia; containing a collection of the most interesting fact, traditions, biographical sketches, anecdotes, &c., relating to its history and antiquities, together with geographical and statistical descriptions. To which is appended an historical and descriptive sketch of the District of Columbia*. Charleston, S.C., Wm. R. Babcock, 1956.

Humphrey, H. B. *Historical summary of coal-mine explosions in the United States,* 1810 – 1958, Bureau of Mines Bulletin 586, Washington, D.C.: U.S. Government Printing Office, 1960.

Hynson, Jerry M. *Baltimore Life Insurance Company Genealogical Abstracts [Maryland]*. Westminster, Md: Willow Bend Books, 2004.

196   Chesterfield County, Virginia

Leigh, Benjamin Watkins. *Reports of cases argued and determined in the Court of Appeals, and in the General Court of Virginia.* Second Edition. Richmond: Gary & Clemmitt, 1867.

Lewis, Ronald. *Black Coal Miners of America, Race Class and Community Conflict 1780 – 1980.* Lexington, Ky: University Press of Kentucky, 1987.

Lewis, Ronald L. *Coal, Iron and Slaves: Industrial Slavery in Maryland and Virginia, 1715-1865.* Westport, Ct: Greenwood Press, 1979.

Lutz, Francis Earle. *Chesterfield, An Old Virginia County Volume I, 1607-1954.* Richmond, Va. Bermuda Ruritan Club, 1954. Reprint, Chesterfield County Historical Society, 2003.

Murphy, Sharon Ann. "Securing Human Property: Slavery, Life Insurance, and Industrialization in the Upper South." *Journal of the Early Republic.* 25 (4): 615-652, 2005.

O'Dell, Jeffrey M. *Chesterfield County: Early Architecture and Historic Sites.* Chesterfield, Va: [Chesterfield County Planning Dept.], 1983.

Salmon, John S., and Margaret T. Peters. *A guidebook to Virginia's historical markers.* Charlottesville: University Press of Virginia, 1994.

Ulery, James P. "Explosion Hazards From Methane Emissions Related to Geologic Features in Coal Mine." National Institute for Occupational Safety and Health, Centers for Disease Control and Prevention Information Circular 9503, Pittsburg, Pa., Department of Health and Human Services, April 2008.

Valentine Museum. *Richmond Portraits in an Exhibition of Makers of Richmond 1737-1860.* Richmond, Va: The William Byrd Press, Inc., 1949.

Weaver, Bettie Woodson. *Midlothian: Highlights of its History*, Midlothian, Va.: [s.n.], 1994.

Wilkes, G. P. *Mining History of the Richmond Coalfield of Virginia,* Virginia Division of Mineral Resources publication 85. Charlottesville: Va: Commonwealth of Virginia, Dept. of Mines, Minerals, and Energy, Division of Mineral Resources, 1988.

Periodicals

Niles' National Register. "Trip to the Coal Mines," Jeter, Rev. J. B., October 14, 1843.

Newspaper Articles

Chicago Tribune. "Entombed." Chicago, Il. February 4, 1882.

Chicago Tribune. "Mine Explosion." Chicago, Il. May 24, 1876.

Daily Dispatch. "A Awful Catastrophe at the Clover Hill Mines." Richmond, Va. April 6, 1867.

Daily Dispatch. "A Shocking Disaster." Richmond, Va. May 23, 1876.

Daily Dispatch. "Coal Mine Explosion!!! Terrible Loss of Life. Twenty People Killed." Richmond, Va. May 16, 1854.

Daily Dispatch. "Coalpit Explosion." Richmond, Va. December 15, 1863.

Daily Dispatch. "Explosion and Loss of Life at the Black Heath Coal Mine." Richmond, Va. November 28, 1855.

Daily Dispatch. "Explosion at the Clover Hill Coal Mines." Richmond, Va. April 5, 1867.

Daily Dispatch. "Fearful Fate." Richmond, Va. February 4, 1882.

Daily Dispatch. "Five Found." Richmond, Va. February 7, 1882.

Daily Dispatch. "From the Pits." Richmond, Va. May 17, 1854.

Daily Dispatch. "Grove Shaft Horror." Richmond, Va. February 5, 1882.

Daily Dispatch. "Latest from the Midlothian Pits." Richmond, Va. March 22, 1855.

Daily Dispatch. "Life Insurance, (White Persons and Slaves)." Richmond, Va. January 21, 1854.

Daily Dispatch. "Terrible Coal Pit Explosion." Richmond, Va. March 21, 1855.

Daily Dispatch. "Terrible Explosion at the Clover Hill Pits – sixty-nine men killed." Richmond, Va. April 5, 1867.

Daily Dispatch. "The Chesterfield Sufferers." Richmond, Va. May 25, 1854.

Daily Dispatch. "The Mine Afire." Richmond, Va. February 8, 1882.

Daily Express. "The Explosion at the Bright Hope Pits." Petersburg, Va. April 15, 1859.

Daily Oregonian. "The Great Colliery Explosion in Virginia – More than Seventy Persons Killed." Portland, Or. May 20, 1867.

Daily Progress. "Coal Pits on Fire." Petersburg, Va. December 28, 1871.

Daily South-side Democrat. "Coal Mine Explosion!!! Terrible Loss of Life." Twenty People Killed. Petersburg, Va. May 17, 1854.

Daily South-side Democrat. "Terrible Explosion at the Black Heath Pitts – Loss of Life." Petersburg, Va. November 29, 1855.

Enquirer. Want ad. Richmond, Va. March 2, 1810.

Fort Wayne Sentinel. "The Coal-pit Explosions at Richmond." Fort Wayne, In. March 24, 1855.

Gettysburg *Republican Compiler.* "The Coal Mine Explosion." Gettysburg, Pa. April 9, 1839.

New-York Daily Times. "Another Explosion at the Virginia Coal Pits." New York, N.Y. November 30, 1855.

New-York Daily Times. "Coalpit Explosion." New York, N.Y. March 22, 1855.

New-York Daily Times. "Four More Deaths from the Midlothian Coal Pits Explosion." New York, N.Y. March 24, 1855.

New-York Daily Times. "Terrible Coal Pit Explosion." New York, N.Y. March 23, 1855.

New-York Daily Times. "Terrific Explosion in Coal Pits at Chesterfield, Va." New York, N.Y. March 21, 1855.

New-York Times. "The Great Colliery Explosion in Virginia – More than Seventy Persons Killed." New York, N.Y. April 7, 1867.

New-York Times. "Thirty-two Men Killed; the Terrible Explosion in the Midlothian Mine. No Hope of Rescuing Any of the Imprisoned Miners Alive –Heartrending Scenes at the Mouth of the Pit – One Body Recovered." New York, N.Y. February 5, 1882. http://www.nytimes.com/ (accessed April 18, 2008).

New-York Times. "Two Men killed in a Mine." New York, N.Y. October 23, 1885.

New-York Tribune. "A Shocking Mine Disaster." New York, N.Y. February 4, 1882.

New-York Tribune. "An Appeal for Help from Midlothian." New York, N.Y. February 8, 1882.

New-York Tribune. "Searching for the Dead." New York, N.Y. February 6, 1882.

New-York Tribune. "The Midlothian Calamity. New York, N.Y. February 5, 1882.

New-York Tribune. The Midlothian Disaster." New York, N.Y. February 7, 1882.

Petersburg Daily Intelligencer. "The Coal Pit Explosion In Chesterfield." Petersburg, Va. April 15, 1859.

Petersburg Index. "The Great Disaster at the Clover Hill Coal Pits." Petersburg, Va. April 6, 1867.

Republican Compiler. "The Coal Mine Explosion." Gettysburg, Pa. April 9, 1839.

Richmond Dispatch. "Death in the Mines." Richmond, Va. October 23, 1885.

Richmond Enquirer. "The Black Heath Coal Mine." Richmond, Va. March 23, 1839.

Richmond Times-Dispatch. Douglas, Frank. "Cemetery transferred, but mystery lingers." Richmond, Va. February 8, 1987.

Rural Messenger. "Terrible Explosion – Eight Men Killed." Petersburg, Va. March 27, 1876.

San Francisco Chronicle. "Thousands online for slave data." San Francisco, Ca. May 2, 2002.

South-side Democrat. "Fearful Coal Pit Disaster at Midlothian, Chesterfield." Petersburg, Va. December 15, 1856.

South-side Democrat. "The Midlothian Coal Pits Accident." Petersburg, Va. December 16, 1856.

INDEX

The names of persons who died in the mines are listed alphabetically in Chapter 2. In this index, those names are listed under the name of the mine in which they perished. When available, race and/or slave status is provided. Four hyphens (----) indicate that no last name was given.
Names of insured slaves can be found in the Slave Insurance Index, immediately following this index.

Baltimore Life Insurance
Company, 64–66
See Slave Insurance List for
details, 68
Slave insurance, 175
Barclay
Lewis, slave, 105
Winston, slave, 105
Barnes, William, Rescued from
Midlothian pit, 155
Barrett, Jim, slave, 105
Bellman
J., Jean?, 22
W., 22
Ben Lomond Coal Company, 101,
113, 115, 121
"An Act to Incorporate", 2, 116
Assets included established
coal mines and slaves, 5
Formation, 2
Lack of tax records, 3
Proposals for Incorporating, 97
Scheme, 111, 114
"Bever Pits," deaths, Simeon,
slave, 51
Bigg___, Tho. B., 122
Black Coal Miners of America, 14
"Black damp", 154, 159
Black Heath Coal Company, 153
Black Heath Coal Mine, 5
1839 explosion, 7, 15
1839 explosion, Newspaper
article, 153
Not considered a good
insurance risk, 65–66, 68,
175, 179
Black Heath Coal Mine, deaths
Burton, Joseph, white, 24
Garland, slave, 33
Hancock, John, white, 36
Jewett, [?], white, 39
Luke, Nicholas [white?], 43
Marshall, John [white?], 44

Black Heath Coal Mine, deaths
(continued)
Rynard, John, white, 51
Thompson, Charles [white?],
53
Unknown (51) "colored men",
57
Black Heath Coal Mine, injured
Cotton, George, white, 60
Wright, William, black, 61
Black Heath Company of Colliers,
102, 111, 124
Blair, Albert, 161
Blount's pits, 101–102
Bolling, Mr., 177
Bowman
A., 23
H., 23
John, 23
Branch
B., 24
Billy, 24
Flemming, 23
Nathan, slave, 105
P., 24
Sie, slave, 105
Brewer, Chas., 58
Bright Hope Mine, deaths
Ainsko, James, white, 21
Ainsko, John, white, 21
Ammonette, Beverley, *See*
Amonette, Beverly, 22
Amonette, Beverly (white), 22
Anderson, Beverly, black, 22
Artis, John, black, 22
Bellman, Robert, black, 22
Berry, Richard, white
(presumed killed), 58
Bertlam, George, white
(presumed killed), 58
Blankenship, Richard, white,
23, 156
Boisseau, Henry, black, 23

SLAVE INSURANCE INDEX

INSURANCE COMPANY	APPLICANT	SLAVE, PAGE NUMBER
Baltimore Life Insurance Company	James L. Porter	Henry, 76
	Tompkins & Co.; James R. McTyre	McTyre, Thomas, 81
	Tompkins & Co.; Jos. T. Tompkins	Horace, 77
	Tompkins & Co.; Michael Duval	Carter, Gilbert, 70
	Tompkins & Co.; Wm. E. Martin	Clay, 70
		Edward, 72
		George, 73
		Henry, 76
		Jefferson, 78
		Peter, 83
		Richard, 85
		Robert, 86
		Stokes, 87
		Watson, 88
Nautilus Insurance Company	A. S. Wooldridge	Maston, William, 80
		Walker, Israel, 88
		Wills, Jim, 89
	Alexander Martin	Porter, Jordan, 85
	Charles Mills	Finley, Nelson, 73
	Chesterfield Mining Co.	Barlett, 69
		Hall, Charles, 74
		Hall, Daniel, 75
	Daniel Wooldridge	Congo, 71
		David, 72
		Henry, 75
	David Moody	Moody, Phill, 83

INSURANCE COMPANY	APPLICANT	SLAVE, PAGE NUMBER
Nautilus Insurance Company (continued)	Edmund A. Lockett	Lockett, Henry, 80
		Lockett, Jim, 80
		Lockett, Joe, 80
		Lockett, Jordan, 80
		Lockett, Ned, 80
	Elias Burnette	Burnette, Dabney, 69
	F. A. Clarke	Swann, Philip, 87
	Haley Cole	Cole, Lewis, 71
	Higginson Hancock	Hewlett, 77
		Pollard, Tom, 84
	James L. Porter	Porter, Frank, 84
		Porter, Henry, 85
	James Moody	Montague, Harry (Henry), 82
		Moody, Henry, 82
		Moody, Joe, 83
	James Moody; Sarah E. Moody	Moody, Robert, 83
	Jefferson Cosby	Isaac, 78
	Jefferson Hancock	Giles, Dick, 73
	John Darracott	Dabney, Davy, 71
		Dabney, London, 71
	John Hobson	Adam, 68
		Barlette, 69
		Peter, 84
	Joseph A. Ellis	Ellis, Peter, 72
	Joseph Mayo	Ligou, Jack, 79
	Mid Lothian Coal Mining Co.	Ampy, 69
		Hall, Bob, 74
		Johnson, Richard, 79
		Porter, Edgar, 84
	Mid Lothian Coal Mining Co.; Elizabeth Wright estate	Wright, Harry, 89
		Wright, Henry, 89
		Wright, Joe, 90
		Wright, Randolph, 90
	Nelson Tumly	Griffin, 74

INSURANCE COMPANY	APPLICANT	SLAVE, PAGE NUMBER
Nautilus Insurance Company (continued)	Nicholas Mills	Anderson, Phill, 69
		Cheatham, Patrick, 70
		Dickenson, Henry, 72
		Flournoy, Anderson, 73
		Godfrey, 74
		Hanes, Henry, 75
		Harrod, Billy, 75
		Hunt, John, 77
		James, Madison, 78
		Jones, Anthony, 79
		Jones, Sam, 79
		Kiner, Sam, 79
		Mills, Cyrus, 81
		Mills, George, 81
		Mills, Harry, 82
		Mills, Jim, 82
		Mills, Lewis, 82
		Mills (Miller), Ned, 82
		Picket, Henry, 84
		Reuben (aka Dutch), 85
		Rid (Red), Sam, 86
		Wilson, 89
		York, Ben, 90
		York (Nork), Nathan, 90
	Richard Archer	Jacob, 78
		Reuben, 85
	Richard Hall	Hall, Bob, 74
	Thomas Marshalls	Smith, Charles, 87
	William M. Watkins	Watkins, Lewis, 88
		Watkins, William, 88
		Watkins, William Henry, 88
	William Winfred, Jr.	Winfred, Jim, 89
	Woodson W. Hancock	Hancock, Jordan, 75

INSURANCE COMPANY	APPLICANT	SLAVE, PAGE NUMBER
Not Listed	Owned by Absolom Martin	Unknown/Name not provided, 91
	Owned by Charles Brewer	Unknown/Name not provided, 90, 91
	Owned by S. D. Wooldridge	Unknown/Name not provided, 91
Virginia Life Insurance Company	H. C. Cox	Alfred, 68
	J. R. Gates	Stephen, 87
	W. H. Wilson	Charles, 70

Made in the USA
Charleston, SC
23 September 2011